ENACTING THE PRESIDENCY

Recent titles in the PRAEGER SERIES
IN POLITICAL COMMUNICATION
Robert E. Denton, Jr., *General Editor*

Enacting
the Presidency

Political Argument, Presidential Debates, and Presidential Character

Edward A. Hinck

Praeger Series in Political Communication

PRAEGER

Westport, Connecticut
London

Copyright Acknowledgment

The author and publisher are grateful for permission to use excerpts from the following:

George F. Bishop, *et al.*, eds., THE PRESIDENTIAL DEBATES: MEDIA, ELECTORAL, AND POLICY PERSPECTIVES (Praeger Publishers, an imprint of Greenwood Publishing Group, Inc., Westport, CT, 1978), pp. 261–281, *passim*. Copyright © 1978. Reprinted with permission.

Library of Congress Cataloging-in-Publication Data

Hinck, Edward A.
    Enacting the presidency : political argument, presidential
debates, and presidential character / Edward A. Hinck.
      p.   cm. — (Praeger series in political communication, ISSN
1062–5623)
    Includes bibliographical references and index.
    ISBN 0–275–93488–8 (alk. paper)
    1. Presidents—United States—Election. 2. Campaign debates—
United States. 3. United States—Politics and
government—1945–1989. 4. United States—Politics and
government—1989– .   I. Title. II. Series.
JK524.H56   1993
324.973'092—dc20   92–19435

British Library Cataloguing in Publication Data is available.

Copyright © 1993 by Edward A. Hinck

Library of Congress Catalog Card Number: 92–19435
ISBN: 0–275–93488–8
ISSN: 1062–5623

First published in 1993

Praeger Publishers, 88 Post Road West, Westport, CT 06881
An imprint of Greenwood Publishing Group, Inc.

Printed in the United States of America

The paper used in this book complies with the
Permanent Paper Standard issued by the National
Information Standards Organization (Z39.48–1984).

10 9 8 7 6 5 4 3 2 1

With appreciation for my teachers:
Karlyn Kohrs Campbell and Donn W. Parson
With gratitude to my family
In memory of my mother, Donna Cravens Hinck
And for Ashley, Robert, and Alexandra

Contents

Series Foreword

Those of us from the discipline of communication studies have long believed that communication is prior to all other fields of inquiry. In several other forums I have argued that the essence of politics is "talk" or human interaction.[1] Such interaction may be formal or informal, verbal or nonverbal, public or private but it is always persuasive, forcing us consciously or subconsciously to interpret, to evaluate, and to act. Communication is the vehicle for human action.

From this perspective, it is not surprising that Aristotle recognized the natural kinship of politics and communication in his writings *Politics* and *Rhetoric*. In the former, he establishes that humans are "political beings [who] alone of the animals [are] furnished with the faculty of language."[2] And in the latter, he begins his systematic analysis of discourse by proclaiming that "rhetorical study, in its strict sense, is concerned with the modes of persuasion."[3] Thus, it was recognized over twenty-three hundred years ago that politics and communication go hand in hand because they are essential parts of human nature.

Back in 1981, Dan Nimmo and Keith Sanders proclaimed that political communication was an emerging field.[4] Although its origin, as noted, dates back centuries, a "self-consciously cross disciplinary" focus began in the late 1950s. Thousands of books and articles later, colleges and universities offer a variety of graduate and undergraduate coursework in the area in such diverse departments as communication, mass communication, journalism, political science, and sociology.[5] In Nimmo and Sanders' early assessment, the "key areas of inquiry" included rhetorical analysis, propaganda analysis, attitude change studies, voting studies, government and the news media, functional and systems analyses, tech-

nological changes, media technologies, campaign techniques, and research techniques.[6] In a survey of the state of the field in 1983, the same
authors and Lynda Kaid found additional, more specific areas of concern
such as the presidency, political polls, public opinion, debates, and
advertising to name a few.[7] Since the first study, they also noted a shift
away from the rather strict behavioral approach.

A decade later, Dan Nimmo and David Swanson argued that "political
communication has developed some identity as a more or less distinct
domain of scholarly work."[8] The scope and concerns of the area have
further expanded to include critical theories and cultural studies. While
there is no precise definition, method, or disciplinary home of the area
of inquiry, its primary domain is the role, processes, and effects of
communication within the context of politics broadly defined.

In 1985, the editors of *Political Communication Yearbook: 1984* noted that
"more things are happening in the study, teaching, and practice of
political communication than can be captured within the space limitations of the relatively few publications available."[9] In addition, they
argued that the backgrounds of "those involved in the field [are] so
varied and pluralist in outlook and approach, . . . it [is] a mistake to
adhere slavishly to any set format in shaping the content."[10] And more
recently, Swanson and Nimmo called for "ways of overcoming the un-
happy consequences of fragmentation within a framework that respects,
encourages, and benefits from diverse scholarly commitments, agendas,
and approaches."[11]

In agreement with these assessments of the area and with gentle
encouragement, Praeger established in 1988 the "Praeger Series in Political Communication." The series is open to all qualitative and quan-
titative methodologies as well as contemporary and historical studies.
The key to characterizing the studies in the series is the focus on communication variables or activities within a political context or dimension.
As of this writing, over thirty volumes have been published and there
are numerous impressive works forthcoming. Scholars from the disci-
plines of communication, history, journalism, political science, and sociology have participated in the series.

Every four years we hear a resounding cry from political pundits and
academics who bemoan the demise of the "quality" of presidential campaigns. Campaigns have become mere "spectacles" consisting of hollow
images, mini-second soundbites, and the preeminence of style over substance. Among the most attacked of American political institutions is
the role and function of presidential debates. Once the cornerstone of
American democracy where issues could be analyzed and candidates
compared, they are now characterized as "joint press conferences," mere
talking heads discussing politics.[12]

For American journalists, presidential debates are the quintessential political battle. For days the media expend a great deal of energy telling us what to look for, who won, who lost, and what it all means. Social scientists, however, are less sure of the power and impact of presidential debates upon voters.[13] Their effects in terms of issue understanding, policy determination, or voter conversion seem to be rather minimal. But we know that debates do matter. Their impact goes beyond statistical analyses of data or sudden shifts of attitudes.

In this study, Edward Hinck challenges traditional assumptions about the role and function of presidential debates. For him, debates are not so much about issues or policy positions as forums for demonstrating images of leadership. This perspective shifts the focus of attention from issues of debate structure, public policy, or argumentative content to issues of argumentative style and enactments of presidential character and leadership. Candidate language choices shape images of presidential character, leadership ability, prudence, and moral excellence. Character and argument are certainly related. Arguments are deliberate acts of language choices that reveal moral qualities and values. Ultimately, the public assesses the candidates on how well they embody community values and leadership potential.

Without question this study is an important and unique contribution to the study of American presidential debates. Written from a communication perspective, Edward Hinck provides genuine insight into the rhetorical functions of debates. Building upon a solid theoretical base, Hinck's excellent analyses of the 1960, 1976, 1980, 1984, and 1988 debates demonstrate how language reveals personal character and leadership values.

I am, without shame or modesty, a fan of this series. The joy of serving as its editor is in participating in the dialogue of the field of political communication and in reading the contributors' works. I invite you to join me.

Robert E. Denton, Jr.

NOTES

1. See Robert E. Denton, Jr., *The Symbolic Dimensions of the American Presidency* (Prospect Heights, IL: Waveland Press, 1982); Robert E. Denton, Jr. and Gary Woodward, *Political Communication in America* (New York: Praeger, 1985, 2d ed., 1990); Robert E. Denton, Jr., and Dan Hahn, *Presidential Communication* (New York: Praeger, 1986); and Robert E. Denton, Jr., *The Primetime Presidency of Ronald Reagan* (New York: Praeger, 1988).

2. Aristotle, *The Politics of Aristotle*, trans. Ernest Barker (New York: Oxford University Press, 1970), p. 5.

3. Aristotle, *Rhetoric*, trans. Rhys Roberts (New York: The Modern Library, 1954), p. 22.

4. Dan Nimmo and Keith Sanders, "Introduction: The Emergence of Political Communication as a Field," in *Handbook of Political Communication*, Dan Nimmo and Keith Sanders, eds. (Beverly Hills, CA: Sage, 1981), pp. 11–36.

5. Ibid., p. 15.

6. Ibid., pp. 17–27.

7. Keith Sanders, Lynda Kaid, and Dan Nimmo, eds. *Political Communication Yearbook: 1984* (Carbondale, IL: Southern Illinois University, 1985), pp. 283–308.

8. Dan Nimmo and David Swanson, "The Field of Political Communication: Beyond the Voter Persuasion Paradigm" in *New Directions in Political Communication*, David Swanson and Dan Nimmo, eds. (Beverly Hills, CA: Sage, 1990), p. 8.

9. Sanders, Kaid, and Nimmo, p. xiv.

10. Ibid., p. xiv.

11. Nimmo and Swanson, p. 11.

12. See Kathleen Hall Jamieson and David Birdsell, *Presidential Debates: The Challenge of Creating an Informed Electorate* (New York: Oxford University Press, 1988), and David Lanoue and Peter Schrott, *The Joint Press Conference* (Westport, CT: Greenwood Press, 1991).

13. See Susan Hellweg, Michael Pfau, and Steven Brydon, *Televised Presidential Debates* (New York: Praeger, 1992), and Lanoue and Schrott, *The Joint Press Conference*.

Acknowledgments

The work on this project began ten years ago during my graduate work at the University of Kansas and has culminated with the final manuscript being completed at Central Michigan University. In the last ten years, I have been fortunate enough to have had the support of many friends as well as a patient and understanding family. While at the University of Kansas, I had the good fortune to work with a large group of graduate students who enriched my intellectual life as well as provided consistent friendship over the years. I am particularly indebted to Robin Rowland, who showed me how to use argument in the context of organizations, contributed to my knowledge of how to employ arguments in scholarly works, and helped me to assimilate what appeared at first to be an alien culture but one which I now hold dear to my heart. I also am very grateful to have shared an office with John Murphy, whose knowledge of history and rhetorical theory has provided me with many insights, some of which have found their way into this work, and I am grateful for his helpful comments on the final chapter. Kevin Barge provided support and encouragement in the course of this project. His friendship as a colleague continued to keep me inspired. John Bart, Claire Jerry, Masayuki Nakanishi, Craig Dudczak, Gregg Walker, Tom Burkholder, Bob Chandler, Jack Hart, Susan Huxman, Bonnie Dow, Mary Lee Hummert, Mary Tonn, Jeff Hobbs, Marty Sadler, Andy Rist, and many other Jayhawks have contributed much friendship over the years. This goes for the many KU debaters, too. I also owe a great deal to Bob Gass, Joyce Flocken, Bob Emry, and Lucy Keele, who provided much encouragement and motivation while I was at California State University, Fullerton. I am especially grateful to Jon Bruschke for teaching me how to use the computer. Karen and Sue Martin provided me with the necessary instruction to use the computers at Central Michigan University. They have also contributed enormous help in managing the disks and producing the final manuscript. The Faculty Research and Creative Endeavors Committee at Central Michigan provided financial support to present previous versions of parts of this manuscript at the 1990 and 1991 SCA conventions. At those SCA conventions Michael Pfau of Augustana College and Susan Hellweg of San Diego State University offered many helpful comments on the work in progress. The Department of Speech Communication and Dramatic Arts has provided generous release time for this project. Nancy Buerkel-Rothfuss, David Ling, and all of the other CMU faculty have been the best colleagues one could hope for. If I have maintained any sense of balance, it is probably due to the wise spirits of Chuck and Onlee Bowden. I owe much to Robert Denton for giving me the opportunity to get work into print. Praeger Publishers has been especially patient and supportive with this project. Anne Kiefer and Jude Grant, my editors at Praeger, were also patient and provided much assistance in getting this work to press. My wife, Shelly, has provided me much support and time to revise and write while Ashley and Robert have made me feel appreciated whenever I have been able to function as a responsible parent. In her own special way, Alexandra was a constant source of motivation in the last few months of working on this project. The CMU debaters and assistant coaches also provided a healthy climate of support. I want to thank Mike Wolf for tracking down articles reporting reactions to the 1984 vice presidential debate between Bush and Ferraro. In the last stages of preparing the final manuscript, Diana Prentice of the University of Kansas provided enormous assistance in acquiring transcripts of the 1988 debates from the Commission on Presidential Debates. I am particularly indebted to Charlotte Amaro, who proofread and double checked for accuracy my use of the debate transcripts. Finally, I want to express my appreciation to Professors Donn Parson and Karlyn Kohrs Campbell. If there is anything interesting or important in what I have presented here, it will be due to the influence that they have had on the development of my skills as a critic.

Chapter One

Political Debates and the Enactment of Leadership

Presidential debates have become one of the most interesting yet criticized events in presidential campaigns. Generally, most scholars agree that debates are important campaign events.[1] However, despite this consensus, much of the commentary concerning debates has focused on how limitations in the format have made it difficult for audiences to see the "real substance" of the candidates' positions and policies.[2] Although several solutions for problems in format have been developed by communication scholars, for the most part, presidential campaign advisers have seemed reluctant to adopt these recommendations.[3] As a result, we have many good recommendations for improving the argumentative content of the debates but very little understanding of debates as rhetorical events.[4]

For the most part, complaints about presidential debates rely on two problematic assumptions: that they should provide the electorate with some form of objective truth and that they are held primarily for the purpose of choosing presidential policies.[5] There are two fundamental problems in this orientation to presidential debates. First, political campaigns are not designed to produce absolute and certain truth about political candidates and their policies. In his review of modern presidential campaigns, Stephen Hess has argued that political campaigns are designed to produce an approximation of the truth through the clash of contending forces.[6] One of those forces is political rhetoric. Within presidential campaigns, candidates must appeal to diverse groups. As Kathleen Jamieson and David Birdsell have noted, specific proposals, although capable of being critically scrutinized, can also constitute rhetorical liabilities for candidates in presidential debates.[7] Even specific treatment of values can create difficulties for candidates.[8] According to Roderick Hart, politicians must by necessity rely on the strategic ambiguities inherent in language to govern effectively a nation of diverse interests, beliefs, attitudes, and values.[9] Thus, specific arguments capable of being carefully analyzed can constitute significant risks to presidential candidates given the varied, often inconsistent forms of rationality operating in the diverse audiences that compose the national community. In this respect, some of the more interesting rhetorical aspects of presidential debates may involve subtle argumentative and stylistic aspects of a candidate's performance. Emphasizing content over style not only leaves critics dependent on campaign advisers who ignore recommendations for improved content but may also neglect consideration for important aspects of the debates. Despite the fact that presidential debates may not measure up to more traditional expectations of form, the rhetorical actions of the candidates are still in need of an adequate account based on a critical approach sensitive to the unique nature of the forum, purpose, and situation.

Second, presidential debates do not have as their primary purpose the presentation and selection of national policy. They are forums designed to present and select candidates for national office; their primary purpose is to provide opportunities for candidates to win over undecided voters, to reinforce voters who have already made a decision concerning whom to vote for, and to change the minds of those who are willing to reconsider their initial judgments concerning which candidate seems more fit to serve as president.[10] In a debate, audiences can learn more about the policies that each candidate is advocating, but the more important issue is how well a candidate's policies stand up to criticisms from the opposing candidate. Even if a candidate offers, initially, what appears to be a desirable program, unless the candidate can defend that program against attack, there would seem to be little reason to believe that the candidate could marshal enough political support to implement that program. From a rhetorical perspective, then, the candidate who displays better advocacy skills demonstrates an ability to persuade others to accept and implement potentially desirable programs. Thus, in a debate, the audience deliberates over the issue of who seems more fit to lead, not which policy to select.

Viewing the purpose of debates as opportunities to present desirable images of leadership shifts the critical focus from a concern for argumentative content to an emphasis on rhetorical action. Although candidates do argue about policies, and their arguments can be analyzed, a useful way to explain what is happening in the debate is to include an analysis of *how* a candidate argues the issues as well as *what* the arguments were. In this respect, examining stylistic aspects of a candidate's performance in relation to the substantive arguments can reveal important information about a candidate's character. Approaching debates from this perspective shifts our attention in debates from considerations about policy to reflections on the nature of presidential character as it is enacted in the course of the debate. Debates are important events in presidential campaigns, then, because they constitute unique opportunities for audiences to observe each candidate's ability to respond to symbolic challenges and because they reveal each candidate's potential for leadership in the way they respond to the rhetorical problems that unfold in the course of the debate.[11]

This conceptualization of presidential debates is developed around four claims: (1) that the purpose behind a candidate's language choices is the need to present a desirable image of presidential leadership; (2) that a useful concept of presidential leadership can be derived from the political and rhetorical theories of Aristotle; (3) that successful debate performances by candidates are ones in which desirable images of presidential character are enacted through discourse; and (4) that these debate performances shape not only the character of the candidates through their unique capacity for revealing important information about a candidate's character but also the character of the national community in the sense that they function epideictically by enacting democratic values and renewing the democratic character of the community.

Although this conceptualization of presidential debates may be applied to other types of political debates, my concern in this study is with presidential debates occurring between those candidates nominated by their party. Despite the possibility of argument in any type of debate, debates between each party's presidential and vice presidential nominee constitute substantially different rhetorical encounters than party forums featuring more than two candidates. Debates between presidential and vice presidential candidates represent a dialectical conflict between two alternatives for the presidency; candidate forums, because of their loosely structured formats designed to ensure that all candidates can participate, represent alternatives for party leadership. Also, debates between presidential and vice presidential candidates occur before audiences who may be sharply divided on issues of value and policy; candidate forums occur before audiences who may share agreement on party values but differ in their preference over who is best equipped rhetorically to represent and defend those party values. The key difference between presidential and vice presidential debates and candidate forums is the nature of the rhetorical situation and purpose: Presidential and vice presidential candidates attempt to shape a favorable image of a national leader, whereas candidates for the nomination search for favorable ways of presenting themselves as party leaders. Because the purposes differ, so does the discourse of the candidates. Accounting for the rhetorical action occurring in candidate forums would require a substantially enlarged theoretical discussion and critical analysis of the candidates' language choices. For the present, my aim is to suggest the value of an alternative perspective on political debates by considering the ways in which debates between presidential and vice presidential candidates who have received the nomination of their party shape images of presidential character.

The theoretical basis for considering a candidate's language choices can be found in the political and rhetorical theories of Aristotle. Leadership ability, according to Aristotle, is measured by how well each candidate's language choices demonstrate both moral excellence (*arete*) and the prudence (*phronesis*) to rule.[12]

Arete and *phronesis* cannot be considered apart from each other in the context of political rhetoric because demonstrative and ethical proofs are tied closely together. In Aristotle's words, "rhetorical persuasion is effected not only by demonstrative but by ethical argument; it helps a speaker to convince us, if we believe he has certain qualities himself, namely, goodness, or goodwill towards us, or both together."[13] In a political debate, character and argument are related. The concept of leadership presumes that the candidates' actions are symbolic of their capacity to lead. According to Aristotle, "We shall learn the qualities of governments in the same way as we learn the qualities of individuals, since they are revealed in their deliberate act of choice; and these are determined by the ends that inspire them."[14] Because arguments are deliberate acts of choice, candidates reveal their moral qualities when they make choices concerning which programs to advocate, what reasons to offer in justifying those programs, and what evidence to offer in support of their claims.

The audience evaluates how well each candidate performs the role of national advocate by using community norms and values to judge a candidate's performance. Candidates must maintain a standard of behavior befitting a national representative. In political debates, when candidates are caught deviating from community norms of political conduct such as lying, deliberately distorting facts, and name-calling, for example, they risk unfavorable evaluations from the audience because these actions give the audience direct evidence of undesirable character. Candidates can also be assessed in terms of how well they embody community values, but these community values must be viewed in the context of political campaigns. Candidates are examined for their ability to defend what is desirable for the community. Thus, argument functions as both a sign of leadership potential and the process by which candidates alter community values in a campaign.[15]

Substantively, candidates' arguments must demonstrate that they know what programs would advance and protect national values. Because they seek ways of appealing to audiences on behalf of their abilities

to act in the national interest, audiences evaluate a candidate's knowledge of community values and goodwill toward the audience. According
to Aristotle, "In a political debate, the man who is forming a judgment
is making a decision about his own vital interests."[16] To be perceived
worthy for national office, candidates must appeal to the audience on
substantive grounds of community interests.

An image of good will is not accomplished by simply claiming to be
in favor of those programs that benefit the country; a candidate must
enact qualities of leadership. Because voters have no control over who
serves in office until the next election, they must make a prediction
about how each candidate will perform as president.[17] Thus, an audience
makes a judgment about a candidate's future behavior based upon the
image of character reflected in the debate. According to Aristotle, the
issue is how a candidate will behave in the future, the possible actions
that a candidate might take while in office,[18] a time during which the
audience has no control over a candidate's actions, except through the
difficult course of impeachment.

The actions of a candidate should provide the audience with reliable
indications of how they will behave in office. The public must have, in
Aristotle's words, confidence in the character of the candidate: "There
are three things which inspire confidence in the orator's own character—
the three, namely that induce us to believe a thing apart from any proof
of it: good sense, good moral character, and good will."[19] Good sense
relates to prudence, or wisdom in decision making and actions. Good
moral character reflects moral excellence, or the capacity to represent
symbolically the moral values of a language community. Good will concerns a politician's motives, whether he is interested in the needs of the
people before whom he argues and whether his actions will support
and protect the community he represents. When these three elements
of character are evident in candidates' language choices, they demonstrate character worthy of national office. A candidate must give evidence of his or her ability to make good decisions, to keep the trust of
the people, and to argue successfully when challenged. For Aristotle, a
candidate's language choices must be perceived as noble acts, those that
are done for the good of the community and that do not contain motives
of individual self-interest.[20]

Finally, the audience evaluates not one act but a candidate's pattern
of response to the questions of the panelists and the answers of the
opposing candidate. Because arguing is linguistic action, the debates
offer the audience an opportunity to examine how a candidate responds
to symbolic challenges.[21] A candidate's arguments give the audience a
basis for assessing how he or she would behave in office—in Aristotle's
words: "Yet the actual deeds are evidence of the doer's character: even
if a man has not actually done a given good thing, we shall bestow praise

on him, if we are sure that he is the sort of man who would do it."[22] Argument, then, is a way of enacting character, of demonstrating the ability to lead, and because political debates call for arguments, they are opportunities to enact a presidential image.[23]

Candidates for the presidency must agree in a way that demonstrates noble character worthy of praise. Because presidents symbolize the rhetorical substance of the nation, their language choices must contain or in some important way reflect the moral excellence of the community and demonstrate prudence to rule. The person who serves as president must be capable of being regarded as a cultural symbol representing not only political values but the moral excellence of the community. One function of the debates, then, is to give the audience an opportunity to evaluate the candidates for their ability to represent national values.

Political debates serve epideictic and deliberative ends by providing the national community with an opportunity to observe how national dissensus is managed symbolically through arguments. Even though audiences cannot participate directly in the policy-making process, they can alter the nature of presidential leadership. During political debates, audiences deliberate over the leadership qualities of the candidates demonstrated in the debates. Even if debates do not change voters' minds, they provide audiences with an opportunity to scrutinize the dialectic created by the political system. Debates, then, provide audiences with an opportunity to observe and evaluate the ability of the political system to produce worthy candidates.

The ability to argue is both a prerequisite of leadership and a sign of a healthy democracy. Arguments function to justify decisions, to legitimize political order, to protect community values, and to solve political problems at a symbolic rather than physical level of force. Arguments preserve political order yet constitute a method by which social change can be managed rhetorically instead of through violence or subterfuge; thus, argument is a form of discourse that represents, alters, and enacts democratic values so that when presidential candidates argue the issues of the day before the community, they enact democracy.

Arguments manage political dissensus in two important respects. Rhetorically, refutation indicates the presence of and the need to appeal to a divided audience.[24] When both candidates argue, they create a national dialogue that represents and resolves political differences rhetorically. Audiences observe and pass judgment on the moral quality of this dialogue. Although the public cannot participate in the dialectic, they can observe the political system functioning properly when political differences are resolved through debates.[25]

Political debates perform an epideictic function by renewing the democratic character of the community. Arguments unify the political community because candidates must shape appeals that transcend political differences. As Aristotle notes, rhetors must take into account their audience when making a speech of praise.[26] Although presidential campaign rhetoric is necessarily an appeal on behalf of a candidate, a candidate's arguments must transcend partisan interests in some way. Because arguments are defining characteristics of democracy, a candidate who argues well provides evidence that he or she can embody and defend the values of the community he or she represents and that the political system is worthy of praise for the strong candidates that it produces.

Presidential campaigns are also opportunities to reexamine political values. In this respect, debates serve as opportunities to reexamine the character of the community because the character of the community is reflected in the moral quality of the candidate's dialogue. Also, because the values and moral qualities of competing political programs are represented by the candidates in a political debate, argument functions as a method for reexamining and altering community values. Presumably, since the audience uses community norms to evaluate the candidates' performances, its choices represent the preferred values and character of the community. Thus, altering the values and character of the community is accomplished through rational discussion of alternatives in debates. In this regard, political debates celebrate and renew the democratic ethos of the community by proving rhetorically that it is through good reason that we alter our values, priorities, or policies, not by force or subterfuge. This element is vital to the character of a democracy.[27]

Regardless of their outcomes, debates reinforce democratic values and reassure audiences that the democratic system is working as it should. Whether audience members make up their minds on the basis of the policies discussed, the positions taken, or the delivery of the candidates is not as significant as the fact that the candidates fight for office rhetorically, by arguing in full view of audiences that expect their leaders to symbolize their most precious democratic value: choice through rational dialogue. When candidates no longer need to justify their actions to an audience made up of members of the community, when candidates can do as they wish in the name of democracy without accountability to the citizenry, or when candidates do what they wish and provide poor accounts to the public, then a serious problem has developed in the system. Political debates serve an epideictic function, then, by renewing the democratic character of the community when it has been severely tested.

Given the use of Aristotelian concepts as a starting point, my critical approach relies on the model of neoclassical criticism developed by Gerald P. Mohrmann and Michael Leff in their analysis of Lincoln at Cooper Union.[28] The most fundamental reason for adopting this approach is their emphasis of purpose as a way of unifying the analysis of a rhetorical text. Since previous analyses of debates have left rhetorical purpose largely unexplored and because debates are composed of a series of short speeches,[29] an approach that seeks ways of making sense of the many textual pieces that constitute presidential debates seemed appropriate.

In their analysis of Lincoln's Cooper Union address, Mohrmann and Leff began with Paul Rosenthal's distinction between nonpersonal persuasion and personal persuasion.[30] Nonpersonal persuasion concerns issues of policy, personal persuasion has as its purpose the promotion of a speaker. Adapting this distinction to campaign discourse, Mohrmann and Leff argued that "the ultimate goal of the campaign orator is to promote himself as a candidate. Both policies and character are in question, but the treatment of issues is subsidiary to the purpose of creating a general identification between the speaker and the audience."[31] This conceptualization of purpose is particularly relevant for political debates given the fact that Rosenthal's original distinction arose from his study of the 1960 debates. Thus, debates involve arguments over policies and character, but in a debate the speaker's primary purpose is to shape a desirable image of presidential character. According to Mohrmann and Leff, "The listeners act as judges of a future event, an election: the end is to effect a judgment of the candidate, a judgment based on character and upon the treatment of issues."[32]

The role of the critic, then, is to reveal the ways in which the language choices of the candidates formulate a favorable image of presidential character. But to do this requires a close examination of the discourse that constitutes the debates. According to Leff, critics who use this approach "must move from what is given in the text to something that they themselves produce—an account of the rhetorical dynamics implicit within it. At a minimum, this act of interpretation requires a means to justify the identification of significant features in the text and to explain the interactions among the features."[33] Because there is no objective procedure to guide the critic, a critical focus must be argued.[34]

Debates pose interesting problems for critics, however. Instead of one integrated unit of discourse authored by a single rhetor, debates are composed of a series of short speeches.[35] Thus, the rhetorical action of a debate is concerned with how well each candidate enacts the role of president, over time, in the course of a debate. The critic's task, then, is to identify the moments in a debate when the dramatic action shaped each candidate's character. A key aspect to understanding how a candidate's image is shaped in a debate is a consideration of time, or the temporal dimension, of a candidate's performance. According to Leff, textual analysis must take into account internal and external dimensions of time.[36] In debates, the internal dimension of time is seen in the progression of dramatic action; the external dimension of time is related to the ways in which the language choices of each candidate are directed toward a fitting or appropriate response to a situation that develops at some point in the debate. Each of these dimensions of time can be understood more fully if one considers the dramatic nature of the debates as dialectical encounters.

There is a relationship between the campaign and the debate reminiscent of Kenneth Burke's concept of container and thing contained.[37] The drama of the campaign contains the debate as the debate contains the larger drama of the campaign. All of the discourse exchanged in the campaign up to the time of a debate may be considered potential options to be exercised in shaping a presidential image. Nomination acceptance speeches feature a number of claims about a candidate's political vision that are tested in the course of the campaign and often find their way into the debate. Throughout the campaign, both candidates try out different ways of creating issues for the opposition and resolving problems with their own political image. Those elements of the campaign that each candidate finds successful may be used in the course of the debate as part of an image strategy.[38] But not all of the arguments of each candidate can be introduced into the debate because the form of the discourse necessitates choices about how to construct and defend the most desirable image. Although discourse during the campaign features many different rhetorical possibilities for the construction of a candidate's image, the debate is the event in which these possibilities can be actualized through dramatic enactment. In the debate, each candidate must choose his or her words in a way that will withstand dialectical scrutiny from the panelists and the opponent.

Also, debates are unique opportunities for assessing presidential qualities because dialectical discourse constrains the rhetorical action of the candidates. When debates pit two candidates against each other for the purpose of presenting and supporting opposing views, and there exists the opportunity for immediate response, conflicts in style and substance create opportunities for argument over campaign issues and qualities of leadership. Conflicts in style and substance are embodied in language, giving form to arguments and creating a dialectic from which an audience chooses a national leader based on rhetorical strengths and weaknesses.[39] A "presidential" image, then, is formed or eroded in a candidate's pattern of response to symbolic challenges from the opposing candidate.[40]

Furthermore, debates invite candidates to rhetorically perform the role of president. As a form of political discourse, arguments are appropriate for presidential campaigns because they require opposing positions, invite attack and defense, and force a choice between alternatives. The clash of contending forces takes form in arguments over the desirability of candidates and their programs. The strength and desirability of competing political programs is directly related to each candidate's ability to argue, to demonstrate what is preferable for the community during the course of the debate. When Democratic and Republican candidates typically represent a choice between two alternatives, the candidate's ability to argue is symbolic of his or her ability to lead. As Gronbeck has argued, the presidential campaign is a symbolic test of a candidate's mettle, and the mettle of candidates is revealed in their language choices in the course of the campaign.[41]

Debates, then, constitute crucial tests for candidates; they summarize dramatically the larger dialectical encounter of the campaign. They are unique opportunities for the dramatic enactment of leadership because candidates are forced to choose what presidential image to offer; because these images are tested in dialectical encounters, they reveal the character of the candidates.[42] In these ways, debates contain the dialectical essence of the campaign.[43]

Time affects the dramatic action in three ways. In an external sense, when a candidate responds to a panelist's question or an opponent's argument, each response can potentially function as a key moment in debate.[44] Not only can the panelists' questions create a rhetorical problem for a candidate in any of the exchanges, but also a candidate can be attacked by the opposing candidate as well. Follow-up questions from panelists and refutation from the other candidate can also constitute threats to a candidate's image. In these situations, the inability to solve a rhetorical problem or respond satisfactorily to a symbolic threat provides important information about a candidate's ability to defend his presidential image. These situations are opportunities to demonstrate, symbolically, a candidate's ability to lead by summarizing in a specific test of presidential character the larger conflicts between the candidates. Thus, these exchanges are potentially significant because they give specific symbolic form to the political images being examined by the audience.[45]

Internally, opening and closing statements can affect the ways in which an audience experiences a candidate's political image. Opening statements give candidates an opportunity to create a favorable context for their language choices in the debate. Candidates can establish the tone, define the central issue of the campaign, or offer a specific vision of leadership for the country and in these ways prepare the audience for what follows. Closing statements are opportunities for candidates to recoup losses by recontextualizing previous language choices. Candidates can correct mistakes, focus the deliberation of the audience on specific issues, or solve rhetorical problems they were unable to remedy earlier in the debate. Opening and closing statements are potentially important moments in political debates because they allow the candidates to select and define the issues they consider crucial to the outcome of the campaign as well as refocusing, redefining, and recontextualizing the internal dynamics of the debate in ways that are most favorable to them.

Examining a candidate's pattern of response to symbolic challenges constitutes a third way in which time affects the development of a candidate's image. A pattern of response can take substantive or stylistic form. By responding to the substantive demands of a question or an opposing argument, a candidate shows that he or she has the intelligence to formulate an argument to defend his or her images or programs. By consistently answering attacks on his or her image, a candidate demonstrates an ability to defend against symbolic attacks.

A candidate's stylistic choices can complement, amplify, and enlarge a particular image of leadership. For example, by responding with words that express an argument concisely and persuasively, a candidate provides stylistic evidence of his or her ability to act decisively. Alternatively, when candidates cannot muster concise explanations of their positions, they give symbolic evidence of faltering in a situation that calls for sure action. Rhetorical style, then, can be as important to understanding the political image of a candidate as substantive appeals.[46] In these ways, debates provide critics with an opportunity to assess candidates' political images by examining their language choices in response to symbolic challenges from panelists and opposing candidates.

All of this means that in a debate, presidential candidates are called upon to perform, rhetorically, the role of president.[47] Watching the debate, an audience experiences a vision of the future; it sees how the candidates perform as president.[48] Approaching debates from the perspective of rhetorical enactment makes sense given Leff and Sachs's most recent use of the concept of iconicity, which asserts that "above the level of the word, discursive form often enacts representational content."[49] Aristotle, too, advised critics to examine not only the content of a speaker's arguments but also the way those arguments are made.[50] Thus, in presidential debates, because of the nature of the situation and the purpose and role played by the rhetors, form and content are related in important ways. Political argument is as much composed of claims, evidence, and reasoning as it is stylistic elements of rhetorical action. Accounting for the ways in which these two aspects of discourse are interrelated in the formation of presidential images can reveal some of the ways in which debates might contribute important information about candidate character.

One further note on how I have approached the debates seems in order. The nature of the discourse makes an objective entry point unfeasible. From an Aristotelian perspective, political rhetoric deals with opinion, not certifiable knowledge, and the substance of the debate concerns future possibility, not certainties concerning policy outcomes.[51]

Presidential candidates argue about who is best fit to be president and whose policies will benefit the nation. Often, the arguments cannot be evaluated with respect to an objective truth criterion. Because the audience evaluates the character of the candidates by watching how they treat issues of policy and character,[52] advocacy skills should be evaluated in relation to the opposing candidate's rhetorical abilities. The criteria for a successful performance, then, must be derived from the debate, between who better responds to the challenge provided by the panelists and the opposing candidate. Although this complicates generalizing across the debates and the campaigns in which they occurred what constitutes a "good" debate performance, what we may find is that enactments of presidential character are very much bound by the context of the debate and campaign in which they occurred. But the absence of objective criteria for evaluating political debates should not stand in the way of studying how candidates use language to present and defend a political image.

What follows is an examination of how presidential and vice presidential candidates' language choices shaped appealing images of political character and solved important problems in these images of character, as well as how some of those language choices failed in these endeavors. This approach is applied to the 1960, 1976, 1980, 1984, and 1988 presidential debates and to the 1976, 1984, and 1988 vice presidential debates. The analysis of each series of debates begins with an introduction and focuses discussion on the most important aspects of political image for each of the candidates and then develops a case for understanding the ways in which the debates revealed the rhetorical strengths and weaknesses of each candidate's performance. I have assumed that the reader is relatively familiar with each of the debates. Even so, I have tried to include as much of the text of the debate as I can in order to create a context for understanding the candidates' discourse and so that my audience can evaluate my claims about each of the candidates' rhetorical choices. Finally, to provide some referent points for those who wish to consider the excerpts that I have quoted in relation to the larger text of the debate, I have used the term "exchanges" to mark off specific portions of the debates. An exchange can be considered one complete unit of the format that usually includes an initial question asked of both candidates by a panelist, their answers to the initial question, a follow-up question asked of both candidates by the same panelist who asked the initial question, their answers to the follow-up question, and each candidate's rebuttal when called for by the format.

NOTES

1. Kathleen Hall Jamieson and David S. Birdsell, *Presidential Debates: The Challenge of Creating an Informed Electorate* (New York: Oxford University Press,

1988), 6. For an exception to this rule see Robert G. Meadow, "A Speech by Any Other Name," *Critical Studies in Mass Communication* 4 (June 1987): 207–210. Sidney Kraus classifies those who evaluate debates in three groups: proponents, conditional, and opponents. See "Voters Win," *Critical Studies in Mass Communication* 4 (June 1987): 214.

2. John Louis Lucaites makes this observation in "Rhetorical Legitimacy, <Public Trust> and the Presidential Debates," *Argumentation and Advocacy* 25 (Spring 1989): 231.

3. For suggestions to improve format, see J. Jeffery Auer, "The Counterfeit Debates," in *The Great Debates*, ed. Sidney Kraus (Bloomington, IN: Indiana University Press, 1962), 142–150; Nelson W. Polsby, "Debatable Thoughts on Presidential Debates," in *The Past and Future of Presidential Debates*, ed. Austin Ranney (Washington, DC: American Enterprise Institute, 1979), 184; Jack Germond and Jules Witcover, "Presidential Debates: An Overview," in *Presidential Debates*, 200; J. Jeffery Auer, "Great Myths about the Great Debates," *Speaker and Gavel* 18 (Winter 1981): 14–21; Lloyd Bitzer and Theodore Rueter, *Carter vs. Ford: The Counterfeit Debates of 1976* (Madison, WI: The University of Wisconsin Press, 1980); Michael Pfau, "Criteria and Format to Optimize Political Debates: An Analysis of South Dakota's 'Election '80' Series," *Journal of the American Forensics Association* 19 (Spring 1983): 205; Robert C. Rowland and Rey Garcia, "The 1984 Democratic Debates: Does Format Make a Difference?" in *Argument and Social Practice: Proceedings of the Fourth SCA/AFA Conference on Argumentation*, ed. J. Robert Cox, Malcolm O. Sillars, and Gregg B. Walker (Annandale, VA: SCA, 1985), 233; Jamieson and Birdsell, *Presidential Debates*, 201. Candidates have been reluctant to adopt recommendations for various strategic and tactical reasons. See Polsby, *The Past and Future of Presidential Debates*, 185; Newton N. Minnow and Clifford M. Sloan, *For Great Debates: A New Plan for Future Presidential TV Debates* (New York: Priority Press, 1987), 35; Dennis K. Davis, "Review and Criticism," *Critical Studies in Mass Communication* 4 (June 1987): 201; Kraus, "Voters Win," 215. Recently, David S. Birdsell has argued that scholars might be better off "dealing with debates as they are, rather than as they might someday be." See David S. Birdsell, "Introduction," *Argumentation and Advocacy* 27 (Winter 1991): 97. Also, Carlin et al. have argued that "those of us interested in political debates should be less concerned with the form of the debates and should perhaps take a more active role in commenting on them in ways which reach the public and enhance their understanding of the events they have witnessed." See Diana Prentice Carlin, Charles Howard, Susan Stanfield, and Larry Reynolds, "The Effects of Presidential Debate Formats on Clash: A Comparative Analysis," *Argumentation and Advocacy* 27 (Winter 1991): 135.

4. Exceptions to this claim can be found in the following studies: Patricia A. Sullivan, "The 1984 Vice-Presidential Debate: A Case Study of Female and Male Framing in Political Campaigns," *Communication Quarterly* 37 (Fall 1989): 329; Donn V. Parson, "Congregation by Segregation: An Analysis of the Argument Strategies in the First 1988 Presidential Debate," in *Spheres of Argument: Proceedings of the Sixth SCA/AFA Conference on Argumentation*, ed. Bruce Gronbeck (Annandale, VA: SCA, 1989), 136–139; Jamieson and Birdsell's list of rhetorical and political functions that debates perform, *Presidential Debates*, chap. 5; Lucaites, "Rhetorical Legitimacy," 231; John Murphy, "Presidential Debates and Cam-

paign Rhetoric: Text Within Context," *Southern Journal of Speech Communication*, 57 (Spring 1992): 219–28.

5. Auer, "The Counterfeit Debates"; Bitzer and Rueter, *The Counterfeit Debates of 1976*.

6. Stephen Hess, *The Presidential Campaign*, rev. ed. (Washington, DC: The Brookings Institution, 1978).

7. Jamieson and Birdsell, *Presidential Debates*, 129; 163.

8. H. McCloskey, "Consensus and Ideology in American Politics," *American Political Science Review* 58 (1964): 361–382.

9. Roderick Hart, "A Commentary on Popular Assumptions about Political Communication," *Human Communication Research* 8 (Summer 1982): 366–389.

10. Jamieson and Birdsell, *Presidential Debates*, 198.

11. E. A. Hinck, "Enacting the Presidency: A Rhetorical Analysis of Twentieth Century Presidential Debates,"(Ph.D. dissertation, University of Kansas, May 1987). See also Jamieson and Birdsell, *Presidential Debates*, 4, 139–142.

12. Aristotle, *Politics* (1277 a–b), trans. Ernest Barker (London: Oxford University Press, 1977), 99. See also Gail Sheehy, *Character: America's Search for Leadership* (New York: William Morrow, 1988), 11–36; James D. Barber, *The Presidential Character*, 3rd ed. (Englewood Cliffs, NJ: Prentice-Hall, 1985).

13. Aristotle, *Rhetoric* (1366a5–15), trans. W. Rhys Roberts (New York: Modern Library, 1954), 55–56.

14. Ibid.

15. Walter Fisher, "Rhetorical Fiction and the Presidency," *Quarterly Journal of Speech* 66 (April 1980): 119–126.

16. Aristotle, *Rhetoric* (1354b30), 21.

17. Jamieson and Birdsell, *Presidential Debates*, 3.

18. Aristotle, *Rhetoric* (1392a1–10), 129.

19. Ibid., 91.

20. Ibid., 58.

21. V. William Balthrop, "Argument as Linguistic Opportunity," in *Proceedings of the Summer Conference on Argumentation*, ed. Jack Rhodes and Sara Newell (Alta, UT: SCA/AFA, 1980), 184–213.

22. Aristotle, *Rhetoric* (1367b30–35), 61.

23. Karlyn Kohrs Campbell and Kathleen Hall Jamieson, "Form and Genre in Rhetorical Criticism: An Introduction," in *Form and Genre: Shaping Rhetorical Action*, ed. Karlyn Kohrs Campbell and Kathleen Hall Jamieson (Falls Church, VA: SCA, 1977), 9–32; Kathleen Campbell, "Enactment as a Rhetorical Strategy in 'The Year of Living Dangerously,' " *Central States Speech Journal* 39 (Fall/Winter 1988): 258; Charles Kauffman, "Poetic as Argument," *Quarterly Journal of Speech* 67 (November 1981): 41; Bruce Gronbeck, "Functional and Dramaturgical Theories of Presidential Campaigning," *Presidential Studies Quarterly* 14 (Fall 1984): 494–495. See also James E. Combs, *Dimensions of Political Drama* (Santa Monica, CA: Goodyear, 1980), 1–17.

24. Gladys Engel Lang, "Still Seeking Answers," *Critical Studies in Mass Communication* 4 (June 1987): 212.

25. S. Michael Halloran, "Doing Public Business in Public," in *Form and Genre: Shaping Rhetorical Action*, ed. Karlyn Kohrs Campbell and Kathleen Hall Jamieson (Falls Church, VA: SCA, 1977), 118–38.

26. Aristotle, *Rhetoric* (1367b10), 60.

27. Jamieson and Birdsell, *Presidential Debates*, 10.

28. Michael C. Leff and G. P. Mohrmann, "Lincoln at Cooper Union: A Rhetorical Analysis of the Text," *Quarterly Journal of Speech* 60 (October 1974): 346; G. P. Mohrmann and Michael C. Leff, "Lincoln at Cooper Union: A Rationale for Neo-Classical Criticism," *Quarterly Journal of Speech* 60 (December 1974): 459.

29. The two problems that debates pose for scholars are how to conceptualize them and how to evaluate them rationally. See Harold D. Lasswell, "Introduction," in *The Great Debates*, ed. Sidney Kraus (Bloomington, IN: University of Indiana Press, 1962), 19.

30. Paul I. Rosenthal, "The Concept of Ethos and the Structure of Persuasion," *Speech Monographs* 33 (June 1966): 114.

31. Leff and Mohrmann, "Lincoln at Cooper Union: A Rhetorical Analysis of the Text," 348.

32. Mohrmann and Leff, "Lincoln at Cooper Union: A Rationale for Neo-Classical Criticism," 464.

33. Michael Leff, "Textual Criticism: The Legacy of G. P. Mohrmann," *Quarterly Journal of Speech* 72 (1986): 378.

34. Lawrence W. Rosenfield, "Anatomy of Critical Discourse," *Speech Monographs* 25 (March 1968): 55; Wayne Brockriede, "Rhetorical Criticism as Argument," *Quarterly Journal of Speech* 60 (April 1974): 171; Karlyn Kohrs Campbell, "The Nature of Criticism in Rhetorical and Communicative Studies," *Central States Speech Journal* 30 (Spring 1979): 10.

35. Jamieson and Birdsell provide an excellent explanation of why debates take the form that they do. See *Presidential Debates*, 118, for a summary of the sources of amalgamation.

36. Leff, "Textual Criticism: The Legacy of G. P. Mohrmann," 383.

37. Kenneth Burke, *A Grammar of Motives* (Berkeley, CA: University of California Press, 1969), 3–15.

38. Myles Martel, *Political Campaign Debates: Images, Strategies and Tactics* (New York: Longman, 1983).

39. Kenneth Burke, *A Grammar of Motives* (Berkeley, CA: University of California Press, 1969), 323–441.

40. Discovering patterns of response reveals much about the speaker. See Roderick Hart, *Verbal Style and the Presidency: A Computer Based Analysis* (New York: Academic Press, 1984), chap. 1 and 2, 1–66; also Jamieson and Birdsell, *Presidential Debates*, 142.

41. Bruce Gronbeck, "The Functions of Presidential Campaigning," *Communication Monographs* 45 (November 1978): 268–280.

42. Gronbeck, "Functional and Dramaturgical Theories of Presidential Campaigning," 484–495.

43. I am grateful to Professor Sam Becker of the University of Iowa for suggesting this relationship between debates and the larger context of the campaign in his critique of an earlier version of my analysis of the 1980 Reagan-Carter debate, "Enacting Leadership through Political Debate: A Rhetorical Analysis of the 1980 Presidential Debate between Ronald Reagan and Jimmy Carter (Paper presented at the Doctoral Honors Seminar, Ohio University, Athens, Ohio, May 1984).

44. Burke, *Grammar of Motives*, 59–62.

45. Ibid., 60.

46. For a discussion of the importance of rhetorical style, see Karlyn Kohrs Campbell and Kathleen Hall Jamieson, "Form and Genre in Rhetorical Criticism: An Introduction," 9–32.

47. Ibid. Campbell and Jamieson also discuss the rhetorical strategy of enactment.

48. Michael Leff and Andrew Sachs, "Words the Most Like Things: Iconicity and the Rhetorical Text," *Western Journal of Speech Communication* 54 (Summer 1990): 256.

49. Ibid., 258.

50. Aristotle, *Rhetoric* (1366a10–15), 61.

51. Ibid., 28.

52. Mohrmann and Leff, 464.

Chapter Two

The First Kennedy-Nixon Debate

The first debate was the key to the campaign in 1960. According to Theodore Sorenson, "The four debates, and the first in particular played a decisive role in the election results."[1] Earl Mazo, a press correspondent who followed the 1960 campaign, noted how the mood in the campaign switched completely after the first debate, leading Kennedy staffers to gain new confidence in the ability of their candidate to handle Nixon.[2] In addition to polls confirming the effect of Kennedy's performance on the audience,[3] Kennedy received the support of southern Democratic governors who were crucial to the campaign and had been holding out to see how the Democratic contender would stand up to Nixon.[4] Because the debate occurred early in the campaign, was witnessed by the largest audience, and featured Kennedy's best performance, it shaped the rest of the 1960 campaign.

This chapter explains how in the opening statement Kennedy enacted a desirable image of presidential leadership and placed Nixon in the position of defending the status quo while simultaneously calling for change. In two key exchanges over leadership and experience, Kennedy eliminated doubts concerning his qualifications for office. In Sander Vanocur's questions concerning Nixon's contributions to the Eisenhower administration, Nixon was unable to suggest himself in a role larger than that of a vice president. In the exchange over farm surplus, teacher's salaries, and legislative enactment, Kennedy was effective in attacking the desirability of the Republican platform. Finally, in the closing statements, Kennedy reinforced his framework for interpreting the debate while Nixon failed to refute Kennedy's concept of presidential leadership. In these ways, Kennedy reshaped the issues and the images of the 1960 campaign in the first debate.

THE OPENING STATEMENTS: KENNEDY BECOMES PRESIDENT

Kennedy began his opening statement by establishing a powerful way of viewing his candidacy. The thesis of the speech, like that of Kennedy's campaign, was that the nation had to get moving again. In presenting this thesis, though, Kennedy implicitly presented himself as contemporary version of Abraham Lincoln:

Mr. Smith, Mr. Nixon. In the election of 1860, Abraham Lincoln said the question was whether this nation could exist half-slave or half-free. In the election of 1960, and with the world around us, the question is whether the world will exist half slave or half free, whether it will move in the direction of freedom, in the direction of the road that we are taking or whether it will move in the direction of slavery.

By stating the issue in dramatic terms reminiscent of Lincoln, Kennedy suggested that he had the same kind of vision that Lincoln had had 100 years earlier. Kennedy then defined the issue for the audience to consider—Are we moving in the direction of freedom?—and then established a criterion for evaluating whether or not the nation was moving in the direction of freedom at a sufficient pace: "I think it will depend in great measure upon what we do here in the United States, on the kind of society that we build, on the kind of strength that we maintain." Kennedy's focus on action—"what we do here in the United States"— and his criterion of strength suggested that the leader who maintained his positions in these debates was stylistically better suited for office. Thus, Kennedy begins a pattern of uniting style and substance to demonstrate strength in action.

Support for the claim that the issue was whether the world would remain half-slave or half-free was evident in Kennedy's reference to Khrushchev: "We discuss tonight domestic issues, but I would not want that to be . . . any implication to be given that this does not involve directly our struggle with Mr. Khrushchev for survival." Kennedy's use of Khrushchev highlighted the symbolic significance of the debate. It was not only a test of the candidate's programs but also a test of their ability to stand up under pressure from threatening forces. When Kennedy directed the audience's attention to Khrushchev's presence in New York, he provided additional evidence of the fact that the public was witnessing a test of leadership ability in the debate: "Mr. Khrushchev is in New York and he maintains the Communist offensive throughout the world because of the productive power of the Soviet Union, itself." So Kennedy's strategy of tying domestic issues to foreign policy and the symbolic threat of Khrushchev highlighted his view that the prestige of American leadership was on trial. One aspect of Kennedy's strategy, then, was to embody American prestige. If Kennedy's language choices reflected a more stylistically appealing candidate, the audience could "try out" Kennedy as the new challenger to Khrushchev.

To substantiate his criticism of the Republican party's programs and leadership, Kennedy offered eight indictments of the Eisenhower administration—each one supporting the claim that we were not doing enough and that "these are all things I think in this country that can make our society strong or can mean that it stands still."

1. Fifty percent of our steel mills are unused (statistic).

2. The United States has the lowest rate of economic growth of any major industrial nation in 1959 (statistical comparison).

   A. Economic growth means strength and vitality.

   B. Economic growth allows us to sustain our defenses.

   C. Economic growth means we are able to keep commitments abroad.

3. $9 billion worth of food is kept—some of rotting while

   A. There is a hungry world.

   B. 4 million Americans wait every month for a food package (statistic).

   C. There are cases in West Virginia where kids take part of their lunch home to feed others (illustration).

4. The Soviet Union is turning out twice as many scientists and engineers as we are (statistical comparison).

5. Many of our teachers are inadequately paid.

   A. Many of our children go to school on part-time shifts (example).

   B. We should have an education system second to none (comparison with the Soviet Union in point four)

6. Criminals like Jimmy Hoffa go free (example of an inadequate criminal justice system).

7. We have failed to develop our natural resources to the fullest (example).

   A. The Soviet Union will surpass us by 1975 (comparison).

   B. Much of a major industrial nation's power is its use of natural resources (hence, by implication, the Soviet Union will be a superior power).

8. Not every American enjoys full Constitutional rights (example).

   A. Negroes, Puerto Ricans, Mexicans have

      1. One-half the chance to get through school as whites.

      2. One-third the chance to get through college as whites.

      3. One-third the chance to be a professional as whites.

4. One-half the chance to own a house.

5. Four times the chance to be out of work than whites (examples of statistical comparison).

Kennedy's strategy of enumerating the problems that the nation faced allowed him to appeal to many different groups of Americans in terms of their professional interests, values, and demographic characteristics. Kennedy's use of statistics enabled him to talk about widespread problems, and the illustrations, comparisons, and examples made the problems vivid and immediate for the audience. The tightly packed brief of particulars, the different forms of evidentiary support, and the various groups to which Kennedy was appealing reflected his attempt to embody "national substance" by arguing on behalf of the various groups that composed the national community.

Kennedy extended this embodiment of national substance by anticipating argument from the opposition, refuting potential criticisms, and appealing in a vivid way to farmers and the aged. In his appeal to the aged, Kennedy invoked the memory of Franklin D. Roosevelt and rehearsed himself in the role of FDR assuming leadership in a time of crisis. By developing historical parallels between the elections of 1860, 1932, and 1960, Kennedy showed the audience that these were similar historical situations and implied that they called for similar instances of leadership. Kennedy's strategy, then, attempted to focus the audience members' attention through the historical lenses of 1860 and 1932 on listening for the candidate whose words came closest to what they remembered about Lincoln and FDR. Kennedy's use of FDR's persona was important in other respects. It connected him to the Democratic tradition, allowed the audience to see him in the role of a president who appealed to members of both parties, and distanced him from potential rhetorical liabilities associated with the Truman administration.

Substantively, the historical parallels developed by Kennedy's opening statement did not constitute an argument that could be analyzed or refuted easily by Nixon, but the references to Lincoln and Roosevelt constituted a powerful symbolic context for interpreting the language choices of the candidates. Roosevelt, like Lincoln, took office in time of great national crisis. If Nixon did not refute the comparison in some way, Kennedy's frame for understanding the campaign would enhance the persuasive impact of his indictments of the Eisenhower administration, create the impression that we were in a similar crisis period in which strong leadership on the domestic front was necessary to maintaining strength in foreign affairs, and suggest himself in the role of a leader ready, willing, and able to get the nation moving again. Whether the nation actually faced such a crisis was less important than the fact that Kennedy's parallels suggested its existence. Kennedy, like Lincoln and Roosevelt, would appear to be campaigning at a time of great crisis, setting the tone of the campaign, and establishing the expectations for leadership.

One aspect of Kennedy's vision of leadership was an appeal to the audience's national pride. When Kennedy stated, "I want people in Latin America and Africa and Asia to start to look to America to see how we're doing things, to wonder what the president of the United States is doing, and not to look at Khrushchev or look at the Chinese Communists," he defined the role of the United States as a leader among nations, focused the audience's attention on the Communist competition, and offered some evidence of the fact that he was qualified for the job by being able to define the problem and explain a solution. Later, in the exchange over Vanocur's question dealing with school construction, Kennedy would enact this role of president more clearly when he stated: "I think that what we have to do, however, is have the president and the leadership set before our country exactly what we must do in the next decade if we're going to maintain our security in education, in economic growth, in development of natural resources."

Kennedy invoked the persona of FDR when he stated, "In 1933 Franklin Roosevelt said in his inaugural that this generation of Americans has a "rendezvous with destiny." I think our generation of Americans has the same rendezvous." In speaking FDR's words, Kennedy tapped the legacy of American history of fortitude under fire, advancement over adversity, and suggested himself in the role of FDR by recognizing a new vision for this generation—triumph over communism. Thus, Kennedy's concluding question was a dramatic and fitting end to the crisis he had suggested for the audience: "The question now is: Can freedom be maintained under the most severe tack—attack it has ever known?" More dramatically, Kennedy's answer—"I think it can be"—reflected confidence, a characteristic quality of the leadership of FDR and of any competent leader during a crisis. If the audience accepted Kennedy's rhetorical frame for interpreting the 1960 campaign, the issues would become as serious as those of 1932. Once established, this framework implied choosing a candidate with the abilities equal to an FDR or Abraham Lincoln, and by fusing their qualities of leadership with his own words, he presented himself as a knowledgeable, confident candidate. Unless Nixon could offer an equally appealing image or an equally convincing use of past presidential rhetoric, Kennedy would appear as the more appealing choice. The emphasis on action was evident throughout the speech and constituted a recurring campaign theme: "I think in the final analysis it depends upon what we do here. I think it's time America started moving again."

Kennedy's opening statement is a good example of how a candidate can constrain an opponent's rhetorical ground by forcing him to enact an established concept of the presidency in a superior way or define a more desirable image of leadership for the nation. At this point, Nixon had to refute Kennedy's characterization of the present system by proving that America was moving with the Republican administration or demonstrate that America would move more quickly and effectively under his leadership. However, Nixon's opening statement did not present a desirable image of leadership for the audience. Nixon's inabilities begin with his introduction in which he accepted Kennedy's definition of the issues for the campaign.

There is no question but that we cannot discuss our internal affairs in the United States without recognizing that they have a tremendous bearing on our international position. There is no question but this nation cannot stand still, because we are in a deadly competition, a competition not only with the men in the Kremlin but the men in Peking. We're ahead in this competition, as Senator Kennedy, I think, has implied. But when you're in a race, the only way to stay ahead is to move ahead, and I subscribe completely to the spirit that Senator Kennedy has expressed tonight, the spirit that the United States should move ahead.

Admitting the existence of problems can be an appropriate strategy especially if the problems are obvious to the audience and the candidate has a defensible solution to propose. But here Nixon accepted Kennedy's definition of the central issue in the campaign—that we need to get America moving again. Stylistically, Nixon was unable to define a favorable point of contrast for his candidacy. Although Nixon tried to restate Kennedy's words to suit his rhetorical needs, the awkward syntax highlighted his inability to define and distinguish his candidacy as Kennedy did. When Nixon tried to establish the differences between them, he stated the contrast ambiguously, implicitly contradicting himself: "I think we disagree on the implication of his remarks tonight and on the statements that he has made on many occasions during his campaign to the effect that the United States has been standing still." Nixon did not explain what he meant by the "implication of his [Kennedy's] remarks," did not offer a comparison between what Kennedy had said in the campaign and in the opening statement, and contradicted his previous words when he said that the United States had not been standing still. In short, Nixon's language choices did not, in a substantive way, distinguish his position in the debate from Kennedy's opening position.

When Nixon chose to refute Kennedy's criticisms of the Eisenhower administration, he failed to attribute the successes to specific contributions he had made. For example, Nixon answered Kennedy's contention that the United States had had the lowest economic growth in gross national product by distinguishing the years of economic recession from those of economic recovery:

We heard tonight, for example, the statement made that our growth and national product last year was the lowest of any industrial nation in the world. Now, last year, of course, was 1958. That happened to be a recession year, but when we look at the growth of GNP this year—a year of recovery—we find that it's 6.9 percent and one of the highest in the world today.

Nixon refuted Kennedy's claim by distinguishing years of economic recovery from recession, but he missed an opportunity to attribute the recovery to specific actions taken by the Eisenhower administration. Even later, Nixon failed to attribute economic growth to any particular action that he or the administration took: "When we compare the growth in this administration with that of the previous administration, that then there was a total growth of 11 percent over seven years; in this administration there has been a total growth of 19 percent over seven years." In both instances, Nixon relied on the audience to attribute these successes to actions taken by the Eisenhower administration.

Stylistically, Nixon's use of language suggested him in the role of a witness or an observer to the accomplishments of the Eisenhower administration. In his transition to a direct refutation of Kennedy's claim that we were standing still, Nixon asked a series of rhetorical questions: "Is the United States standing still? Is it true that this administration, as Senator Kennedy has charged, has been an administration of retreat, of defeat, of stagnation? Is it true that as far as this country is concerned in the field of electric power, and all of the fields that he has mentioned, we have not been moving ahead?" All of these questions would be answered negatively by a Republican audience and although Nixon was making use of Eisenhower's popularity to counter Kennedy's charge of retreat and defeat, the strategy did little to enhance Nixon's image as an effective leader. Nixon was defending the Eisenhower administration, not his proposed administration and in this sense, Nixon's image as vice president dominated his attempt to embody the Republican spirit. Unable to demonstrate a rhetorical style reflecting his own presidential qualities, Nixon presented himself in the more limited role of Eisenhower's vice president.

In addition to presenting himself in the more limited persona of Eisenhower's vice president, Nixon's refutation of Kennedy's claims was meager. First, Nixon failed to substantiate a number of claims addressing Kennedy's charges. For example, Nixon suggested that the ways to answer Kennedy's question—are we doing enough?—was to compare the seven and a half years under Truman with the seven and a half years under Eisenhower. The comparison focused on schools, hydroelectric power, construction of hospitals, and highways. In each of these examples, Nixon stated only that Eisenhower's administration built more than Truman's. No statistics were offered, leaving the probative value of the evidence resting on Nixon's credibility to make accurate comparisons.

Second, Nixon did not explain why Kennedy's programs were retreads of Truman's. This argument was one of Nixon's most important contentions. If Nixon could substantiate this claim, he would do serious damage to Kennedy's frame for understanding the campaign and undercut the use of Kennedy's appeal to the tradition of FDR. On this issue, Nixon's use of evidence was disappointing. In attacking Kennedy's assertion that his programs could improve on the Republican record, Nixon stated, "When we look at the various programs, that he [Kennedy] offers, they do not seem to be new. They seem to be simply retreads of the programs of the Truman administration which preceded him." No examples, illustrations, or statements from Nixon were offered. Nixon's message appealed only to Republican members of the audience. Nixon's choice to use the word "seem" communicated an element of uncertainty: If the programs were not retreads in substance, but only in appearance, he had not supported his claim with sufficient evidence to prove Kennedy heir to Truman. Further, Nixon's argument was weak because he challenged Kennedy to refute that which was as yet unproven: "And I would suggest that during the course of the evening he [Kennedy] might indicate those areas in which his programs are new, where they will mean more progress than we had then." However, Kennedy had already distinguished himself apart from the Truman administration by borrowing the words of FDR and Lincoln. Nixon's challenge, then, begged the question and failed to refute the frame of reference established by Kennedy.

Overall, Nixon's opening statement added more support for Kennedy's claim, did not draw a sharp distinction between the policies advocated by the two candidates, failed to refute the perception of imminent crisis established by Kennedy, and accepted Kennedy's terms for measuring the progress of the nation. Although Nixon did a good job of refuting Kennedy's claims that the economy had not fared well under Republican leadership and did a good job of appealing to his Republican constituency, he was unable to develop more than a vice presidential persona. Most importantly, almost nothing was done to counter Kennedy's use of the personae of FDR and Lincoln. Thus, the opening statements contrasted Kennedy as FDR and Lincoln, Nixon as Eisenhower's vice president; whereas Kennedy used much better evidence of various kinds appealing to many groups composing the electorate, Nixon's most important contentions had to be accepted on his credibility. Substantively and stylistically, then, Kennedy's opening statement offered a more coherent and desirable image of presidential leadership than Nixon's did.

KEY EXCHANGES: LEADERSHIP AND EXPERIENCE

Bob Fleming's opening question was an important opportunity for both candidates. Whereas Kennedy was invited to demonstrate that he was, indeed, qualified for the presidency, Nixon was offered an opportunity to press his attack before a national audience. Fleming's question explicitly defined the issue in terms of leadership: "Senator, the vice president in his campaign has said that you were naive and at times, immature. He has raised the question of leadership. On this issue, why do you think people would vote for you rather than the vice president?"

Kennedy provided two reasons to support his claim that he was an effective leader. First, Kennedy indicated that the amount of time that they had served in Congress was the same, that they both had served in the labor committee, that they both had fourteen years of experience in government. Kennedy concluded that their experience was comparable based on the amount of time served and committees on which they worked.

Second, Kennedy indicated that another means of comparison was in the programs they advocated. Here Kennedy shifted the comparison from specific programs to "party record." Kennedy invoked the tradition of the Democratic party by claiming the legacies of Woodrow Wilson, Franklin Roosevelt, and Harry Truman, and added that the Democratic party had supported and sustained the programs he discussed that night. In these respects, Kennedy's defense of his ability to lead was grounded in his understanding of national values and history. To the extent that the audience saw Kennedy in the tradition of Wilson, FDR, and Truman, and accepted these presidents as representatives of national values, Kennedy embodied a desirable tradition of national leadership.

Pointing out that Nixon embodied the Republican party, Kennedy attacked the Republican leadership and by implication, Nixon, on four specific grounds:

Mr. Nixon comes out of the Republican party. He was nominated by it, and it is a fact that through most of these last twenty-five years the Republican leadership has opposed federal aid for education, medical care for the aged, development of the Tennessee Valley, development of our natural resources. I think Mr. Nixon is an effective leader of his party. I hope he would grant me the same. The question before us is: Which point of view and which party do we want to lead the United States?

Using the four attacks, Kennedy proved he understood the rhetorical requirements of office by arguing that the public must choose one leader representing one party embodying the most desirable vision of leadership for the nation. Phrasing the issue in terms of "a point of view" and a political party to lead the nation, Kennedy challenged Nixon to substantiate his credentials by defending the Republican vision of leadership. Defending the record of the Democratic party presented Kennedy in the role of its best proponent; criticizing Nixon and the Republican party on the grounds that they opposed education, the aged, economic development, and the utilization of natural resources demonstrated the desirability of the Democratic program.

When given the opportunity to respond, Nixon said: "I have no comment." Although Nixon could have defended the record of the Republican party and attacked Kennedy on other grounds of leadership ability, perhaps he thought it best not to pursue the charges of immaturity and naivete. Whatever Nixon's thinking was, choosing not to answer constituted a retreat from one of his strongest arguments against Kennedy. Not substantiating this claim in Kennedy's presence implied that it was unsupportable. Future criticism on this ground would appear ignoble and unpresidential. In contrast to Nixon, Kennedy rose to the challenge by defending himself and the Democratic vision of leadership. Nixon's retreat helped solve Kennedy's rhetorical problem.

When Stuart Novins asked whether Nixon's experience was as an observer or participant in the Eisenhower administration's policy-making, Nixon had an opportunity to recoup his losses from the previous question by demonstrating his qualifications for the presidency. Offering three examples of recommendations he had made and pointing to his role as chairman of the President's Committee on Price Stability and Economic Growth, Nixon gave some evidence of participating in the policy-making of the Eisenhower administration. Nixon's answer, however, did not define a specific concept of presidential leadership apart from his role as vice president. In each of Nixon's examples, he was acting in a vice presidential capacity for President Eisenhower, not as a president. This was a problem for Nixon because, historically, vice presidents have had a limited role in presidential policy-making; thus, to appear presidential, Nixon needed to redefine the terms of the question and discuss his qualifications in terms of his own platform. Because Kennedy had the opportunity to respond, his criticism of Nixon's role in the Eisenhower administration diminished the persuasive force of Nixon's presidential qualities. By raising this issue, Novins highlighted Nixon's limitations by creating doubts about Nixon's rhetorical qualifications for the presidency.

NIXON FAILED TO SOLVE HIS RHETORICAL PROBLEM

When Vanocur asked Nixon about Eisenhower's comment criticizing the significance of his contribution to the Eisenhower administration,

Nixon faced a formidable rhetorical problem. Solving it would provide symbolic evidence of his ability to solve complex problems, a significant qualification for the office given the complexity of the problems faced by presidents. Vanocur stated:

Now, in his news conference on August 24, President Eisenhower was asked to give one example of a major idea of yours that he adopted. His reply was, and I'm quoting: "If you give me a week, I might think of one. I don't remember." Now, that was a month ago, sir, and the president has not brought it up since, and I'm wondering, sir, if you can clarify which version is correct—the one put out by Republican campaign leaders or the one put out by President Eisenhower.

The credibility of Eisenhower and of the Republican campaign leaders was at stake. Nixon needed both to win the election. Handling this sticky rhetorical situation in a competent way would have defused a major campaign issue and connected Nixon even more closely to Eisenhower's popularity. Nixon failed to accomplish either of these goals.

Nixon's limitation can be analyzed in five parts. First, by acknowledging Eisenhower's humor in a defensive tone, Nixon gave the audience evidence of a rift existing between him and Eisenhower. "Well, I would suggest, Mr. Vanocur, that—if you know the president, that that was probably a facetious remark." Explaining the level at which the humor operates was a sign that the audience probably did not understand the joke. This reflected the seriousness of the damage done by Eisenhower's statement. Nixon needed to provide a more personalized defense. He was perhaps one of the few individuals who could have known Eisenhower well enough to prove that the statement was humorous. Had Nixon been able to give a quick hearty laugh, then redefine the issue in more favorable terms, he would have confirmed the humorous tone and dismissed the issue. But he was unable to do this. Thus, what might have seemed humorous at first became more serious.

Second, by claiming that he had provided valuable input to the president but being unable to offer examples because he thought it was "improper for the president of the United States to disclose the instances in which members of his official family had made recommendations," Nixon forced the audience to take his word on the question of his contribution to the Eisenhower administration. This was problematic for Nixon because his credibility was a source of doubt for some members of the audience. Additionally, the purpose behind the debate was to identify these contributions so that they could be examined for clues about Nixon's presidential potential. Without any examples to consider, Nixon's qualifications for presidential leadership could not be assessed by the audience.

Third, when he attempted to demonstrate his qualifications for office by explaining his role in the National Security Council to which he offered advice on Lebanon, Quemoy, and Matsu, Nixon was unable to indicate what advice or suggestions the president had followed: "The president had asked for my advice, I have given it—sometimes my advice has been taken, sometimes it has not." Absent examples supporting his claim, the audience had no basis on which to formulate an opinion, and Nixon's word on this matter was insufficient given the fact that Eisenhower had not confirmed Nixon's contribution to his administration.

Fourth, Nixon missed an opportunity to redefine Vanocur's question in more favorable terms: "As far as what experience counts and whether that is experience that counts, that isn't for me to say." Contradicting the Republican leadership and main theme of the Republican campaign, Nixon implied either that he could not or would not explain why his experience as vice president was superior to Kennedy's senatorial experience. Although Nixon noted that their experience had been in different branches of the government, he made no further case for his own abilities as a leader.

Finally, Nixon accepted Kennedy's terms for assessing experience. This underscored his inability to define the qualifications for office in his words and in terms favorable to his candidacy:

—I can only say that my experience is there for the people to consider, Senator Kennedy's is there for the people to consider. As he pointed out, we came to Congress in the same year—his experience has been different from mine, mine has been in the executive branch, his has been in the legislative branch. I would say that the people now have the opportunity to evaluate his as against mine.

This statement did not build a case for Nixon's candidacy. Although Nixon noted a difference in experience, he drew no implications from this fact and failed to give the audience a reason to consider him more qualified for office than Kennedy.

In summary, Nixon reacted defensively to the question, provided no basis for evaluating his contribution to the Eisenhower administration, offered no way to assess his contribution to the National Security Council, was unable to redefine the terms of the question more favorably, and acknowledged Kennedy's earlier claim that both he and Kennedy had very similar experience. If Nixon's advantage in the campaign was experience, at this point he had failed to live up to the claims made on his behalf by the Republican leadership when he failed to distinguish his experience from Kennedy's.

In vivid contrast to Nixon's answer, Kennedy captured the theme of the Republican party and expanded the question of experience to include his campaign theme of future goals: "Well, I'll just say that the question is of experience . . . and the question also is uh—what our judgment is of the future and what our goals are for the United States and what ability we have to implement those goals." Accepting experience as the major issue that separated them, Kennedy used Nixon's poor answer to prove that he had the experience Nixon lacked. Taking the dispute one step further, Kennedy expanded the consideration of experience to include the future of the nation and ability to implement those goals that bring about a desirable order for the nation.

Second, Kennedy provided a historical anecdote relating Lincoln's rise to the presidency. Strategically, this story countered the audience's expectation that Nixon had a natural right to the office because of his experience as vice president and it implied that Kennedy was the appropriate choice for office because, like Lincoln, he followed a similar course at a crucial time in our national history.

Kennedy refocused the audience's attention on the future by concluding with a rhetorical question: "The question really is, which candidate and which party can meet the problems that the United States is going to face in the sixties?" Nixon's answer did not address this question and by placing this question before the audience, Kennedy allowed the audience to compare them in the role of president. To the extent that Kennedy continued to ask this question and tailor his answers to reflect concern for the future, Kennedy presented himself not only as the candidate with a more coherent vision of leadership for the nation but also as a candidate more willing and ready to lead.

KENNEDY DISMANTLED THE REPUBLICAN VISION

Nixon's candidacy was placed in jeopardy from a third perspective in this debate when he was unable to defend the Republican vision of leadership reflected in his programs. Alternatively, Kennedy's qualifications for office were enhanced when he demonstrated his ability to defend the Democratic programs in the exchanges over Charles Warren's questions concerning farm surpluses and Nixon's tie-breaking vote in the Senate against legislation providing higher teacher salaries, and Fleming's query on the nature of political leadership.

Farm Surpluses

The answers to Warren's question on farm policy provided a good comparison of the candidates' ability to defend a major program. Warren's question asked the candidates to justify what appeared to be unfair governmental support of the farmer. Placing the candidates in the position of justifying governmental policy required them to act as national leaders by demonstrating the desirability of a partisan policy in terms of national interests.

Kennedy began his justification of farm surpluses by asserting a relationship between the farmer and the economy of the nation: "If the federal government moved out of the program and withdrew its support uh—then I think you'd have complete economic chaos." This suggested that Kennedy understood the implications of federal action, especially the act of discontinuing policies that had been in effect for some time. Two related claims were developed in support of this statement. First, Kennedy argued that because the farmers were not in a position to control their market very well, they could not bargain effectively: "The farmer plants in the spring and harvests in the fall." A second reason that farmers did not control their market well was found in the fact that relatively few purchasers composed the market for a large number of farmers:

There are hundreds of thousands of them [farmers]. They really don't—are not able to control their market very well. They bring their crops in or their livestock in, many of them, about the same time. They have only a few purchasers . . . that buy their milk or their hogs—a few large companies, in many cases—and, therefore, the farmer is not in a position to bargain very effectively in the market place.

The implication of the argument was that the federal government should help those who were at a disadvantage in the marketplace. The answer indicated that farmers were different from automobile manufacturers and factory owners in that they did not control their market, hence could not bargain effectively as could those who control their market and were justified in receiving assistance.

A second reason for supporting Kennedy's contention was developed from the interrelationship between the farmer and the steel and automobile industries. Kennedy used historical experience to support his view: "I think the experience of the twenties has shown what a free market could do to agriculture." Enthymematically, Kennedy used the audience's memory of the depression to bolster the importance of the farmer in the national economy. For those who could not recall the depression, Kennedy explained:

And if the agricultural economy collapses, then the economy of the rest of the United States sooner or later will collapse. The farmers are the number one market for the automobile industry of the United States, the automobile industry is the number one market for steel. So, if the farmer's economy continues to decline as sharply as it has in recent years, then I think you would have recession in the rest of the country.

Kennedy's answer featured a second move by which he attacked the Eisenhower administration's policy. "Secondly, my objection to present farm policy is that there are no effective controls to bring supply and demand into better balance." The first part of the argument indicated that the present policy was one of lowering price supports. When Kennedy said that "dropping of the support price in order to limit production does not work," he supported his assertion with two facts: "and now we have the highest uh—surpluses—$9 billion worth, we've had a uh—higher tax load from the treasury for the farmer in the last few years with the lowest farm income in many years." From these facts Kennedy concluded, "I think that this farm policy has failed." The audience could see Kennedy making a claim, providing evidence to support the claim, and then drawing a conclusion for the audience.

Attacking the opposition was insufficient to demonstrate desirable programs and leadership. Kennedy now had to show why his program was more desirable than Nixon's: "In my judgment, the only policy that will work will be for effective supply and demand to be in balance." Although Kennedy's use of the word "judgment" implied careful consideration of the alternatives, his policy was really a state of economic affairs rather than a course of action capable of bringing about desirable economic equilibrium. In this respect, Nixon could have criticized this aspect of Kennedy's answer.

After indicating what his judgment of the problem revealed and defining a role for the federal government in this area, Kennedy spoke as though he had the power to enact policy, as though he were an official policymaker, and in this way, fulfilled the expectations of Warren's question: "I, therefore, suggest that in those basic commodities which are supported, that the federal government, after endorsement by the farmers in that commodity, attempt to bring supply and demand into balance—attempt effective production controls—so that we won't have the 5 or 6 percent surplus which breaks the price 15 or 20 percent." In this statement, Kennedy can be seen criticizing one policy, recommending another, then arguing for the superiority of his approach to the problem.

Kennedy's final move tied Nixon to the program of Eisenhower's Secretary of Agriculture, Ezra Benson. The connection forced Nixon to defend the current administration or distinguish himself apart from the Eisenhower administration in such a way as to make the criticism irrelevant without distancing him from desirable elements of Eisenhower's program. Kennedy said:

I think Mr. Benson's program has failed, and I must say, after reading the vice president's speech before the farmers, as he read mine, I don't believe that it's very much different from Mr. Benson's. I don't think it provides effective government controls. I think the support prices are tied to average market price of the last three years, which was Mr. Benson's theory. I, therefore, do not believe that this is a sharp enough breach with the past to give us any hope of success for the future.

Kennedy compared the two solutions to see how well they fit the needs of the future. Substantively, the comparison revealed Kennedy's ability to apprehend, scrutinize, and evaluate options. But a reflective tone was also evident throughout the conclusion: "I think . . . I must say . . . I don't believe . . . I don't think . . . I think . . . I therefore do not believe." Thus, Kennedy's argument and the stylistic quality of relying on his "thoughts" reinforced each other, and in this sense, style and substance were related in ways that suggested that Kennedy was thoughtful and rational in his approach to policy-making.

In summary, Kennedy's answer to Warren's question on farm surpluses justified price supports for the farmer, implicitly argued for equality in economic transactions, employed cause and effect reasoning to demonstrate the disaster of removing price supports for farmers, attacked the incumbent administration's policy on price supports, recommended his own policy for price supports, defined the role of the federal government in this area, called for farmers to cooperate in developing his policy of price controls, tied Nixon to the administration policy he had attacked on historical and theoretical grounds, and offered an alternative vision of hope after criticizing the vision of the Republican contender. In doing these things, Kennedy used facts, statistics, historical evidence, and economic theory to support his claims. He used cause-effect reasoning and reasoning from experience. The structure of the answer involved two major contentions with a number of subclaims functioning to support his major claims. The microstructure of his support materials took the form of arguments featuring claims, evidence, and the drawing of conclusions for the audience. At a macro level, this answer explained why farmers received price supports, defined the role of government in this area, indicted the opposition's policy, and offered an alternative view of leadership. The answer was a model argument refuting one alternative to substantiate another using various types of support materials in the process. Because arguments reveal the character of candidates as well as the qualities of those programs they advocate, Kennedy's skill in using argument suggested symbolically that he and his programs, specifically this one, would be more desirable than Nixon and his programs.

Nixon's answer to Kennedy opened with a clear contrast in positions, arguing that he had called for more government controls: "I, of course, disagree with Senator Kennedy insofar as his suggestion as to what should be done uh—with re—on the farm program. He has made the suggestion that what we need is to move in the direction of more government controls, a suggestion that would also mean raising prices uh—

that the consumers pay for products and im—and imposing upon the farmers uh—controls on acreage even far more than they have today."[5] Stylistically, Nixon's syntax was awkward. The vocalized pauses were too numerous to create the impression of a polished candidate. Lacking substantive support, the opening argument compared unfavorably with Kennedy's more clearly developed line of thought. Nixon continued his attack by asserting without support, "I think this is the wrong direction. I don't think this has worked in the past. I don't think it will work in the future." By the time Nixon moved to defend his program, he had indicted Kennedy twice without evidence and thus, his argument, as a form of discourse, was incomplete. The implication that one could draw from this excerpt was that Nixon's image, compared to Kennedy's, needed further refinement.

Potentially, Nixon could have demonstrated his knowledge by explaining the history of the policy. Instead, Nixon previewed an attack on FDR's administration that never developed and explained that the farm program "recognizes that the government has a responsibility to get the farmer out of the trouble he presently is in because the government got him into it, and that's the fundamental reason why we can't let the farmer go by himself at the present time." Then Nixon added: "The farmer produced these surpluses because the government asked him to, through legislation, during the war." Nixon gave no evidence nor drew a conclusion for the audience, leaving them to wonder whether this policy was still desirable. In this regard, Nixon's answer did not fulfill the expectations of Warren's question as well as Kennedy's did.

The remainder of Nixon's answer revealed stylistic limitations. After the stunted attack on FDR, Nixon said: "Now that we have these surpluses, it's our responsibility to indemnify the farmer during that period that we get rid of the farmer uh—the surpluses." The verbal slip and immediate interruption underscored Nixon's own awareness of his syntactical error. A similar problem was also evident in his conclusion: "But I would propose holding that income up, not through a type of program that Senator Kennedy has suggested that would raise prices, but one that would indemnify the farmer, pay the farmer, in kind, uh—from the products which are in surplus." Nixon's position was made unnecessarily complex by stressing that a positive effect could not be achieved through one action, but through another. His use of the term "indemnify" and his description of the policy of paying the farmer through "in-kind" surpluses were too technical to constitute appealing descriptions for the audience. In short, Nixon's stylistic and substantive limitations prevented a more persuasive defense of his farm policy.

In summary, Nixon's answer made claims without providing support, was ambiguous with respect to the program that he was advocating, was confusing structurally, and featured a verbal slip that the audience could interpret unfavorably. None of the answer functioned as a satis-fying response to Kennedy's position. From this exchange, one could conclude that Kennedy had successfully questioned Nixon's ability to answer attacks on his policy and that Nixon was unable to substantiate his attacks on Kennedy's farm policy.

Teachers' Salaries

Kennedy's attack on Nixon's justification for vetoing higher teacher salaries was a good example of a candidate's ability to defend a legislative program. Answering first, Nixon attempted to preempt criticism by aligning himself with Kennedy:

—I think that the reason that I voted against having the federal government uh—pay teachers' salaries was probably the very reason that concerned Senator Kennedy when, in January of this year, in his kick-off press conference, he said that he favored aid for school construction, but at that time did not feel that there should be aid for teachers' salaries—at least, that's the way I read his remarks. Now, why should there be any question about the federal government aiding s—teachers' salaries? Why did Senator Kennedy take that position then? Why do I take it now? We both took it then and I take it now for this reason: We want higher teachers' salaries; we need higher teacher salaries; but we also want our education to be free of federal control.

Nixon's strategy was to appear in favor of teacher salaries by quoting Kennedy and to claim that his reasons for opposing the legislation were Kennedy's at the beginning of the campaign, at the time of the vote on the legislation, and even now in the course of the debate. Continuing, Nixon stated: "But, as Senator Kennedy said in January of this year in this same press conference, the way that you get higher salaries for teachers is to support school construction, which means that all the local school districts in the various states then have the money which is freed to raise the standards for teachers' salaries." The only defense of his vote came when Nixon said that "once you put the responsibility on the federal government for paying a portion of teachers' salaries, your local communities and your states are not going to meet the responsi-bility as much as they should." Given these difficulties, Nixon needed an effective conclusion for this answer but again fell short. By arguing that teachers' salaries had gone up 50 percent compared to 34 percent in other areas over the past eight years, Nixon hoped to prove that there was no problem with teachers' salaries. However, Nixon stated that this was not enough, that the salaries should be increased, but that the federal government should not be the agent of change. Then Nixon indicated that his objection to federal support for teachers' salaries was not on the basis of cost, but control—on the basis of preventing eventual control of education by the government. Despite the fact that Nixon presented strong evidence to justify his claim, his conclusion was fraught with qualifications, diminishing the persuasive force of his justification. It was unnecessarily complex, confusing structurally, and hence ineffective as a summary for his justification in opposing the legislation.

In his turn, Kennedy refuted Nixon's explanation for action by distinguishing between the policy discussed in January and the policy considered in the Senate in February:

When uh—the vice president quotes me in January '60, I do not believe the federal government should pay directly teachers' salaries but that was not the issue before the Senate in February. The issue before the Senate was that the money would be given to the state; the state could then determine whether the money would be spent for school construction or teachers' salaries.

Here, Kennedy showed a superior command of facts by distinguishing between the issue at different points in time. Remembering the facts more accurately than Nixon enhanced Kennedy's argument, and by fulfilling the formal qualities of an argument in a superior way, Kennedy enhanced his image as an advocate. Kennedy's superior use of argument spotlighted Nixon's inability to recall the facts accurately, and diminished Nixon's image as a credible advocate for national policy.

Redefining the issue, Kennedy then drew a distinction between himself and Nixon: "On that question the vice president and I disagreed. I voted in favor of that proposal and supported it strongly because I think that that provided assistance to our teachers for their salaries without any chance of federal control and it is on that vote that the—Mr. Nixon and I disagreed and his tie vote uh—defeated . . . his breaking the tie defeated the proposal." Using the public record, Kennedy chipped another piece off Nixon's image as a credible advocate by attributing responsibility to Nixon for preventing the passage of legislation that Nixon claimed to be favoring. Either Nixon could not distinguish between policies worthy of support, or his previous statements about supporting teachers' salaries were untrue. The former conclusion disqualified Nixon on the grounds of poor leadership; the latter revealed a candidate out of touch with the facts on this issue.

Kennedy went on to defend the legislation on the grounds that it would meet the goal of enhancing teachers' salaries while protecting local authority: "I don't want the federal government paying teachers' salaries directly—but if the money will go to the states and the states can then determine whether it shall go for school construction or for teachers' salaries, in my opinion you protect the local authority over the school board and the school committee. And, therefore, I think that was a sound proposal and that is why I supported it and I regret that it did not pass." Kennedy completed the dialectical form by refuting the opposing view and then defending his. By suggesting that the policy he voted for would have enacted the goals that both he and Nixon supported, Kennedy demonstrated a consistency and sincerity of character that Nixon lacked. The nature of each candidate's character, however, was measured not only in terms of available facts, but also by how well the candidates used the facts and the form of argument to refute the opposing candidate's argument.

Legislative Enactment

The final example of Kennedy's ability to defend his program can be found in Fleming's question, coming immediately after Vanocur asked Kennedy to explain how he would get legislation passed under less favorable circumstances than he enjoyed in August. In the exchange over Vanocur's question, Kennedy provided a well-organized, well-reasoned, and well-supported answer. He refuted charges of ineffectiveness by demonstrating that the Republican party was responsible for blocking action on important social legislation. Nixon questioned Kennedy's ability to unite all Democrats in Congress but did not justify the role of the Republicans in blocking passage of these bills and did not substantiate the criticism that these laws were ineffective. Instead, Nixon based his defense on the grounds that the American people thought these laws were too extreme. No support was offered for this claim. When Nixon tried to direct the audience's attention to his proposals, no explanation was provided to draw a distinction between his proposals and those of the Democrats. When Nixon asserted that his programs were superior to the Democrat's, no support was offered. The exchange over Vanocur's question, then, set up Fleming's question: "Mr. Vice President, do I take it, then, you believe that you can work better with Democratic majorities in the House and Senate than Senator Kennedy could work with Democratic majorities in the House and Senate?"

Nixon tried to do five things in his answer to Fleming. First, Nixon predicted that the Republicans would win control of the House but not the Senate. Second, he said that popular support was necessary to move a legislative program through Congress: "I would say that a president will be able to lead—a president will be able to get his program through—to the effect that he has the support of the country, the support of the people." Third, Nixon disputed the view that getting programs through Congress was purely a question of finagling: "Sometimes we—we get the opinion that in getting programs through the House or the Senate it's purely a question of legislative finagling and all of that sort of thing. It isn't really that. Whenever a majority of the people are for a program, the House and Senate responds to it." This created doubt about the value of Kennedy's experience as a legislator and effectiveness as a leader in Congress. If "finagling" was not the means, but the support of the people, Nixon's words implied that Kennedy lacked the support that would have defined him as a leader. Fourth, Nixon said that Congress would respond favorably to whoever was president because that individual would have the popular endorsement of the public: "And whether this House and Senate in the next session is Democratic or Republican, if the country will have voted for the candidate for the presidency and for the proposals that he has made, I believe that you will find that the president, if it were a Republican, as it would be in my case, would be able to get his program through that Congress."

Nixon's evidence of ability was not defined in terms of his capacity to lead but in terms of his chances for victory in the election. Translated, Nixon's answer seemed to be saying, "Trust me, vote for me, and I think I will be able to accomplish the job." The problem with the answer was that Nixon relied on the assumption that he had a credible image as a strong candidate, which was not necessarily the case, given previous exchanges. Nixon's final move was to argue that Kennedy's proposals did not have popular support, and hence would be rejected by Congress and the president:

Now I also say that as far as Senator Kennedy's proposals are concerned, that again the question is not simply one of uh—a presidential veto stopping programs. You must always remember that a president can't stop anything unless he has the people behind him, and the reason President Eisenhower's vetoes have been sustained—the reason Congress does not send up bills to him which they think will be vetoed—is because the people and the Congress, the majority of them, know the country is behind the president.

Here, Nixon premised his idea of leadership on opinion polls rather than taking the opportunity to define leadership in terms of specific actions. This approach was problematic given the fact that Nixon did not enjoy overwhelming support in the polls and given his previous inability to solve the doubts created by Vanocur's question concerning his contributions to the Eisenhower administration.

Kennedy's answer took advantage of the opportunity to appeal to the audience on the basis of public interest by first attacking the claim that the Democratic legislation was too extreme. In the first example, Kennedy used a comparison between the wealth of a company and the cost of the minimum wage to refute the charge of extremity: "One was a bill for $1.25 an hour for anyone who works in a store or company that has a million dollar-a-year business. I don't think that's extreme at all." Extending his previous attack on the Republicans, Kennedy stated that "nearly two-thirds to three-fourths of the Republicans in the House of

Representatives voted against that proposal." This pattern of refutation and attack continued in the second example on federal aid to education. Again, Kennedy used a comparison to demonstrate that the bill was not extreme: "The fact of the matter is it was a bill that was less than you recommended, Mr. Nixon, this morning in your proposal." After answering the charge of extremity on federal aid to education, Kennedy used the legislative history of the bill to prove there was no Republican support in the House: "It was not an extreme bill, and yet we could not get one Republican to join; at least, I think, four of the eight Democrats voted to send it to the floor of the House—not one Republican—and they joined with those Democrats who are opposed to it." Kennedy went on to answer Nixon's previous criticism of Democratic disunity: "I don't say the Democrats are united in their support of the program, but I do say that a majority are, and I say a majority of the Republicans are opposed to it." At this point, Nixon's previous charge that Kennedy was ineffective in leading the Democrats became irrelevant. Kennedy had not claimed that the Democrats were united, only that a majority supported these policies. Thus, Nixon's criticisms of Kennedy's leadership no longer had factual basis.

Arguing that medical care should be tied to Social Security, Kennedy attacked Nixon's proposal with reluctant testimony: "The proposal advanced by you and Mr. Javits would have cost $600 million—Mr. Rockefeller rejected it in New York; he said he didn't agree with the financing at all; said it ought to be on Social Security." Quoting Rockefeller was an effective use of evidence because it showed Nixon out of step with a member of the Republican leadership. When Kennedy concluded for the audience, "so these are three programs which are quite moderate," his conclusion seemed well supported by the evidence, and the charge of extremism appeared to have been refuted.

Kennedy drew one further conclusion for the audience: "I think it shows the difference between the two parties. One party is ready to move in these programs; the other party gives them lip service." The answer functioned to support Kennedy's main issue: Which party will get America moving again? If this was the central issue of the campaign, Kennedy proved that Democratic leadership would be more likely to get America moving again because his performance on this question constituted a superior defense of programs. Nixon's answer did not feature a concise argument demonstrating his ability to lead. Moreover, Nixon revealed his misunderstanding of the nature of leadership when he argued that it was a function of popular support. In short, Kennedy's answer suggested his ability to justify positions, generate political support for controversial policies, and build the political coalitions necessary to govern a democracy.

In these exchanges over farm surpluses, teachers' salaries, and legislative enactment, Kennedy appeared more willing to act while Nixon appeared not only to be blocking these programs but also limited in his ability to justify his opposition. In many of these exchanges, Kennedy had proven only that Democrats vote differently than Republicans. The difference between Kennedy and Nixon, however, was that Kennedy had done a better job of interpreting what these votes meant for the audience and Nixon had not done a particularly effective job of justifying Republican opposition to the legislation Kennedy supported. Comparatively, then, the argumentative style and substance of Kennedy's discourse suggested that he would be the more likely candidate to get America moving again. Also, in these exchanges, Kennedy's performance seemed to measure up to the standard of leadership that he had presented in the opening statement much better than Nixon did. In these respects, Kennedy had presented his concept of presidential leadership and then used his answers to show how he would fulfill the expectations for office. Even if Nixon's answers could be interpreted as strong arguments in defense of his positions on these programs, they could not be interpreted in terms of an equally persuasive context for understanding what constituted leadership for this election.

CLOSING STATEMENTS

Nixon did four things in his closing statement. First, he tried to put the issue of economic growth in perspective through the use of statistics. The evidence admitted that the Soviets were moving faster but refuted the implication that we were threatened by their growth by pointing out that we were further ahead than we had been twenty years before. Had Nixon stopped here and turned his attention to the specific means by which this administration would maintain the lead over the Soviets, his closing statement would have been more effective. But Nixon went further to agree with Kennedy, that the Soviets were to be feared. When Nixon took this position, it became important for him to illustrate the ways in which the Republican leadership had been responsible for and would continue to maintain the lead over the Soviets.

Next, Nixon distinguished himself from Kennedy on the basis of the means by which they would maintain a strong economy. Unfortunately, Nixon repeated many of the claims that he had made earlier in the debate—that Kennedy would rely too much on the federal government to solve problems and stimulate growth and that Kennedy's proposals were not as effective as his. These statements did not extend previous arguments that Nixon had made and they did not answer any of Kennedy's analysis. Here, Nixon's appeal was limited to a partisan audience.

Third, instead of closing the debate on specific issues or summarizing his criticisms of Kennedy in a persuasive way, Nixon opened up two new areas for discussion, health insurance and inflation. This was a strategic mistake because Kennedy had the final closing statement in which to answer these attacks.

Finally, in a short, undramatic conclusion, Nixon said that he stood for growth, an abrupt transition from his criticism of the Truman administration's inflationary policies: "It is essential that a man who is president of this country, certainly stand for every program that will mean for [sic] growth, and I stand for programs that will mean growth and progress. But it is also essential that he not allow a dollar spent that could be better spent by the people themselves." Nixon's claim that he stood for growth was vulnerable to criticism. Kennedy, too, could argue that he stood for growth. Nixon needed to explain to the audience why he was a better choice than Kennedy. Nowhere in the closing statement did Nixon mention the ways in which the platform could provide for greater economic growth than Kennedy's. Thus, little evidence was offered for Nixon's most important contention in the closing statement.

Kennedy began his closing statement by offering a historical vision of the future. Reinforcing Nixon's statement that Soviet production was only 45 percent of ours, Kennedy offered this statement of resolve: "I want to make sure that it stays in that relationship. I don't want to see the day when it's 60 percent of ours and 70 and 75 and 80 and 90 percent of ours, with all the force and power that it could bring to bear in order to cause our destruction." No evidence was offered to support the hypothetical vision of Soviet economic growth, but the dramatic style created an image of threat and underscored the concept of the presidency Kennedy intended to develop in his closing statement.

Second, Kennedy blunted Nixon's last competent attack on his platform by distinguishing between the Kerr bill, which Nixon attacked, and the amendment to the bill, which was Kennedy's policy. At this point, Nixon had carried few attacks through the debate, Kennedy had answered those attacks that Nixon was able to construct, and Nixon had failed to sustain his criticism of the Democratic platform. Kennedy had also done a superior job of using the legislative history of these bills to support his claim that Republicans had consistently opposed legislation to solve these domestic problems.

Kennedy returned to the issue of getting America moving again by assessing the choice confronting the audience:

If you feel that everything that is being done now is satisfactory, that the relative power and prestige and strength of the United States is increasing in relation to that of the Communists, that we are—gaining more security, that we are achieving everything as a nation that we should achieve, that we are achieving a better life for our citizens and greater strength, then I agree. I think you should vote for Mr. Nixon.

Returning to the theme of getting America moving again was a particularly effective strategy because it created an unfavorable standard for evaluating Nixon's ability to lead. Kennedy performed better in the exchange on each of these issues in the debate. If the audience accepted this standard, it would conclude that Kennedy was more fit for the presidency.

Kennedy took the strategy one step further. Reflecting FDR's words, Kennedy defined the role of the president:

But if you feel that we have to move again in the sixties, that the function of the president is to set before the people the unfinished business of our society, as Franklin Roosevelt did in the thirties, the agenda for our people—what we must do as a society to meet our needs in this country and protect our security and help the cause of freedom—as I said at the beginning, the question before us all that faces all Republicans and Democrats is: Can freedom in the next generation . . . conquer or are the Communists going to be successful?

Kennedy's theme in the opening statement was tied nicely to the closing, creating a favorable context for interpreting his exchanges with Nixon. The sense of crisis was reinforced and the contrast between Kennedy's vision of the future and Nixon's was sharpened. Having defined the role of the presidency in terms of unfinished business for the future, Kennedy enacted himself in the role by presenting the unfinished business before society, articulating his vision for the future, and defending the desirability of that vision.

SUMMARY

In the first debate, Kennedy revealed his ability to present and enact a concept of the presidency but Nixon could not articulate his vision of presidential leadership or fulfill Kennedy's concept of the presidency. Nixon's rhetorical style and substance suggested him in the more limited role of vice president. Alternatively, Kennedy used argumentative form more competently than Nixon did enhancing his image of a vigorous and capable leader.

Kennedy organized his refutation clearly and concisely, suggesting an image of a candidate who had control of the situation. Additionally, Kennedy's superior use of evidence fulfilled the form of the argument in a more satisfying way than did Nixon, who relied more on his credibility to support his claims. Because argumentative style and substance reflexively enhance a rhetor's credibility, Kennedy's character appeared strong while Nixon, unable to fulfill the formal expectations for an argument, appeared weak.

The analysis of the first debate also shows how advocacy skills reflexively affect perceptions of a candidate's political program. Candidates who cannot defend their programs appear weak, and their programs appear less desirable than the alternative candidate's. Candidates' advocacy skills reveal that which is desirable, worthy of the audience's support, just as their ability to defend that which is desirable reveals comparable traits of character. When Nixon revealed that he was unable to defend the Republican programs against Kennedy's attacks and could not sustain similar criticisms of Kennedy's programs, he failed to demonstrate the value of his programs. By implication, Nixon's performance revealed that he was unable to defend what was desirable for the community.

Finally, if one accepts the idea that the ways in which candidates attempt to solve rhetorical problems provides symbolic evidence of leadership ability, then Nixon revealed his limitations when he failed to solve the rhetorical problem presented to him by Vanocur. One possible inference was that if Nixon were unable to solve this rhetorical problem, he might also be limited in his ability to solve real problems of presidential leadership while in office.

This chapter has illustrated how a critic can locate tests of character in presidential debates. By examining the opening statements, it was possible to compare each candidate's concept of the presidency. Examining the closing statements revealed how well each candidate achieved his objectives or recouped his losses in previous exchanges. The exchanges over farm surpluses, teacher salaries, and legislative enactment contrasted substantive and stylistic elements of Kennedy's and Nixon's images. By identifying these differences, it was possible to explain how argument altered the perception of Kennedy and his programs so that they enjoyed a more credible appeal than prior to the debate. Analysis of key exchanges that summarized essential differences between the candidates focused on how Kennedy solved his problem of inexperience and revealed how Nixon contributed to that solution. This conceptual lens also located Nixon's inability to dissolve the rhetorical problem of Eisenhower's dubious support in Vanocur's question about Nixon's contribution to the Eisenhower administration.

NOTES

1. Theodore C. Sorenson, *Kennedy* (New York: Harper & Row, 1965), 197.

2. Earl Mazo, *Great Debates* (Santa Barbara, CA: Center for the Study of Democratic Institutions, 1962), 3.

3. Elihu Katz and Jacob Feldman, "The Debate in the Light of the Research: A Survey of Surveys," in *The Great Debates*, ed. Sidney Kraus (Bloomington, IN: Indiana University Press, 1962), 169. See also Earl Mazo, *Great Debates*, 4–5.

4. *New York Times*, September 28, 1960, 1.

5. The vocalized pauses of the debaters were best transcribed by Theodore Clevenger Jr., Donn W. Parson, and Jerome B. Polisky in their verification of the transcripts of the 1960 debates. See "The Problem of Textual Accuracy," in *The Great Debates*, ed. Sidney Kraus (Bloomington, IN: Indiana University Press, 1962), 341–347, and the transcript of the first debate, 348–368.

Chapter Three

The Second, Third, and Fourth Kennedy-Nixon Debates

After the first debate, the difference between Kennedy and Nixon was Kennedy's development of a coherent and appealing concept of presidential leadership. Nixon needed to develop an alternative concept of leadership equally appealing as Kennedy's in the remaining debates. Although Nixon's performance in the specific exchanges improved, he was unable to develop a competing image of leadership as desirable as Kennedy's and he was unable to criticize successfully Kennedy's appeal as a vigorous, vibrant candidate, ready to get America moving again.[1] The discussion of the last three debates examines Nixon's opportunities to exploit Kennedy's weaknesses, Nixon's strategy of challenging Kennedy's ethics as a responsible advocate, and Nixon's use of Kennedy's campaign theme. Each of these issues constituted important opportunities for Nixon to rebound from his performance in the first debate, but in each instance, Nixon's words continued to reflect his rhetorical limitations.[2]

THE SECOND DEBATE

Analysis of the second debate focuses on the role of party labels and the issue of responsible advocacy. For most of the second debate, Nixon performed well in his answers. On these two issues, however, he faltered. The significance of the exchanges over party labels and responsible advocacy lay in what they revealed about Nixon's character. Although one could argue that, from a political and historical perspective, Nixon's performance in the debates matched Kennedy's, such a position emphasizes the effects of the performances over the image of political character that resides in the texts. My argument concerning the last three debates is that Kennedy's performance in the first debate established a frame of reference for understanding the campaign and subsequent discourse exchanged in the last three debates. To argue that Nixon presented an image of presidential leadership that was as appealing as Kennedy's would require a critic to locate crucial exchanges that suggested a dramatic reversal in character. I found no such exchanges in the last three debates. I did find important exchanges that seemed to confirm my conclusions regarding the images of presidential leadership developed in the first debate. Thus, to demonstrate the fact that in potentially threatening exchanges Kennedy avoided significant errors, the analysis in this chapter emphasizes exchanges that tested impressions from Chapter 2. In short, in the second debate, Nixon's skills as an advocate improved, but he still lacked an alternative vision of presidential leadership equal to Kennedy's.

Responsible Advocacy

Paul Niven's question to Nixon inviting criticism of Kennedy's claims that America was weak set up the issue of responsible advocacy. At this point, Nixon raised the ethical issue: "As far as Senator Kennedy's comments are concerned, I think he has a perfect right and a responsibility to criticize this administration whenever he thinks we're wrong; but he has a responsibility to be accurate and not to misstate the case." Nixon had identified an important element of national leadership and the way in which each candidate handled this issue would reveal sharp differences in his ability to manage appealing images of national character. If Nixon could substantiate his claim, Kennedy would appear unworthy of office; despite favorable performances in other exchanges, Kennedy would have failed a prerequisite for leadership—reliability, or the fact that he could be trusted to see the facts and use them accurately. The issue had reciprocal burdens for Nixon: Having charged Kennedy with irresponsible advocacy, he needed to prove his case or appear as though he lacked judgment concerning sensitive and important issues, such as ethics.

Nixon provided insufficient evidence to support his claim. Initially, he stated his opinion without supporting facts: "I don't think he [Kennedy] should say that our prestige is at an all-time low. I think this is very harmful at a time Mr. Khrushchev is here—harmful because it's wrong." Evidence of the inaccuracy came on the issue of hunger in America: "I don't think it was helpful when he suggested—and I'm glad he has corrected this to an extent—that 17 million people go to bed hungry every night in the United States. Now this just was not true."

Nixon made a comparison on two levels, arguing that there are fewer starving under the Eisenhower administration than there were under the Truman administration and that the United States had fewer starving people than any other country. The comparison was a much stronger use of evidence. Kennedy now had to refute these facts or appear as an irresponsible advocate. Kennedy proved the existence of a hunger problem with reluctant testimony:

Well, Mr. Nixon uh—I'll just give you the testimony of Mr. George Aiken— Senator George Aiken, the ranking minority member—Republican member— and former chairman of the Senate Agricultural Committee, testifying in 1959— said there were 26 million Americans who did not have the income to afford a decent diet. Mr. Benson, testifying on the food stamp plan in 1957, said there were 25 million Americans who could not afford a elementary, low-cost diet, and he defined that as someone who uses beans in place of meat. Now, I've seen a good many hundreds of thousands of people who are uh—not adequately fed. You can't tell me that a surplus food distribution of five cents po—per person—and that n—nearly six million Americans receiving that—is adequate. You can't tell me anyone who uses beans instead of meat in the United States— and there are 25 million of them according to Mr. Benson—is well fed or adequately fed.

The refutation was particularly vivid because Kennedy worked back and forth between statistics from Republican sources and illustrations from his own observations. Nixon's statistical comparisons between the United States and other countries were also refuted: "I believe that we should not compare what our figures may be to India or to some other country that has serious problems, but to remember that we are the most prosperous country in the world and that these people are not getting adequate food and they're not getting, in many cases, adequate shelter, and we ought to try to meet the problem." If the most prosperous nation in the world could not feed and shelter its people, Kennedy's campaign theme appeared true: Vigorous leadership was needed to get America moving again. Thus, Kennedy's use of evidence answered Nixon's charge of irresponsible advocacy and suggested that the Republicans had not fulfilled their responsibility to the hungry and homeless. The issue of responsible advocacy would develop again in the fourth debate in which Kennedy refuted Nixon's charge even more vividly.

The Role of Party Labels

Harold Levy closed the second debate on strong grounds for Kennedy by pressing Nixon to explain why he was urging voters to disregard party labels in the election. Levy focused the debate on Nixon's attempt to claim Kennedy's themes when he set up the following question for the vice president: "Mr. Vice President, you are urging voters to forget party labels and vote for the man. Senator Kennedy says that in doing this you are trying to run away from your party on such issues as housing and aid to education by advocating what he calls a 'me-too program.' Why do you say that party labels are not important?"

Attempting to place himself in the tradition of great presidents, Nixon stated, "I have found that in the history of this country we've had many great presidents. Some of them have been Democrats, and some of them have been Republicans. The people some way have always understood that, at a particular time, a certain man was the one the country needed." In place of party labels, Nixon suggested that the audience compare the candidates on the basis of what they stood for: "It isn't the label that he wears or that I wear that counts, it's what we are. It's what we believe."

Nixon defined the issue in terms of leadership, a good strategy given his limited performance in defending what was desirable for the nation. He stated: "What's involved here is the question of leadership for the whole free world. Now, that means the best leadership. It may be Republican, it may be Democratic, but the people are the ones that determine it. The people have to make up their minds." Although a nonpartisan tone was important for a candidate aspiring to national office, Nixon did not defend his candidacy in terms of the programs he offered for the nation. By indicating that the best leadership might be Republican or Democrat, he took no position. The implication was either (1) he did not know, disqualifying him for office on the grounds that he could not articulate what was desirable for the community or (2) he could not defend the Republican program for which he stood—and presumably held dear—disqualifying him for office on the basis of his inability to defend that which the community would entrust him to safeguard as their leader.

The most awkward moment came when Nixon asked Kennedy to lend him the credibility he lacked. First, Nixon argued without evidence that the Republican programs would move America forward faster than those of Kennedy. Nixon stated that his programs "will move America forward. They will move her forward faster and they will move her more surely than his [Kennedy's] program. This is what I deeply believe." Then, sensing that his belief was not enough to warrant support from the audience, Nixon said: "I'm sure he [Kennedy] believes just as deeply that his will move that way. I would suggest, however, that in the interest of fairness, that he could give me the benefit of also believing as he believes." Ingratiating in tone and confusing structurally, Nixon's words awkwardly asked Kennedy for the support he himself could not muster and suggested that he was unable to defend the Republican cause.

Kennedy's final comments followed two lines of attack. First, he said that "parties are important in that they tell something about the program and something about the man." Then Kennedy did what Nixon could not, he enacted himself in the role of Lincoln, Wilson, Roosevelt, and Truman while casting Nixon in the role of McKinley, Harding, Coolidge, Dewey, and Landon. Finally, Kennedy closed with an attack on the Republican party, stating: "And the Republicans in recent years—not only in the last twenty-five years, but in the last eight years—have opposed housing, opposed care for the aged, opposed federal aid to education, opposed minimum wage, and I think that record tells something."

In this exchange, Nixon chose not to substantiate the appeal of the Republican platform but instead argued that the people would somehow know whom to choose. Kennedy gave the audience a basis for choosing him over Nixon by challenging the Republican record on social issues and by using Levy's question as an opportunity to defend the desirability of the Democratic party.

Summary of Findings in the Second Debate

In the second debate, Kennedy was performing as a superior advocate mainly because, in contrast, Nixon was unable to sustain his attacks on these two issues dealing with presidential character. When Nixon tried to present himself in the tradition of great presidents, Kennedy turned the tables on him. When Nixon raised the charge of irresponsible advocacy, Kennedy used Republican testimony and vivid illustrations from his own experience to refute Nixon's statistics. When Nixon tried to feature America's strengths by comparing our nation to other countries, Kennedy suggested the comparison was unworthy for a nation of such great wealth claiming to be the best in the world community. Kennedy's use of argument, then, on these two key tests of presidential character was more satisfying than Nixon's. No vision of leadership cohered for Nixon, no attack on Kennedy's character was sustained, and no suggestion of presidential tone appeared in Nixon's words. Finally, understanding the limited appeal of his credibility, Nixon asked Kennedy to lend him his approval, a clear sign of Nixon's inability to defend his own image. Despite Nixon's improved performance in the first half of the second debate, on these matters of significant rhetorical action, Kennedy's performance was still superior on issues that defined presidential character.

THE THIRD DEBATE

Analysis of the third debate revealed Kennedy's ability to avoid rhetorical traps, Nixon's inability or reluctance to attack Kennedy, and Nix-

on's inability to develop his own sense of presidential style and substance in his answers. When Kennedy sidestepped the snares provided
by the panelists, Nixon had opportunities to press his attack but due to
reluctance or inability, did not, which allowed Kennedy's answers to
appear as plausible solutions to the rhetorical problems set by the panelists. In the exchanges over labor unions and economic growth, Nixon's
inability to develop his own presidential style and substance was revealed in his contradictory argument calling for change and maintenance
of the status quo. In contrast, Kennedy's answers continued to reflect
an image of a vigorous candidate running for office.

Avoiding Pratfalls, Missed Opportunities

In the third debate, the panelists had designed more difficult questions
to test the candidates. When Frank McGee opened up the third debate
by asking Kennedy if he would use military action to defend Berlin,
Kennedy gave evidence of our right to be in Berlin, then moved to
answer indirectly: "I don't think that there is any doubt in the mind of
any American; I hope there is not any doubt in the mind of any member
of the community of West Berlin. I am sure there isn't any doubt in the
minds of the Russians." Then, Kennedy redefined the issue. Instead of
revealing what actions he would take, Kennedy indicated only that he
thought our nation was committed to West Berlin. Because the audience
could insert any meaning they wanted for the phrase "meet our commitment," Kennedy's language choices allowed him to reassure the audience while avoiding an explicit commitment to a specific course of
action. The answer artfully dodged McGee's question.

Later in the debate, McGee constructed this situation for Kennedy:

Now, your running mate, Senator Lyndon Johnson, is from Texas, an oil-
producing state and one that many political leaders feel is in doubt in this election
year, and reports from there say that oil men in Texas are seeking assurances
from Senator Johnson that the oil depletion allowance will not be cut. The
Democratic platform pledges to plug loopholes in the tax laws and refers to
inequitable depletion allowance as being conspicuous loopholes. My question
is, do you consider the 27.5 percent depletion allowance inequitable, and would
you ask that it be cut?

If Kennedy accepted the terms of the question, he was placed in the
position of alienating Texas—a crucial state in the election—or appearing
inconsistent in his support of the Democratic platform. When Kennedy
said he would review the 104 depletion allowances and then decide, he
altered the terms of the question and redefined the situation from one
of apparent inconsistency to one in which he determined the choices
before him.

Kennedy's skill was also demonstrated in his use of humor. In Charles Von Fremd's second question during the third debate, he told Kennedy, "The Chairman of the Republican National Committee, Senator Thruston Morton, declared earlier this week that you owed Vice President Nixon and the Republican party a public apology for some strong charges made by former President Harry Truman, who bluntly suggested where the vice president and the Republican party could go." When Von Fremd asked Kennedy if he thought that he owed them an apology, Kennedy defended the right of Truman to express himself as he pleased and then took this as an opportunity for a bit of humor: "Perhaps Mrs. Truman can [change his manner of speaking], but I don't think I can. I'll just have to tell Mr. Morton that, if you'd pass that message on to him." Although Nixon took a more serious tone in arguing that children look to the president as a role model, Kennedy had defused the issue as a basis for disqualifying him for office.

As Kennedy steered around these obstacles, Nixon had an opportunity to probe weaknesses. On the Berlin question, he did not criticize Kennedy's failure to answer directly and changed the focus of the question to an underdeveloped comparison of the two parties in terms of the wars for which they had been responsible. On the oil depletion issue, Nixon slipped into the trap Kennedy avoided, had the ladder with which he could climb out, but failed to use it. First, by stating that he clearly supported the "present depletion allowance," Nixon assured the oil constituency at the expense of offending his Democratic and undecided audience. Because Johnson was from Texas, it would seem that that state had more to gain from a Democratic ticket than a Republican one. Nixon had the statistic to refute Kennedy's previous answer when he stated: "I should point out, that as far as depletion allowances are concerned, the oil depletion is one that provides 80 percent of all those involved in depletion, so you're not going to get much revenue insofar as depletion allowances are concerned, unless you move in the area that he indicated." But when Nixon used "move in the area he indicated" in place of a specific reference to Kennedy's program, the force of his criticism was diminished. Nixon was not connecting Kennedy clearly, specifically, and unambiguously to the need to cut oil depletion allowances. In this respect, his answer did not force Kennedy away from the tentative position of studying the issue. Further, Nixon could have argued that studying the issue was irrelevant, that Kennedy would be required to cut the oil depletion allowance because of the problem posed by the mathematics of depletion allowances. Placing the statistic at the conclusion of the answer and not pressing the implication meant that the audience was left to do the analysis on its own. Although Nixon had the information to construct a good attack, he did not illustrate very well why Kennedy's position on oil depletion allowances was indefensible. Here Nixon was right, but did not do enough to illustrate for the audience why Kennedy was wrong.

Labor Unions and Economic Growth

His answer to McGee's question on labor unions revealed Nixon's inability to distinguish himself from Kennedy stylistically when he adopted Kennedy's campaign theme: "In this critical year—period of the sixties we've got to move forward; all Americans must move forward together, and we have to get the greatest cooperation possible between labor and management. We cannot afford stoppages of massive effect on the economy when we're in the terrible competition we're in with the Soviets." In the fourth debate, Nixon's use of Kennedy's theme would be more pronounced. His use of Kennedy's theme in the third debate suggested that even at this point in the campaign, he was still unable to develop his own style and themes with which he could appeal to the audience. Later in the debate, answering Roscoe Drummond's follow up of the second debate in which the issue of who can achieve the greatest amount of economic growth developed, Nixon used the Kennedy campaign theme but without the corresponding argumentative substance of Kennedy's previous answers: "Mr. Drummond, I am never satisfied with the economic growth of this country. I'm not satisfied with it even if there were no communism in the world, but particularly when we're in the kind of race we're in, we have got to see that America grows just as fast as we can, provided we grow soundly." The repetition of the phrase "I'm not satisfied" was reminiscent of Kennedy's charges against the Eisenhower administration. Also, Nixon reminded the audience of an argument he made in the first debate, but the reminder evoked an image of Kennedy, not Nixon: "Because even though we have maintained, as I pointed out in our first debate, the absolute gap over the Soviet Union; even though the growth in this administration has been twice as much as it was in the Truman administration, that isn't good enough."

From this point, Nixon, like Kennedy in his opening statement, listed the reasons that we needed more economic growth: to take care of our domestic needs such as education, housing, and health and to maintain our forces abroad. After completing the essential steps of Kennedy's opening charges, Nixon returned to his opening theme: "Now what all this of course adds up to is this: America has not been standing still." After speaking in the persona of Kennedy, after constructing a case for greater economic growth in the same organizational pattern as Kennedy, and after covering some of the same areas of need for economic growth as Kennedy, Nixon then argued inconsistently that all of this meant that America was not standing still. Here, Nixon's attempt to present himself in the image of Kennedy was unconvincing; returning to his own platform revealed the inconsistent appeal. Concluding his answer, Nixon tried on Kennedy's image once again. "We have been moving. We have been moving much faster than we did in the Truman years, but we can and must move faster, and that's why I stand so strongly for programs that will move America forward in the sixties, move her forward so that we can stay ahead of the Soviet Union and win the battle for freedom and peace."

Kennedy's response followed the pattern he had established earlier. He used none of Nixon's campaign messages and featured no contradiction. He repeated Nixon's opposition to aid to education in the way of teacher salaries. He created doubt about Nixon's sincerity on the issue of aid to distressed areas when he provided evidence indicating that the incumbent administration vetoed legislation of that type passed by Congress. To refute Nixon's criticism of the Truman administration, Kennedy argued that the United States had had the lowest rate of economic growth compared to all industrialized societies during the Eisenhower administration. The most important aspect of Kennedy's performance was the fact that he avoided Nixon's contradiction, that the United States needed to move but that it had been moving. Finally, Nixon's performance seemed less appealing than Kennedy's because he had used Kennedy's campaign themes at two places in the answer. Thus, Nixon appeared to be embracing Kennedy's original claims.

Summary of Findings in the Third Debate

The third debate showed Kennedy as being adept in solving rhetorical problems and more capable of defending the Democratic ticket as a program for economic growth. In contrast, Nixon was unable to maintain his indictments of Kennedy's programs, could not explain why the Republican ticket was a superior program for growth, and failed in his attempt to enact Kennedy's persona of a strong candidate.

THE FOURTH DEBATE

Nixon's inability to discover his own style of leadership was evident in stylistic and substantive choices during the fourth debate in which his desire to shape an image similar to Kennedy's was evident in his use of Kennedy's words and theme in the opening statement. This problem persisted in the closing statement. Because Nixon's use of Kennedy's style and theme constituted strong evidence to suggest his inability to develop his own style and concept of leadership for the 1960 campaign, the opening and closing statements are given extended consideration. Also, in the fourth debate, Nixon repeated his charge that

Kennedy was an irresponsible advocate. Because responsible advocacy was an essential prerequisite for presidential reliability, and because Nixon was given another opportunity to make his case against Kennedy on this important issue, the question about American prestige was given consideration.

The Opening Statements

In his opening statement, Nixon boiled the contest down to one issue: "There is one issue that stands out above all the rest; one in which every American is concerned, regardless of what group he may be a member and regardless of where he may live. And that issue, very simply stated, is this: How can we keep the peace—keep it without surrender. How can we extend freedom—extend it without war?" Nixon had been gaining support with the "peace" issue and to feature it here in the opening statement in the last debate, his last chance to perform better than Kennedy, was a good strategy. However, Nixon did not explain how Kennedy's programs upset peace in the status quo. Because Kennedy's theme to get America moving again did not obviously imply war, the burden of proof was on Nixon to demonstrate why the Democratic platform would lead to war.

Alternatively, Kennedy had been attacking the Eisenhower administration for its lack of vigorous leadership in its failure to move America forward. During the campaign and especially within the debates, Nixon had been unable to answer the charge that America could move forward in many areas. This forced the burden of rebuttal on Nixon. In this debate, he had two objectives: demonstrate how Kennedy's program risked war and demonstrate how Eisenhower's policies maintained peace at an acceptable rate of economic growth, the essential quality Kennedy claimed was lacking in the Republican program.

Nixon used rhetorical questions to shape the answer to his question, "How do we keep the peace? "Who threatens freedom in the world?" According to Nixon, the problem was international communism and the solution was the Republican candidate, Richard Nixon. The criterion for leadership was the ability to deal with Communists: "And therefore, if we are to have peace, if we are to keep our own freedom and extend it to others without war, we must know how to deal with the Communists and their leaders."

Nixon's strategy in this final debate was potentially effective. Unlike Kennedy, Nixon had more experience in the executive branch. Nixon stated one of this best credentials for office: "I know Mr. Khrushchev. I also have had the opportunity of knowing and meeting other Communist leaders in the world." This reference to personal experience should have heightened Nixon's credibility, especially since the reference to Khrushchev would recall Nixon's "Kitchen debates" with the Soviet leader. In these ways, Nixon was defining leadership in terms of the ability to handle oneself in conflict with the Soviets. Nixon outlined a number of principles he believed were necessary to follow when dealing with the Communists: "I believe there are certain principles we must find in dealing with him [Khrushchev] and his colleagues—principles, if followed, that will keep the peace and that also can extend freedom." But by failing to define these principles of presidential leadership in a direct way, Nixon missed an opportunity to enact the role of president on his own terms.

The remainder of the opening statement made two well-developed arguments: We could not return to the past Democratic policies of Truman and we had to move ahead in the future to stay ahead of the Communists. Both of these claims were well supported. However, they did not answer the charge that had been leveled by Kennedy, that we needed to get America moving again. In granting Kennedy the first opportunity to speak in the first debate, Nixon had allowed Kennedy to create a rhetorical problem for him. Whenever Nixon agreed that America needed to get moving again, he appeared as though he was acquiescing to the younger, less experienced candidate. This theme forced Nixon into the position of explaining why it was necessary to get America moving if the current administration had been doing a satisfactory job. Each time Nixon attempted to discuss areas for improvement, he was confronted with a contradictory set of statements. Finally, because of Kennedy's simple phrasing of his theme—the need to get America moving again—each time Nixon used the word "move," it reminded the audience of Kennedy's opening statement in the first debate in which he argued that the nation had not been moving vigorously enough under the Eisenhower administration. When Nixon discussed the need to look to the future in the opening statement, he appeared to be acquiescing to the opposing candidate, searching for an appropriate rhetorical stance to avoid contradicting himself on the record of his previous opponent's criticisms. In these ways, Nixon's rhetoric revealed a less vibrant image of leadership than that of Kennedy.

Nixon's first point was that we must learn from the past, an implicit attack on the Truman administration. What was missing from this argument was a step explaining why Kennedy should be identified with the Truman administration. In earlier debates, Nixon had asserted that Kennedy's programs were "retreads" of Truman's programs but was unable to establish the similarity in a substantive way. One might infer from the lack of well-developed arguments that Nixon's image of his audience was composed primarily of Republican constituents. Absent supporting evidence, however, Nixon's charge was unappealing to undecideds and conservative Democrats. The most important step in the argument, then, the step requiring Kennedy to defend the Truman administration, was lacking in Nixon's appeal.

Nixon's strategy, to defend the Eisenhower administration by comparing it to the Truman administration, was made in terms of a retrospective outlook. No discussion of how Eisenhower's policies addressed concerns of the future was developed by Nixon. When Nixon did discuss the future, it was in Kennedy's words, of needing to get America moving. Hence, the crucial question of how the Republican platform, an outgrowth of the Eisenhower administration, could best deal with the future—compared to the Democratic platform represented in Kennedy's words—was not directly answered by Nixon's opening address. And the part of Nixon's opening statement that addressed the future echoed Kennedy's vision, not Nixon's.

Nixon developed his attack on the Truman administration by repeating his argument from the third debate: "First, we have to learn from the past because we cannot afford to make the mistakes of the past. In the seven years before this administration came to power in Washington, we found that 600 million people went behind the iron curtain, and at the end of that seven years we were engaged in a war in Korea which cost over thirty thousand American lives." Having developed the shortcomings of the Truman administration, Nixon bolstered the Eisenhower administration: "In the past seven years, in President Eisenhower's administration, this situation has been reversed. We ended the Korean war by strong, firm leadership. We have kept out of other wars and we have avoided surrender of principle or territory at the conference table." Although his statements supported the Eisenhower administration, a sense of strong leadership ability was still undeveloped. Nixon's words described Eisenhower's leadership as strong, firm, and effective, but not his own.

Nixon reviewed the errors of the Truman administration leading to the Korean War and then contrasted this mistake with the Republican attitude toward arms control. Nixon used this point as a justification for Eisenhower's refusal to apologize for the U–2 flights prior to the summit conference and to raise the issue of Quemoy and Matsu again.

Nixon then moved from his defense of the Eisenhower administration to a discussion of the future: "And so I say that the record shows that we know how to keep the peace, to keep it without surrender. Let us now move to the future." Nixon's use of the pronoun "we" rather than "I" reinforced the feeling that he was not defending a record to which he contributed, but rather that he was defending a record with which he was associated. The difference was important. In other places, Nixon had given the impression that he could defend Eisenhower's past record but not his own proposals for the future. Finding this stylistic choice in the opening statement provided more evidence for the claim that Nixon was able to present himself only in the role of the vice president.

Nixon's transition to a discussion of the future was stylistically reminiscent of Kennedy's opening statement in the first debate in which he argued that the country needed to get moving again. When Nixon used the verb five times in the last third of his opening statement, he conjured up images of Kennedy: "Let us move now to the future"; "That is why I say that in this period of the sixties, America must move forward in every area"; "We have to move forward to stay ahead"; "I have made recommendations which I am confident will move the American economy ahead—move it firmly and soundly."

Two other stylistic elements reminiscent of Kennedy were present in Nixon's opening statement. Nixon used Kennedy's framing of the sixties as a crucial decade and he used Kennedy's claim that America had a destiny: "We must have a great goal, and that is: not just to keep freedom for ourselves but to extend it to all the world. To extend it to all the world because that is America's destiny."

Nixon's two connections were in tension with each other. In the first point, he defended the status quo. In the second, he called for America to move ahead of the Soviet Union. How could Nixon justify the need to move ahead if the record of the Eisenhower administration was acceptable? Essentially, Nixon's position was that we were in a deadly race with the Soviets and that we could not become complacent. But in the three instances in which Nixon said that the accomplishments of the Eisenhower administration were not enough, he followed with Kennedy's stylistic call to move America in the sixties: "It is not enough to stand on this record because we are dealing with the most ruthless, fanatical . . . leaders that the world has ever seen. That is why I say in this period of the sixties America must move ahead in every area." Referring to the economy, Nixon said: "And the reason it [the economy] must grow—even more is because we have things to do at home, and also because we're in a race for survival—a race in which it isn't enough to be ahead; it isn't enough simply to be complacent. We have to move ahead in order to stay ahead. And that is why, in this field I will move the American economy ahead—move it firmly and soundly." Finally, calling for a dedication to a great goal, Nixon stated: "But all this, by itself, is not enough. It is not enough for us simply to be the strongest nation militarily, the strongest economically and also to have firm diplomacy. We must have a great goal, and that is: Not just to keep freedom for ourselves but to extend it to all the world. To extend it to all the world because that is America's destiny." The theme, although similar in content to Kennedy's message, lacked an equally appealing personal style and thus Nixon's second point reflected a dim image of Kennedy's more vibrant and vigorous character.

One reason for Nixon's use of Kennedy's position might have been to integrate it into the appeals of the Republican campaign. By incorporating the essential aspects of Kennedy's programs, Nixon could have claimed that the difference between the two programs was in his experience and in his inheritance of the successful Eisenhower administration. Although this was a sensible strategy, it assumed that Nixon could meld the opposition's arguments with the party line in such a way that made opposition difficult, rhetorically. But Nixon's use of Kennedy's key words and Kennedy's arguments revealed that he had not formulated an effective alternative to the more charismatic, more credible, and more effective image embodied in Kennedy's rhetoric.

Kennedy's opening statement refocused the issue of the debate from a comparison of the Truman and Eisenhower administrations to whether other nations would want to be identified with us in the future. Kennedy's opening statement was strong in its substantive appeal, featuring extensive refutation of Nixon's claims. To support his arguments, Kennedy used various kinds of evidence, a strategy of enumeration, and was specific in his use of evidence. What was most characteristic of Kennedy's opening statement was that he sought a basis for comparing the candidates.

Kennedy adopted the persona of "any American" or the "average American" at strategic points to bolster his arguments. He used personal witnessing to create identification between himself and his audience. Because vigor and vitality were qualities of leadership the average American would endorse, Kennedy's image seemed preferable to Nixon's.

Kennedy's opening statement also refuted Nixon's criticisms. To support his claim that he had accurately described the administration's policy in his statements throughout the debates, Kennedy used his own expertise as a member of the Senate Foreign Relations Committee and said that he had reread the testimony of General Twining to make sure he had been correct in his statements: "In the last week, as a member of the Senate Foreign Relations Committee, I reread the testimony of General Twining, representing the administration in 1959, and the assistant secretary of state, before the Foreign Relations Committee in 1958, and I have accurately described the administration policy and I support it wholeheartedly." In previous exchanges, Nixon had never been specific about when, where, and how Kennedy might have gone on record opposing the Eisenhower policy. In this statement, Kennedy offered a specific source, the testimony of the Eisenhower administration's representative to the Foreign Relations Committee. If Nixon desired to prove that Kennedy had been inconsistent, he needed to be specific about when and where in the public record Kennedy opposed the policy he now claimed to support. Kennedy's argument was substantively more appealing than Nixon's unsupported indictment.

From Quemoy and Matsu, Kennedy made a transition to what he defined as the central question in the campaign. The transition was exclusive. Kennedy pared away Quemoy and Matsu, then eliminated Nixon's definition of the issue to offer his own:

So that [Quemoy and Matsu] really isn't an issue in this campaign. It isn't an issue with Mr. Nixon, who now says he also supports the Eisenhower policy. Nor is the question that all Americans want peace and security an issue in this campaign. The question is: Are we moving in the direction of peace and security? Is our relative strength growing? Is—as Mr. Nixon says—our prestige at an all time high, as he said a week ago, and that of Communists at an all time low?

Controlling the question before the audience, Kennedy refocused the comparison and acknowledged the need to demonstrate that U.S. prestige was low. Kennedy then forecast the remainder of his case in terms of three issues: peace and security, strength relative to that of the Soviet Union, and national prestige. These three points formed the basis for Kennedy's later attack on Nixon's definition of the issues. Later Kennedy would argue that he too wanted peace and security, that he too believed America was great, and that the kind of society we build here determined our prestige overseas. Kennedy would take issue, however, with the way these goals had been pursued in the Eisenhower administration. The key element here was the argument of direction that Kennedy was building.[3] Kennedy's contention was that the nature of the Eisenhower administration lacked vigor and vitality. In contrast, Kennedy offered a more vigorous style of leadership. This strategy controlled the development of the opening statement.

Kennedy's method of proving his indictments of the Eisenhower administration offered an image of a candidate with a wide range of rhetorical forms for proving his points, and this suggested in a stylistic way that he was a candidate capable of approaching problems with a variety of resources. Adopting the persona of the average American, Kennedy presented facts supporting the claim that the nation's prestige was at an all-time low. Moving from the series of rhetorical questions above, Kennedy answered them negatively: "I don't believe it [American prestige] is [at an all-time high as Nixon stated]. I don't believe our relative strength is increasing, and I say that, not as the Democratic standard-bearer, but as a citizen of the United States who is concerned about the United States." Stating that he was a common citizen, though, was not the same as speaking like one. To provide the audience with evidence of the similarity, Kennedy witnessed historical events as they might have:

I look at Cuba, ninety miles off the coast of the United States. In 1957 I was in Havana. I talked to the American ambassador there. He said that he was the second most powerful man in Cuba, and yet even though Ambassador Smith and Ambassador Gardner, both Republican ambassadors, both warned of Castro, the Marxist influences around Castro, the Communist influences around Castro, both of them have testified in the last six weeks that in spite of their warnings to the American government, nothing was done.

Republican ambassadors provided reluctant, recent, and consistent testimony to the fact that the Eisenhower administration did not act to prevent Cuba from turning to the Communists when it had its chance.

Using the same way of "looking" at world affairs through the eyes of the average American, Kennedy turned to Latin America:

Our d—security depends upon Latin America. Can any American, looking at the situation in Latin America, feel contented with what's happening today, when a candidate for the presidency of Brazil feels it necessary to call—not on Washington during the campaign—but on Castro in Havana, in order to pick up the support of the Castro supporters in Brazil?

Appealing to national pride, the answer was obvious: Americans should feel ashamed that political candidates in Latin American countries looked to Castro for support rather than the United States. Both the Cuba and the Brazil examples had been used in previous debates. In this debate, Kennedy added another example to illustrate how United States prestige had declined in the region: "At the American Conference—inter-American conference this summer, when we wanted them to join together in the denunciation of Castro and Cuban Communists, we couldn't even get the inter-American group to join together in denouncing Castro. It was a rather vague statement that they finally made." If America could not persuade Latin American states to denounce Castro, Kennedy's charge that American prestige was low seemed true.

Kennedy's fourth example in Latin America dealt with broadcasts to Cuba and Latin America. Kennedy used a rhetorical question to reveal that the Russians broadcast ten times as many programs in Spanish to Latin America as the United States did. The tone was personal, almost as though Kennedy was a neighbor, and thus created identification between him and his audience.

Africa was the third area in world affairs Kennedy addressed, arguing that the Eisenhower administration had given it little attention: "Africa is now the emerging area of the world. It contains 25 percent of all the members of the General Assembly [in the United Nations]." Kennedy added, "And yet last year we gave them less than 5 percent of all the technical assistance funds that we distributed around the world."

Next Kennedy argued that we had lost influence in the Middle East: "We relied in the Middle East on the Baghdad Pact, and yet when the Iraqi government was changed, the Baghdad Pact broke down. We relied on the Eisenhower Doctrine for the Middle East which passed the Senate.

There isn't one country in the Middle East that now endorses the Eisenhower Doctrine."

When Kennedy turned his attention to Asia, he asked a series of rhetorical questions. It was in this section that Kennedy attempted to shift the focus of comparison from the Truman and Eisenhower administrations to a comparison of the Eisenhower administration with Kennedy's program of invigorating national leadership. Kennedy stated: "We look to Europe uh—to Asia because the struggle is in the underdeveloped world. Which system, communism or freedom, will triumph in the next five or ten years? That's what should concern us, not the history of ten or fifteen or twenty years ago. But are we doing enough in these areas? What are freedom's chances in these areas?" This section was expanded into a series of rhetorical questions leading back to Kennedy's main theme:

By 1965 or 1970, will there be other Cubas in Latin America? Will Guinea and Ghana, which have now voted with the Communists frequently as newly independent countries of Africa—will there be others? Will the Congo go Communist? Will other countries? Are we doing enough in that area? And what about Asia? Is India going to win the economic struggle, or is China going to win it? Who will dominate Asia in the next five or ten years? Communism? the Chinese? Or will freedom?

These questions created a sense of uncertainty about the future. Since both Kennedy and Nixon agreed that the major issue in the campaign was how to meet the threat of communism, these questions were appropriate for the candidates to pursue. But the conclusion to this section highlighted Kennedy's approach to the problem, not Nixon's: "The question which we have to decide as Americans—Are we doing enough today? Is our strength and prestige rising? Do people want to be identified with us? Do they want to follow United States leadership? I don't think they do, enough, and that's what concerns me." Again Kennedy was focusing the issue in terms of his campaign theme.

Kennedy began a second list of examples that illustrated the lack of vigor in the Eisenhower administration. One example was the voting patterns on accepting the People's Republic of China into the United Nations previously discussed in the third debate. After this example, Kennedy's style changed from an argumentative stance to a more emotional means of expressing his evidence. It was characterized by the opening phrase, "I have seen, . . . " a form of witnessing: "I have seen Cuba go to the Communists. I have seen Communist influence and Castro influence rise in Latin America. I have seen us ignore Africa." The statements served as an internal summary to Kennedy's arguments and constituted a good example of how Kennedy used his credibility as a rhetor to bolster the substantive appeal developed in prior passages.

In supporting his claim that we have ignored Africa, Kennedy related the story of how, after Guinea achieved independence, the Soviets moved quickly to have an ambassador there while we did not recognize the nation for two months. He also stated that "there are six countries in Africa that are members of the United Nations. There isn't a single American diplomatic representative in any of those six." The implication of these charges was summarized in Kennedy's characterization of Eisenhower's leadership: "I believe that the world is changing fast, and I don't think this administration has shown the foresight, has shown the knowledge, has been identified with the great fight which these people are waging to be free, to get a better standard of living, to live better." This was one of two sections that characterized the Eisenhower administration. Kennedy had to attack the character of leadership to establish the argument of direction portraying the Eisenhower administration as static, unresponding, without vigor in a world that demanded prompt and vigorous response to Communist challenges.

Kennedy offered a second example to demonstrate that the Eisenhower administration had ignored the world situation: "The average income in some of those countries is $25 a year. The Communists say, 'Come with us; look what we've done.' And we've been in—on the whole, uninterested." Though Kennedy offered no evidence to support the claim beyond this illustration, its rhetorical function was potentially effective because it attempted to characterize the attitude of the Eisenhower administration.

Kennedy's next move was to seek agreement on values and indicate areas of disagreement. Kennedy addressed three issues that had been discussed in previous debates: military strength, economic growth, and prestige. Kennedy took Nixon's contention, gave assent to it, and then illustrated why Nixon's view of the issue was not satisfactory.

Mr. Nixon talks about our being the strongest country in the world. I think we are today, but we were far stronger relative to the Communists five years ago. And what is of great concern is that the balance of power is in danger of moving with them. They made a breakthrough in missiles, and by 1961, 2, and 3, they will be outnumbering us in missiles. I'm not as confident as he is that we will be the strongest military power by 1963.

Kennedy's second section followed the same pattern of the first:

He [Nixon] talks about economic growth as a great indicator of freedom. I agree with him. What we do in this country, the kind of society that we build: That will tell whether freedom will be sustained around the world and yet in the last nine months of this year we've had a drop in our economic growth rather than a gain. We've had the lowest rate of increase of economic growth in the last nine months of any major industrialized society in the world.

By agreeing with Nixon, he used his standards for evaluating the Eisenhower administration. Because the evaluation was unfavorable, Kennedy forced Nixon into a defensive position. Either Nixon had to change the standards or he had to refute the facts. Kennedy closed this section with another example supporting his claim concerning U.S. prestige.

Kennedy's conclusion to the opening statement was effective because it summarized his case, reviewed what both candidates agreed on, pointed to the question on which they differed, and enacted him in the role of a vigorous leader concerned about the future of the country:

The point of all this is: This is a struggle in which we are engaged. We want peace. We want freedom. We want security. We want to be stronger. But I don't believe, in these changing and revolutionary times, this administration has known that the world is changing—has identified itself with that change. I think the Communists have been moving with vigor—Laos, Africa, Cuba—all around the world they're on the move. I think we have to revitalize our society. I think we have to demonstrate to the people of the world that we are determined in this free country of ours to be first—not first "if" and not first "but" and not first "when"—but first. And when we are strong, and when we are first, then freedom gains. Then the prospects for peace increase. Then the prospects for our security . . . gain.

This was a fitting conclusion for Kennedy's opening statement. It stressed the need for being first and foremost among nations without qualification. Structurally, the simple, direct syntax gave the impression of an active, vibrant personality. The tone was firm, enhancing Kennedy's appeal as a strong leader. Stylistically, the elements of the opening statement revealed Kennedy to be a formidable advocate, knowledgeable of what it meant to represent America in the international arena, and capable of defending national interests in the upcoming struggle with communism. In these regards, Nixon offered a much less desirable alternative.

In summary, Nixon had not developed a coherent and appealing image to offer the nation in his opening statement in the fourth debate. Although Kennedy did not specifically extend his use of FDR's persona, it might be that he had successfully developed his own sense of style, that although it had been necessary to borrow the persona of FDR at the outset of the debates, it was no longer necessary given Kennedy's superior performance in crucial exchanges. In this opening statement, Kennedy's style and substance reflected a vigorous leader, appropriate for the campaign because Nixon was unable to defend against Kennedy's substantive attacks on the Eisenhower administration. When Nixon tried to defend the Republican platform, he did so only as an extension of the Eisenhower administration, a serious problem for Nixon because he was placed in the position of defending inconsistent positions. When

Nixon tried to answer Kennedy's claim that the nation was not moving fast enough, he used Kennedy's style and campaign theme, presenting a dim and undesirable image of leadership compared to Kennedy's.

Kennedy Refutes Nixon's Ethical Charge

In the fourth debate, Walter Cronkite raised the issue of U.S. prestige when he asked: "Mr. Vice President, Senator Fulbright and now tonight Senator Kennedy maintains that the administration is suppressing a report by the United States Information Agency that shows a decline in United States prestige overseas. Are you aware of such a report, and if you are aware of the existence of such a report, should not that report because of the great importance this issue has been given in this campaign, be released to the public?" In response to Cronkite's question, Nixon offered the following refutation:

I want to point out that the facts simply aren't as stated. First of all, the report to which Senator Kennedy refers is one that was made many, many months ago and related particularly to the uh—period immediately after Sputnik. Second, as far as this report is concerned, I would have no objection to having it made public. Third, I would say this with regard to this report, with regard to Gallup Polls of prestige abroad and everything else that we've been hearing about "what about American prestige abroad?" America's prestige abroad will be just as high as the spokesman for America will allow it to be.

Only the first point dealt with the report in question. Nixon cast doubt on the recency of the evidence by implying that the low estimation of U.S. prestige was attributable to the Sputnik shot, not to Eisenhower's programs. Nixon's third point set up an attack on Kennedy's claim that American prestige was low. By arguing that American prestige was as high as America's spokesperson will allow, Nixon could then use evidence to refute Kennedy's claim, prove America's prestige was high because the facts supported that claim, and offer himself in the role of America's spokesperson.

Nixon refuted Kennedy's claim that American prestige was low by charging that Kennedy had not stated the facts correctly:

Now, when we have a presidential candidate, for example—Senator Kennedy— stating over and over again that the United States is second in space, and the fact of the matter is that the space score today is twenty-eight to eight—we've had twenty-eight successful shots; they've had eight. When he states that we're second in education, and I have seen Soviet education and I have seen ours, and we're not. That we're second in science because they may be ahead in one area or another, when overall we're way ahead of the Soviet Union and all other categories in science.

Nixon shifted the comparison of space programs from a criterion of manned orbit to a criterion of total number of successful shots and he shifted the criterion of evaluating science from some areas to an overall comparison. On education, he provided no evidence beyond his own observation. This claim depended on Nixon's credibility.

Nixon continued to list areas of criticism but offered no evidence to refute them: "When he [Kennedy] says, as he did in January of this years, [sic] that we have the worst slums, that we have the most crowded schools, when he says that 17 million people go to bed hungry every night—when he makes statements like this, what does it do to American prestige? Well, it can only have the effect, certainly, of reducing it." Nixon's claim, then, was that Kennedy, not the Eisenhower administration, was the instrument of battered prestige. Nixon extended this attack to question Kennedy's ethics as a responsible advocate: "Senator Kennedy has a responsibility to criticize those things that are wrong but he also has a responsibility to be right in his criticism. Every one of these items that I have mentioned he's been wrong—dead wrong. And for that reason he has contributed to any lack of prestige." Nixon indicted Kennedy's ability to present facts accurately, an important skill for a prospective president. When Nixon asserted that Kennedy was irresponsible, he assumed a superior stance in passing judgment on Kennedy's behavior. The passage is a good focus for evaluating the candidates because one may presume that a challenge to one's integrity is the best test of an individual's ability. If Kennedy could demonstrate that he was right on the issue of American prestige, he could prove that he was capable of managing his own image and would give symbolic evidence of his ability to protect community values.

Nixon's final move was to refute Kennedy's claim that prestige was low by presenting evidence that the United States enjoyed great support in the United Nations. His examples were votes taken on China, Hungary, and Khrushchev's behavior. Then he concluded with another reference to Kennedy's irresponsibility: "The president gained [after Khrushchev's behavior in the United Nations]. America gained by continuing the dignity, the decency that has characterized us and its that that keeps the prestige of America up—not running down America the way Senator Kennedy has been running her down."

Kennedy's first move was to acknowledge Nixon's attempts to assert a one-up relationship and then refute it. Kennedy did not argue that it was not Nixon's right to do so but instead did not need Nixon's assistance to define what his responsibility was. Kennedy said, "I really don't need uh—Mr. Nixon to tell me about what my responsibilities are as a citizen. I've served this country for fourteen years in the Congress and before that in the service. I have just as high a devotion, and just as high an opinion." Second, Kennedy made a distinction between attacking the nation and the nation's leadership. "What I downgrade, Mr. Nixon, is the leadership the country is getting, not the country." The distinction forced Nixon to defend the leadership or provide an adequate explanation for the problems Kennedy has listed. Third, Kennedy refuted Nixon's statements by arguing that Nixon had misrepresented him. "Now, I didn't make most of the statements that you said I made. The s—I believe the Soviet Union is first in outer space. We have—may have made more shots, but the size of their rocket thrust and all the rest—you yourself, said to Khrushchev, 'You may be ahead of us in rocket thrust but we're ahead of you in color television' in your famous discussion in the kitchen." Next, Kennedy refuted Nixon's comments on slums: "Secondly, I didn't say we had the worst slums in the world. I said we had too many slums, that they are bad, and we ought to do something about them and we ought to support housing legislation which this administration has opposed."

The same pattern of refutation was applied to the example of education. Kennedy said that what Nixon quoted was incorrect, corrected Nixon, and then advanced to attack the Eisenhower administration: "I didn't say we had the worst education in the world. What I say was that ten years ago we were producing twice as many scientists and engineers as the Soviet Union, and today they're producing twice as many as we are and this affects our security around the world." Kennedy's fourth point was an example of how he visualized his leadership in contrast to Nixon's. "And fourth, I believe that the polls and other studies and votes in the United Nations and anyone reading the paper and any citizen of the United States must come to the conclusion that the United States no longer carries the same image of a vital society, on the move, with its brightest days ahead as it carried a decade or two decades ago." The argument was not advancing by this late point in the debate. Kennedy had presented most, if not all of the evidence he had to support this point. He relied on his credibility as a candidate when he stated, "I believe," and his lack of specificity in referring to polls, studies, and votes suggested that the audience must decide for themselves based on the evidence presented.

Kennedy concluded by arguing that the explanation for the lack of a vital society was in the fact that "we've stood still here at home," reinforcing the attack on the Eisenhower administration's leadership and economic policy. Kennedy also answered Nixon's claim that we were ahead in science by arguing that we were not ahead in space science, which Kennedy claimed was the new science.

In summary, Kennedy's answer revealed Nixon's inability to cite facts accurately. Nixon's charge that Kennedy was irresponsible was refuted. In this respect, Kennedy appeared to be more capable of responsible leadership than Nixon because he demonstrated his ability to defend his character against attack.

Closing Statements

Kennedy's closing provided an appropriate conclusion to his campaign. Kennedy returned to the theme of needing to get America moving again. To support this broad claim, Kennedy attacked Nixon and the Republican party, and then contrasted these two aspects of the opposition with the desirable elements of the Democratic party. Then Kennedy offered his vision of leadership for the nation: "I believe it my responsibility as the leader of the Democratic party in 1960 to try to warn the American people that in this crucial time we can no longer afford to stand still. We can no longer afford to be second best." The second element of the closing statement was a positive message:

I want people all over the world to look to the United States again, to feel that we're on the move, to feel that our high noon is in the future. I want Mr. Khrushchev to know that a new generation of Americans who fought in Europe, in Italy, and the Pacific for freedom in World War II have now taken over in the United States, and that they're going to get this country back to work again.

In these two excerpts from the closing statement, Kennedy's language represented an active image of leadership. Anticipating crisis, Kennedy tried "to warn" that "we can no longer afford to stand still," "no longer afford to be second best." Relieving the tension of anticipated crisis, Kennedy desired that people "look to the United States," "to feel we're on the move," "to feel that our high noon is in the future." Kennedy's repeated use of the infinitive verb form suggested active leadership. By giving the audience a sense of how he viewed the world, how he felt about these issues, and how he responded symbolically to these challenges, Kennedy presented an image of a strong, vibrant leader.

Kennedy's sense of confidence, optimism, and resolve was unmistakable in these words presaging the inaugural: "I don't believe that there is anything this country cannot do. I don't believe there is any burden or any responsibility that any American would not assume to protect his country, protect our security, to advance the cause of freedom." In his conclusion, Kennedy returned to the words of FDR: "Franklin Roosevelt said in 1936 that that generation of Americans had a "rendezvous with destiny." I believe in 1960 and 61 and 2 and 3 we have a rendezvous with destiny, and I believe it incumbent upon us to be the defenders of the United States and the defenders of freedom, and to do that we must give this country leadership, and we must get

America moving again." By returning to his opening statement in the first debate, Kennedy completed the process of placing before the nation its unfinished business, and by borrowing the words of Franklin Roosevelt, as well as portraying the election as a decision at a time of great national crisis, suggested that he, like Roosevelt, possessed the requisite qualities of presidential leadership needed by the country.

Nixon's closing statement was disappointing. His final position was that America was not standing still but had to move faster, two points that were inconsistent in the context of this campaign and which have been analyzed previously for the ways in which they limited Nixon's appeal as an alternative to Kennedy. Finally, Nixon reviewed the charges he had made against Kennedy but failed to provide further evidence to support his arguments. In short, Nixon's closing statement did not solve his rhetorical problems, did not offer a concept of leadership, and did not develop a distinct style of presidential character.

Summary of Findings in the Fourth Debate

The fourth debate revealed Nixon's weaknesses and Kennedy's strengths in the opening and closing statements and in the exchange over responsible advocacy. Although Kennedy gave his most disappointing answers in the specific exchanges, the key issue of responsible advocacy showed Kennedy's superior command of the facts on that key issue. Nixon's closing statement did not solve his problem of locating a particular idiom in which to address the public. In contrast, Kennedy's opening and closing arguments highlighted his strong performances in earlier debates, closing the series nicely with Kennedy's enactment of FDR's persona.

SUMMARY

In all four of these debates, candidates had their credibility at stake. By credibility, I mean not only their believability but their character as responsible advocates, as worthy advocates for the programs they represented, and as reliable advocates for the nation they desired to lead. If a candidate could not defend his integrity, he could hardly be expected to defend the integrity of the democratic system that he represented. The same would be true of a candidate's program that makes claims about what would be desirable for the nation. The analyses illustrated how candidates can be compared in terms of the substantive and stylistic ways in which they used argument. The more completely the candidate could satisfy the form of attack and defense, or vice versa, the more able he appeared to defend himself and the language community he represented. Using argument to select candidates also celebrated the democratic decision-making process of rational dialogue. Because arguments test candidates and because the public witnesses this symbolic ordeal, arguments were appropriate forms of discourse for examining the rhetorical qualifications of the candidates. Also, in each of these debates, the candidates were confronted with rhetorical problems that were symbolic of the complex problems they might face in office. The ability to solve these rhetorical problems provided the audience with evidence of the candidate's ability to use language effectively, an important aspect of presidential competence. Finally, in each of these debates, the candidates had an opportunity to enact a concept of leadership. Whereas Nixon never did develop his own particular approach to the office, Kennedy used the words of FDR in the opening and closing debates to create a particular context for viewing the campaign and to present himself in the role of a candidate who sets the unfinished business before the nation. This particular way of viewing the campaign was never countered by Nixon and helped the audience to see Kennedy in terms of a strong, dynamic candidate ready to complete the unfinished business before the nation.

NOTES

1. See Theodore C. Sorenson, *Kennedy* (New York: Harper & Row, 1965), 202, who argued that the last three debates were anticlimactic compared to the dramatic victory achieved by Kennedy in the first.

2. Ibid., 202. According to Sorenson, the last three debates preserved and reinforced Kennedy's gains from the first debate.

3. For a discussion of the type of argument known as argument of direction, see Chaim Perelman and L. Olbrechts-Tyteca, *The New Rhetoric*, trans. John Wilkinson and Purcell Weaver (Notre Dame, IN: Notre Dame University Press, 1969), 266–287.

Chapter Four

The 1976 Presidential Debates: Gerald Ford Versus Jimmy Carter

The 1976 presidential debates were significant because for the first time an incumbent president running for reelection agreed to debate his opponent.[1] Because incumbent presidents campaign on the grounds that their policies are more desirable than those proposed by the challenger, the appropriate focal point for analyzing these debates should be an examination of how well each candidate developed and defended his presidential programs. But in 1976, the issue was not whose policies were more desirable. In the wake of Watergate and Gerald Ford's pardon of Richard Nixon, voters were trying to assess whom to trust and who would be most effective in restoring an image of integrity to American leadership.[2]

Ford needed to solve two rhetorical problems in the debates. First, he needed to perform competently in the debates to remove doubts about his intellectual ability.[3] Ford was perceived as a "bumbler," physically and intellectually, as someone who had played football without his helmet. Although these were not substantive issues to which Ford could respond, they were part of the public's image of him as a candidate. Although the debates presented an opportunity for him to dispel doubts about his competency, they also created the conditions for magnifying errors.

Second, Ford needed to satisfy continuing curiosity about Watergate and eliminate doubts about the wisdom of Nixon's pardon.[4] Since Ford had been appointed vice president by Nixon, and then pardoned Nixon for unadmitted crimes, the public questioned Ford's motives for seeking the presidency.[5] In Robert Reinhold's words, "However honest he may be, however effective he may be in managing the economy, Mr. Ford appears to be saddled with the past, unable to shake the ghosts of Herbert Hoover and Richard Nixon."[6] The pardon constituted an issue for Ford from the beginning of the campaign. Commenting on a *Times/ CBS* survey conducted in early September, Reinhold noted that "the survey contains signs that Watergate remains a strong undercurrent against Mr. Ford. As they have since the *Times/CBS* survey first monitored the issue last May, more voters disapproved of the pardon Mr. Ford gave former President Richard M. Nixon than approved it, and this was clearly linked to the vote."[7] More important, resolving doubts about Ford's character was the key to winning independent undecided voters, and the debates played a critical role in shaping opinions about the candidates. The *New York Times* reported on October 15, 1976, that after the first two debates, three issues helped Carter regain the dominant position he held among independents at the outset of the campaign: unemployment and inflation, foreign policy, and the populism/Watergate issue.[8] Of the three, the populism/Watergate issue was most important to independent voters. By the end of the campaign, domestic and foreign policy issues had become secondary to the "character and personality of the two candidates."[9] Thus, Ford needed to distinguish himself from the Nixon administration and develop a concept of presidential character apart from Nixon's. Such an image could have been used as a rhetorical resource to answer questions about Watergate and the pardon and to direct the audience's attention to a comparison of his qualifications for leadership with Carter's. Unfortunately, when Ford had opportunities to solve these problems, he was unable to accomplish either of these goals.[10]

THE FIRST DEBATE

The first debate was held on September 23, 1976, in Philadelphia. The format featured twelve questions on different topics divided evenly between the candidates. The analysis of this debate is developed in two sections. The first shows how Ford could perform competently as an advocate, defending his record and attacking the qualifications of his opponent. This argument is developed to demonstrate that Ford could muster a persuasive case for his candidacy on policy issues. However, the second portion of the analysis reveals that Ford was unable to present himself as a candidate who would use his presidential power in a fair and just way. Thus, the debates defined Ford's inability to muster a defense of his character and made him vulnerable throughout the campaign on the issues of trust and fairness.[11]

Ford's Refutative Skills

Ford's refutative skills are most evident in the last half of the debate. In the fifth and seventh exchanges, Ford presented strong attacks on two of Carter's major qualifications for office: that he reduced the size of government in Georgia and that he was a leader in proposing an energy policy for the country. In the sixth and eighth exchanges when Ford was pressed to explain how he would reduce the deficit, fund new programs, return money to the public in the form of tax relief, and reduce unemployment, he presented a plausible defense of his platform and noted that Carter had argued from inconsistent positions. In the ninth exchange, when Elizabeth Drew challenged Carter's campaign promise to cut taxes for middle and low income groups, Ford pointed out another inconsistency on the part of Carter, defended his proposal for tax relief, and attacked Carter for his charge that Ford had used his veto power excessively. The analysis in this section begins with Ford's attack on Carter's qualifications for office and then examines Ford's defense of his administration in the sixth, eighth, and ninth exchanges.

Can Carter Reduce the Size of the Government?

In the fifth exchange, James Gannon asked about Carter's promise to overhaul the federal government. Carter reviewed his actions in Georgia, prompting Gannon to ask in follow up if Carter would really reduce the number of federal employees or "merely put them in different departments and relabel them." In his follow-up answer, Carter admitted that the number of employees went up by 2 percent but asserted that the reorganization improved the delivery of services.

Ford's refutation was evenly divided between an attack on Carter and a defense of his own actions. Although Ford's refutation did not focus on the specific claims in Carter's answer, the facts suggested that the size of government in Georgia had increased during Carter's administration and that the effects of Carter's leadership were unfavorable.

I think the record should show, Mr. Newman, that the Bureau of Census—we checked it just yesterday—indicates that in the four years that Governor Carter was governor of the State of Georgia, expenditures by the government went up over 50 percent. Employees of the government in Georgia during his term of office went up over 25 percent. And the figures also show that the bonded indebtedness of the state of Georgia during his Governorship went up over 20 percent. And there was some very interesting testimony given by Governor Carter's successor, Governor Busbee, before a Senate committee a few months ago, on how he found the Medicaid program when he came into office following Governor Carter. He testified, and these are his words, the present Governor of Georgia—he says he found the Medicaid program in Georgia in shambles.

Ford completed the dialectical form of attack and defense when he listed what he had done to reduce the size of government:

Now, let me talk about what we've done in the White House as far as federal employees are concerned. The first order that I issued after I became president was to cut or eliminate the prospective forty thousand increase in federal employees that had been scheduled by my predecessor. And in the term that I've been president—some two years—we have reduced federal employment by eleven thousand. In the White House staff itself, when I became President we had roughly 540 employees. We now have about 485 employees. . . . So, I think our record of cutting back employees, plus the failure of the part of the governor's program to actually save employment in Georgia, shows which is the better plan.

Here Ford demonstrated his ability to argue and to refute attacks. By refuting Carter's claims of success, then proving how his policy met the goals of the challenger's proposal in a more desirable way, Ford fulfilled the dialectical form of political argument in a more satisfying way than Carter did. And Carter never answered these criticisms at a later point in the debate, so we never get a defense of his leadership in Georgia. The impression left by Ford's evidence was that if Carter's accomplishments were true, they came only at the expense of increasing expenditures and debt, two attacks Carter had been leveling at Ford in the campaign. It is also important to note that comparatively, Ford's action to reduce the size of the federal government captured the proactive tone of leadership Carter had developed in the first part of his answer. On these grounds, then, Carter's claim to control the size of government seemed in doubt.

Developing a National Energy Policy

In the seventh exchange, Frank Reynolds asked Carter why he would use nuclear power as a last priority in an energy policy. Carter used his answer to develop the charge that "the energy policy of our nation is one that has not yet been established under this administration." In summarizing, Carter sketched this brief outline of an energy policy:

So, shift from oil to coal; emphasize research and development on coal use and also on solar power; strict conservation measures—not yield every time the special interest groups put pressures on the president, like this administration has done; and use atomic energy only as a last resort with the strictest possible safety precautions. That's the best overall energy policy in the brief time we have to discuss it.

In his rebuttal, Ford refuted Carter's claim that no energy policy had been established:

Governor Carter skims over a very serious and a very broad subject. In January of 1975, I submitted to the Congress and to the American people the first comprehensive energy program recommended by any president. It called for an increase in the production of energy in the United States. It called for conservation measures so that we would save the energy that we have.

Here Ford pointed out that Carter was simply wrong in his criticism. Moreover, there was little difference between what Carter and Ford had proposed. Further, Ford defended the desirability of his program:

In my program for energy independence, we have increased, for example, solar energy research from about $84 million a year to about $120 million a year. We are going as fast as the experts say we should. In nuclear power we have increased the research and development under the Energy Research and Development Agency very substantially to ensure that our nuclear powerplants are safer, that they are more efficient, and that we have adequate safeguards. I think you have to have greater oil and gas production, more coal production, more nuclear production, and in addition, you have to have energy conservation.

In both of these exchanges, Ford seemed to be more in command of the facts than Carter. When Carter asserted that he had reorganized the government in Georgia, Ford proved that he had done so only at the expense of increasing its size and cost. When Carter claimed that Ford had no energy policy, Ford revealed that he had presented an energy similar to Carter's in 1975. On these two campaign issues, then, Ford demonstrated effective refutational skills.

Ford Defends the Republican Platform

Ford underwent a challenging test of his ability to defend his platform in the sixth and eighth exchanges. In the eighth exchange, Drew asked Ford to reconcile his campaign promises with his answers to Carter in the debate:

Mr. President, at Vail, after the Republican convention, you announced that you would now emphasize five new areas. Among those were jobs and housing and health, improved recreational facilities for Americans, and you also added crime. You also mentioned education. For two years you've been telling us that we couldn't do very much in these areas because we couldn't afford it, and in fact, we do have a $50 billion deficit now. In rebuttal to Governor Carter a little bit earlier, you said that if there were to be any surplus in the next few years, you thought it should be turned back to the people in the form of tax relief. So, how are you going to pay for any new initiatives in these areas you announced at Vail you were going to now stress?

Ford answered by saying that in the last two years things had been very tough but that they had started to improve. Additionally, Ford indicated that he expected receipts to improve, disbursements to decrease, and the deficit to be lower in 1978. Finally, Ford discussed ways to improve the quality of life programs that necessitated only small cost increases. Drew was not satisfied with Ford's answer, prompting her to follow up with: "Sir, in the next few years would you try to reduce the deficit, would you spend money for these programs that you have just outlined, or would you, as you said earlier, return whatever surplus you got to the people in the form of tax relief?" Again, Ford answered that all of this goals were achievable because of expected improvement in the economy. Ford also attempted to argue that Carter would be less likely to accomplish these objectives given the estimated costs of his platform. In an optimistic tone, Ford concluded: "We feel that you can hold the line and restrain federal spending, give a tax reduction, and still have a balanced budget by 1978."

Carter's refutation in this exchange was strong in the sense that he presented numerous facts to show how the economy had deteriorated over the last few years. However, only some of the refutation was relevant to the Ford administration. Carter attempted to tie Ford to Nixon when he stated that "the best thing to do is to look at the record of Mr. Ford's administration and Mr. Nixon's before his." However, when Carter presented his evidence indicting the Nixon administration, the audience could discount it as irrelevant to the claim that Ford was ineffective. And when Carter's evidence did apply to Ford, it lacked persuasive force because Ford had already admitted that the economy had not done well over the last two years. What was missing in Carter's rebuttal was evidence to refute Ford's claims that things were improving. So although Carter was correct in his assessment of how things had worsened over the last eight years, the degree of blame that should be attached to Ford was unknown. And in not arguing that, contrary to Ford's claim that things were getting better, the future looked bleak under continued Republican leadership, Carter missed an opportunity to refute the premise of Ford's rather unrealistic claim that he could accomplish his goals.

Ford Defends His Vetoes

In the eighth exchange, James Gannon asked Ford to justify his veto on a number of job bills passed by a Democratic controlled Congress. Ford did an excellent job of justifying his actions. He argued that the bill would not have solved the unemployment problem, that proponents of the bill admitted no more than 400 thousand jobs would be made available, that each job would have cost the taxpayers $25,000, and that the jobs would not have been available for about nine to eighteen months. Ford argued that the solution to unemployment was to stimulate the economy so that the jobs were produced in the private sector, not the public sector.

When asked by Gannon in the follow-up question if he intended to veto legislation just passed by Congress that authorized a $3.7 billion public works program, Ford indicated again why such programs were not as desirable for the country as policies that stimulated economic growth: "But that is an extra $4 billion that would add to the deficit, which would add to the inflationary pressures, which would help to destroy jobs in the private sector, not make jobs where the jobs really are. These make-work, temporary jobs, dead end as they are, are not the kind of jobs that we want for our people." In the last part of this follow-up answer, Ford did an excellent job of answering Carter's charge that he had used his veto power excessively and failed to stop the deficit from increasing:

I think it's interesting to point out that in the two years that I've been president, I've vetoed fifty-six bills. Congress has sustained forty-two vetoes. As a result we have saved over $9 billion in federal expenditures. And the Congress by overriding the bills that I did veto—the Congress has added some $13 billion to the federal expenditures and to the federal deficit. Now, Governor Carter complains about the deficits that this administration has had, and yet he condemns the vetoes that I have made that have saved the taxpayer $9 billion and could have saved an additional $13 billion. Now, he can't have it both ways. And, therefore, it seems to me that we should hold the lid as we have to the best of our ability so we can stimulate the private economy and get the jobs where the jobs are—five out of six—in this economy.

In his rebuttal, Carter hammered at the unemployment statistics, repeating that we have 500 thousand more people out of work than three months earlier, that we had 2.5 million more out of work than when he took office, and that the unemployment rate at 7.9 percent was a terrible tragedy in this country. But this did not square with Ford's claim in his first answer in this exchange that

we have added some 4 million jobs in the last seventeen months. We have now employed 88 million people in America—the largest number in the history of the United States. We've added 500 thousand jobs in the last two months. Inflation is the quickest way to destroy jobs. And by holding the lid on Federal spending, we have been able to do a good job, an affirmative job in inflation and, as a result, have added to the jobs in this country.

The debate over unemployment statistics was never resolved for the audience. From the exchange, it seemed clear that the economic situation was unfavorable for the country but whether Ford had performed poorly as president was less certain. In Ford's answers, we see him making choices and justifying his actions. In his attacks on Ford's leadership, Carter failed to explain why Ford's vetoes were unjustified, why reducing the deficit was less important than signing the jobs bills, and why stimulating the economy to produce jobs in the private sector was an inappropriate solution to the nation's economic ills. Thus, by ignoring Ford's justification for his vetoes, Carter left the audience with the impression that Ford might have been doing as good a job as any president could given the circumstances.

Tax Reform: Carter Is Inconsistent and Plays "Fast and Loose" with the Facts

The last example of Ford's refutational skill occurred in the ninth exchange over tax reform when Drew asked Carter how we would provide tax relief to the middle class. Carter reviewed his proposal, identifying a number of ways to generate revenue for tax relief. In the follow-up, Drew noted that Carter would need $10 billion to provide tax relief but identified ways to generate only $5 billion, leaving him $5 billion short. In his answer to the follow-up, Carter did little to suggest that he could come up with the additional 5 billion but charged "that the present tax benefits that have been carved out over a long period of years—fifty years—by sharp tax lawyers and by lobbyists have benefitted just the rich."

Ford's refutation was particularly thorough. First, Ford pointed out that Carter had changed his position from one week earlier. "Governor Carter's answer tonight does not coincide with the answer that he gave in an interview to the Associated Press a week or so ago. In that interview Governor Carter indicated that he would raise the taxes on those in the medium—or middle-income brackets or higher." After describing his proposal for tax relief and repeating the charge that "Mr. Carter wants to increase taxes for roughly half of the taxpayers of this country," Ford refuted Carter's claim that "we've never had a president since the War Between the States that vetoed more bills":

Now, the governor has also played a little fast and loose with the facts about vetoes. The records show that President Roosevelt vetoed on an average of fifty-five bills a year. President Truman vetoed on the average, while he was President, about thirty-eight bills a year. I understand that Governor Carter, when he was governor of Georgia, vetoed between thirty-five and forty bills a year. My average in two years is twenty-six, but in the process of that, we have saved $9 billion.

Finally, Ford answered the charge that the tax structure was a result of sharp lawyers and lobbyists by pointing out that "the Democrats have controlled the Congress for the last twenty-two years, and they wrote all the tax bills."

These exchanges clearly demonstrated Ford's refutative skills. Ford created doubt about Carter's ability to control the size of government in Georgia, proved Carter wrong in his claim that no energy policy had been established, provided a plausible defense of his platform, justified his vetoes, and showed how Carter's use of the facts was suspect. On these grounds, it seems appropriate to conclude that Ford was capable of defending his record, and the analysis of these exchanges helps explain why Ford was perceived as the winner of the first debate.

Ford Failed to Polish His Tarnished Image

But policy issues were subsidiary to the question concerning Ford's fairness. In the first debate, Ford had two opportunities to remove doubts about his integrity. Both questions came from Reynolds and asked Ford to explain or justify inconsistencies in the way the government treated its citizens. This section shows how Ford was unable to solve doubts about himself and government in general.

The first opportunity to address the doubts stemming from the Nixon pardon came when Reynolds asked:

Mr. President, when you came into office, you spoke very eloquently of the need for a time for healing. And very early in your administration you went out to Chicago and you announced, you proposed, a program of case-by-case pardons for draft resisters to restore them to full citizenship. Some fourteen thousand young men took advantage of your offer, but another ninety thousand did not. In granting the pardon to former President Nixon, sir, part of your rationale was to put Watergate behind us—to, if I may quote you again, "truly end our long national nightmare." Why does not the same rationale apply now, today, in our Bicentennial Year, to the young men who resisted in Vietnam and many of them still in exile abroad?

Reynolds' question tested the plausibility of Ford's explanation for pardoning Nixon. The question presumed that both situations required application of the same principle, thus creating a rhetorical problem for Ford: He needed to explain why similar circumstances brought forth different policies. Reynolds' question also reinforced one of Carter's campaign themes, that there must be fairness in government's treatment of citizens, and implied that Ford's treatment of draft evaders was inconsistent with his pardon of Nixon. Although this question created a rhetorical problem for Ford, it was also an opportunity for him to distinguish between the two situations and provide an explanation that would satisfy continued doubts about his sense of fairness. Had Ford been able to solve this problem, Carter would have had to make a stronger case for mistrusting Ford, or shift the issue from a question of trust to one of competence—a shift that might have been more desirable for Ford given Carter's limited credentials for national office. Ford's response to Reynolds' question was ineffective on the issue of fairness and trust. Ford stated that he thought he gave the draft evaders "ample time" to take advantage of the program he offered, then took the position that he was "against an across-the-board pardon of draft evaders or military deserters." No explanation was offered by Ford to justify his opposition to an across-the-board pardon for those who resisted the draft.

When Ford tried to justify pardoning Nixon, his case was unpersuasive. First, he tried to distinguish between the two situations: "Now in the case of Mr. Nixon, the reason the pardon was given was that when I took office this country was in a very, very divided condition. There was hatred; there was divisiveness: people had lost faith in their government in many, many respects." But the problem with this statement was that Ford did not distinguish effectively between the divisiveness caused by the Vietnam conflict and that caused by Nixon. Without a clearer contrast between the two circumstances, Ford's position seemed to embrace a double standard. And as long as this double standard was implicit in Ford's response to the issue, his ability to apply principles of justice consistently remained in doubt. Next, Ford stated his reason for pardoning Nixon but did not explain why Nixon deserved a pardon while draft resisters did not: "Mr. Nixon resigned, and I became president. It seemed to me that if I was to adequately and effectively handle the problems of high inflation, a growing recession, the involvement of the United States still in Vietnam, that I had to give 100 percent of my time to those two major problems." The key words in this answer were "it seemed to me." Ford's explanation was not formulated in terms of a rational appeal but one based on his credibility as a trustworthy leader. Because his sense of fairness was in question, his appeal begged the question. Ford provided no rationale for the differences in the way he viewed the two situations and, thus, his image as a fair candidate who could be trusted to administer justice according to community values was still in question.

Finally, Ford tried to explain his pardon of Nixon on the grounds that Nixon had suffered enough humiliation and that a pardon was a deserved relief from the disgrace that had been heaped on the former president: "Mr. Nixon resigned: that is disgrace—the first president out of thirty-eight that ever resigned from public office under pressure." The problem with this answer was that it presumed Nixon's innocence or at least that the disgrace experienced by Nixon was out of proportion to the crime he had committed. But because Nixon had resigned, a full investigation was never completed, and the public was unable to determine whether the penalty Nixon paid was appropriate for his crime. Thus, the audience needed to take Ford's word that his treatment of

Nixon and draft evaders was appropriate. But because Ford could not explain his inconsistency, he failed to present himself as a fair candidate who could be trusted to protect and dispense justice.[12] Ford's summary on this answer went no further than to repeat the two reasons without adding any further support:

So, when you look at the penalty that he [Nixon] paid, and when you analyze the requirements that I had—to spend all of my time working on the economy, which was in trouble, that I inherited, working on our problems in southeast Asia, which were still plaguing us—it seemed to me that Mr. Nixon had been penalized enough by his resignation in disgrace. And the need and necessity for me to concentrate on the problems of the country fully justified the action that I took.

Reynolds' follow-up question gave Ford another opportunity to balance his treatment of Nixon with a fairer treatment of draft resisters. Again, Ford stated that "I think we gave them a good opportunity—I don't think we should go any further" but provided no reason that we should not go any further. Ford's answer, then, presupposed a credible leader who was fair—who could be trusted to administer the laws justly—all of which were qualities that were, for him, in question.

If Ford was unable to solve his rhetorical problem concerning the consistent application of principles of justice, all Carter needed to do in his response was remind the audience of Ford's failure. And this was Carter's first move: "Well, I think it's very difficult for President Ford to explain the difference between the pardon of President Nixon and his attitude toward those who violated the draft laws." Carter's observation made Ford's failure obvious for the audience. Although Carter's criticism of Ford was undeveloped, there was little need for further refutation given the fact that Ford was unable to justify his limited offer of a pardon to draft resisters.

Carter used this opportunity to advocate his proposal for pardoning draft resisters. Carter's justification for pardoning draft evaders, like Ford's pardon for Nixon, was to heal the divisiveness in the nation. But unlike Ford, Carter developed the theme of fairness in his answer:

And I think that what the people are concerned about is not the pardon or the amnesty of those who evaded the draft, but whether or not our crime system is fair. We have got a sharp distinction between white-collar crime. The big shots who are rich, who are influential, very seldom go to jail. Those who are poor and who have no influence quite often are the ones who are punished.

Carter's statement did not name Ford or Nixon, but the indictment evokes an image of a powerful person who was in trouble and decides to cut a deal with the man he was to name as his successor. Carter did not need to develop a case to prove injustice in the nation because Ford's answer did not develop a substantive explanation for different treatment of ordinary citizens and influential officeholders. When Carter stated that "the fairness of it is what is the major problem that addresses our leader, and this is something that hasn't been addressed adequately by this administration," he connected the doubts about Ford's reasons for pardoning Nixon to the larger issue of presidential character, defined the key question that remained to be answered by Ford, and spotlighted the most important blemish on Ford's presidential image, his association with Richard Nixon.

Ford's Second Opportunity to Overcome Suspicions of Unfairness

Ford had a second opportunity to overcome memories of Watergate when Reynolds asked him to respond to another inconsistency in the way government had treated its citizens. According to Reynolds, the House Ethics Committee had just completed what was to him an unjustified investigation of a United States senator alleged to have been receiving corporate funds illegally over a number of years. Reynolds wanted to know if "events like this contribute to the feeling in the country that maybe there is something wrong in Washington." He gave Ford an opportunity to evince leadership when he added, "And I don't mean just in the executive branch, but throughout the whole government."

If Ford could have answered in a way that suggested that these were not appropriate responses to the problems facing the country, he could have shaped an appealing image of presidential character. Ford needed to refute the assumption underlying the question, that there was something wrong with Washington, with government in general, and to argue that the decision to postpone the investigation of alleged wrongdoing, and the decision to investigate Daniel Schorr, were character flaws of isolated individuals unable to fulfill the trust of the American communities they represented. Had Ford developed this line of argument, he could have demonstrated his understanding of the expectations for presidential office. Moreover, he could have applied this line of thinking to the country's experience with Nixon, arguing that Nixon was uncharacteristic of leaders in general, and thus distanced himself from the Nixon administration. But Ford pointed the finger of blame at Congress, arguing that they were responsible for the anti-Washington attitude of the public. First, Ford acknowledged the dissatisfaction: "There is a considerable anti-Washington feeling throughout the country but I think the feeling is misplaced." He then argued without evidence that he had reestablished trust in the presidency: "In the last two years we have restored integrity in the White House and we have set high standards in the executive branch of the government." Then he placed the blame on Congress: "The anti-Washington feeling, in my opinion, ought to be focused on the Congress of the United States." Two-thirds of the way through his answer—after attacking Congress for spending $1 billion for its housekeeping, salaries, and expenses, and after attacking Congress for hiring more employees—Ford realized that Republicans work in Congress too, and narrowed the blame to the Democratic majority in Congress. Finally, Ford attempted to redirect doubts about integrity from the executive to the legislative branch.

They spend too much money on themselves. They have too many employees. There is some question about their morality. It seems to me that in this election the focus should not be on the executive branch, but the correction should come as the voters vote for their Members of the House of Representatives or for their United States senator. That's where the problem is. And I hope there'll be some corrective action taken, so we can get some new leadership in the Congress of the United States.

Ford's answer failed to refute Reynolds' assumption that the public was dissatisfied with government leadership in general. Ford's answer also relied on his credibility when he argued without evidence that he had restored integrity to the White House. When Ford prefaced his blame for Congress with the phrase, "it seems to me," his ability to locate accurately the source of the anti-Washington attitude relied on his credibility as a judge of character. The problem with this criticism of Congress was that Ford presumed, erroneously, that the audience believed he possessed the authority and integrity to recognize good character. There was little evidence to suggest that was the case, and the question from Reynolds indicated the presence of doubt. Finally, the rhetorical situation called for a noble response, not an answer motivated by selfish interests. Ford did not appear presidential because he presumed, incorrectly, that his good character did not need to be established and because he did not understand that his attempt to shift the blame to others might appear self-serving. His answer failed to solve doubts about his character and implicitly confirmed an undesirable perception of a self-serving motive for seeking office.

Summary of Findings in the First Debate

Although both candidates demonstrated strong advocacy skills on the various policy issues, Carter's credentials as an experienced national leader were not strong. Ford needed to develop a concept of presidential character apart from Nixon and use that to defend himself against Carter's attempts to associate him with Nixon. Had Ford been able to remove doubts about his fairness and to shape a desirable image as a candidate who could be trusted to safeguard community values of justice, he could have emphasized his experience in contrast to Carter's record in Georgia. Further, had Ford been able to provide the public with an appealing context or framework for understanding his past actions as president, or had Ford been able to develop a concept of leadership under which he could defend his policies, including Nixon's pardon, he could have appealed to the audience on the basis of a broader vision of leadership, a vision of leadership that could regain the trust of the American people. In the first debate, there was not enough reason to vote for either candidate, but there was enough doubt about both to justify tuning in for the second debate.

THE SECOND DEBATE

The second debate occurred on October 6, 1976, in San Francisco and concerned foreign policy. Carter argued that Ford did not act in the public interest by conducting foreign policy in secrecy, a charge that reminded the audience of questions about Ford's trustworthiness. Ford's refutation of Carter's criticism was surprisingly strong, except for an unfortunate choice of words in a response to Max Frankel, associate editor of the *New York Times*. The analysis begins with a discussion of Ford's error and concludes by arguing that Ford's trustworthiness remained an important issue in the second debate, as it had been in the first.

Ford's Error

Frankel's inquiry about Ford's view of the relationship between the United States and the Soviet Union was straightforward:

They [the Soviets] used to brag, back in Khruschev's day, that because of their greater patience and because of our greed for business deals, that they would sooner or later get the better of us. Is it possible that, despite some setbacks in the Middle East, they've proved their point? Our allies in France and Italy are now flirting with communism; we've recognized a permanent Communist regime in East Germany; we've virtually signed, in Helsinki, an agreement that the Russians have dominance in eastern Europe; we've bailed out Soviet agriculture with our huge grain sales; we've given them large loans, access to our best technology; and if the Senate hadn't interfered with the Jackson amendment, maybe you would have given them even larger loans. Is that what you call a two-way street of traffic in Europe?

Ford began by arguing that his administration had been negotiating with the Soviets from a position of strength. However, two-thirds of the way through his answer, he addressed Frankel's mentioning of the Helsinki agreement. Concluding his response, Ford blundered by asserting that "there is no Soviet domination of eastern Europe, and there never will be under a Ford administration."

In the context of his answer, Ford's assertion that the Soviets did not dominate eastern Europe made some sense. Just prior to his claim, he explained how the Warsaw Pact forces needed to notify the United States and NATO forces of any military maneuvers undertaken in eastern Europe. One could argue that if the Warsaw Pact forces needed to notify NATO forces, the Soviet Union did not, in an absolute sense, dominate the region. However, Frankel followed Ford's statement with a request for clarification: "I'm sorry, could I just follow—did I understand you to say, sir, that the Russians are not using eastern Europe as their own sphere of influence and occupying most of the countries there and making sure with their troops that it's a Communist zone, whereas on our side of the line the Italians and the French are still flirting with the possibility of communism?"

Ford reasserted his belief that the Soviets did not dominate eastern Europe. In this statement, there was no ambiguity about Ford's view of eastern Europe.

I don't believe, Mr. Frankel, that the Yugoslavians consider themselves dominated by the Soviet Union. I don't believe that the Rumanians consider themselves dominated by the Soviet Union. I don't believe that the Poles consider themselves dominated by the Soviet Union. Each of those countries is independent, autonomous; it has its own territorial integrity. And the United States does not concede that those countries are under the domination of the Soviet Union. As a matter of fact, I visited Poland, Yugoslavia, and Rumania, to make certain that the people of those countries understood that the president of the United States and the people of the United States are dedicated to their independence, their autonomy, and their freedom.

In one respect, this was a noble answer. Ford's statement could have been interpreted to mean that, although these countries were confronted daily with Soviet domination, the people of these nations did not see themselves dominated by the Soviet Union, and that the United States should not acknowledge the Soviet Union's claim over these nations. But stylistically, Ford's answer was simply a statement of his beliefs and in the context of Frankel's questions, those beliefs seemed to be substantially different from the beliefs of most Americans.

Carter's response highlighted the discrepancy between Ford's view of eastern Europe and that of the average American when he stated:

In the case of the Helsinki agreement, it may have been a good agreement at the beginning, but we have failed to enforce the so-called Basket Three part, which ensures the right of people to migrate, to join their families, to be free to speak out. The Soviet Union is still jamming Radio Free Europe. . . . We've also seen a very serious problem with the so-called Sonnenfeldt Document, which apparently, Mr. Ford has just endorsed, which said that there is an organic linkage between the eastern European countries and the Soviet Union. And I would like to see Mr. Ford convince the Polish Americans and the Czech Americans and the Hungarian Americans in this country that those countries don't live under the domination and supervision of the Soviet Union.

Carter's answer not only reflected a more accurate understanding of the relationship between the Soviet Union, eastern Europe, and the United States, but highlighted how Ford's perception of eastern Europe was widely off the mark.

But it was only when media criticism identified Ford's statement as a major error that the mistake became magnified and constituted a major difference between the two candidates.[13] By itself, Ford's mistake was insufficient to alter his image of competence. Because of his image as a politician who often errs, the audience could have interpreted the mistake as one more example of Ford's faux pas. Given this context, it is difficult to argue that the public was unwilling to tolerate some error on Ford's part. Supporting Carter on these grounds required the public to accept him as qualified for office, a judgment that was difficult given Carter's limited credentials, and given Carter's campaign strategy stressing that he was an outsider to Washington mainstream politics. Finally, the decision to support Carter on the narrow grounds that Ford was incompetent in foreign policy because of his statement on Poland assumed that the audience accepted the press as reliable critics of presidential campaign discourse. Because the polls did not signal an immediate shift of landslide proportions to Carter after the second debate, doubts about Ford's competence constituted a slowly developing, and only partial, aspect of his presidential image.[14] Rhetorical factors other than competence were important in the second debate.

Trustworthiness as a Key Issue

An alternative explanation for the lack of a shift in support for Carter appears to be related to the more important issue of fairness and trust as dimensions of presidential character that took precedence over questions of competence. Ford's qualifications for office were simply better than Carter's: Ford had been president for more than two years; Carter possessed no comparable experience. On these grounds, Carter's case for office was not strong despite the widely known jokes concerning Ford's intellect. Thus, it seems plausible to argue that the audience needed to resolve whether Ford embodied the character of the community or represented the type of character embodied by Richard Nixon before it considered Ford's qualifications as a candidate who could defend American values through argument.

Carter continued to raise questions about Ford's trustworthiness in the second debate by weaving charges of secrecy in the Ford administration into four of his seven answers. In his response to his first question from Frankel, Carter connected desirable foreign policy decision making to the character and participation of the American people: "We've lost, in our foreign policy, the character of the American people. We've ignored or excluded the American people and Congress from participation in the shaping of our foreign policy. It's been one of secrecy and exclusion."

Carter's answer to the third question from Richard Valeriani, diplomatic correspondent of the *Baltimore Sun*, concerning his concept of the national interest in foreign policy, developed the relationship between the character of the nation's foreign policy and the character of the people by arguing that the character of the people had not been represented in Nixon and Ford's foreign policy:

I've traveled the last twenty-one months among the people of this country. I've talked to them, and I've listened. And I've seen at first hand, in a very vivid way, the deep hurt that's come to this country in the aftermath of Vietnam and Cambodia and Chile and Pakistan and Angola and Watergate, CIA revelations. What we were formerly so proud of—the strength of our country, its moral integrity, the representation in foreign affairs of what our people are, what our Constitution stands for—has been gone. And in the secrecy that has surrounded our foreign policy in the last few years, the American people, the Congress have been excluded.

Through the strategy of enumeration, Carter reminded the audience of reasons to distrust Ford and then argued that he understood the requirements for office: "I believe I know what this country ought to be. I've been one who's loved my nation, as many Americans do. And I believe that there is no limit placed on what we can be in the future if we can harness the tremendous resources—militarily, economically— and the stature of our people—the meaning of our Constitution—in the future." Although the relationship between the Constitution and foreign policy was not developed in detail, Carter's strategy was to develop only a connection between foreign policy and character. If Carter could make this connection plausible for the audience, he could establish character and, by implication, trust, as the primary concerns in deliberating over a candidate's ability to represent and enact community values in the conduct of foreign policy.

Carter took the strategy one step further by arguing that recent mistakes in foreign policy were due to the failure of the leaders to include the American people in the decision-making process:

Every time we've made a serious mistake in foreign affairs, it's been because the American people have been excluded from the process. If we can just tap the intelligence and ability, the sound commonsense, and the good judgment of the American people, we can once again have a foreign policy to make us proud instead of ashamed. And I'm not going to exclude the American people from that process in the future, as Mr. Ford and Mr. Kissinger have done.

Carter's reasoning on this issue was that American foreign policy should reflect the character of the American people; under the Nixon and Ford administrations, it had not, and the result was poor policy. Although this runs counter to classical rhetorical theory,[15] Carter's argument presumed that the character of the community was the defining element of expedient policy, and because Carter was trying to make Ford's character, not his competence, the primary issue in this debate, Carter wanted the audience to judge Ford's integrity before they evaluated his competence.

This strategy controlled much of Carter's discourse throughout the debate. For example, in Valeriani's follow-up question asking Carter what he would do to bring people into the foreign policy decision-making process, Carter began his answer by asserting that Ford conducted his foreign policy in secrecy: "First of all, I would quit conducting the decision making in secret, as has been characteristic of Mr. Kissinger and Mr. Ford." The remainder of the answer was substantively unsatisfying because Carter mentioned only fireside chats as one way to include the people and then argued that previous administrations worked with Congress more closely than had Ford. Neither of these approaches appeared to increase substantially the participation of the public in the decision-making process. In short, Carter was unable to discuss specific ways to include the people in the policy-making process because the nature of the office required that the decision-making process be conducted by the president, as a representative of the people in conjunction with presidential advisers, not with the direct participation of the national community. But because Ford had not developed a concept of presidential character with which to defend and interpret his record, even the strongest refutation of Carter's claims seemed unpersuasive. Ford's presidential image depended first on his ability to present himself as a fair and trustworthy candidate and second on the audience's perception of him as a competent executive. Because Ford never solved his initial problem of credibility, doubts about his ability to represent the community in foreign policy remained.

Ford's refutation of Carter's claims of secrecy was good. Ford identified an inconsistency in Carter's statements about conducting an open decision-making process and holding unpublicized meetings with the Soviet Union about a Middle-East settlement. Ford also presented strong evidence that he had been very open about his approach to the Sinai II agreement and that he and his administration had maintained close contact with the Congress on various issues. But this response was his only direct attack on Carter's repeated charges of secrecy, and Ford ignored Carter's contention that his foreign policy did not reflect the character of the people. Ford's refutation was, by itself, insufficient to remove the doubts created by Carter's consistent charges of secrecy.

In the next question, Carter pursued the indictment of secrecy again in his rebuttal to Ford's answer to Frankel's question concerning the relationship between the Soviet Union and the United States: "We also have seen Mr. Ford exclude himself from access to the public. He hasn't had a tough, cross-examination–type press conference in over thirty days. One press conference he had without sound." Later, responding to Frankel's question concerning arms reduction, Carter inserted again in his answer the issue of the integrity of the community by arguing that we needed to reestablish ties with our allies because "they have felt neglected. And using that base of strength, and using the idealism, the honesty, the predictability, the commitment, the integrity of our own country—that's where our strength lies. And that would permit us to deal with the developing nations in a position of strength." When Valeriani asked Carter if he really believed that America was not strong, Carter admitted that he thought the nation was strong militarily, but argued that the element of community character was a defining quality of strength: "But as far as strength derived from commitment to principles; as far as strength derived from the unity within our country; as far as strength derived from the people, Congress, the secretary of state, the president sharing in the evolution and carrying out of our foreign policy . . . in those respects, we are not strong." In responding to Ford's justification of his actions in the *Mayaquez* incident, Carter implied that Ford kept the details from the American public for too long:

The only thing I believe is that whatever the knowledge was that Mr. Ford had should have been given to the American people eighteen months ago, immediately after the *Mayaquez* incident occurred. This is what the American people want . . . after the immediate action is taken, I believe the president has an obligation to tell the American people the truth and not wait eighteen months later for the report to be issued.

Finally, in his closing statement, Carter asked this rhetorical question: "Will we have a government of secrecy that excludes the American people from participation in making basic decisions and therefore covers up mistakes and makes it possible for our government—our government—to depart from the principles of our Constitution and Bill of Rights?" All other issues in the second debate were subsidiary to this question. Carter had woven this concern about secrecy and trust through four of seven questions directed to him, made the charge in two of his rebuttals to Ford, and identified it in the closing statement as a key question for the audience to resolve in deliberating over the two choices for office. For Carter, the argument against Ford was that he did not represent the character of the community in his foreign policy, not that Ford was incompetent to conduct foreign policy.

Summary of Findings in the Second Debate

I have been arguing that concerns about Ford's fairness and trustworthiness took precedence over concerns about his ability to conduct foreign policy. In this respect, the analysis points to a different conclusion than that arrived at by the press: Ford's mistake on Poland was not the deciding fact between the candidates. Despite the attention devoted by the press to Ford's error, the capacity of Ford's foreign policy to reflect the character of the national community was a more potent issue for the Carter campaign. Although there might have been doubts about Ford's competence after the second debate, the primary question that still needed to be resolved in the voters' mind was whether Ford could be trusted to safeguard the integrity of the nation, at least in the conduct of foreign policy. To establish this conclusion, it is necessary to consider the last debate as Ford's final opportunity to present an image of trustworthy presidential character and to see if Ford was able to shift the dialectical focus of the campaign to Carter's limited qualifications for office.

THE THIRD DEBATE

The third debate was held on October 22, 1976, at Williamsburg, Virginia. Trust and integrity remained important issues for both Carter and Ford. Carter continued to question Ford about his integrity throughout the first half of the debate. When Jack Nelson, Washington bureau chief for the *Los Angeles Times*, provided Ford with his last opportunity to dispel doubts about his character, Ford failed. The analysis begins by summarizing the instances in which Carter questioned Ford's character to demonstrate that integrity remained an important issue. Then I provide a close examination of Ford's failure to present evidence of desirable presidential character. I conclude by indicating that both candidates perceived presidential integrity to be a key issue in the closing statements and summarize the findings of this section and the chapter.

Continued Questions about Ford's Integrity

In the first question, Joseph Kraft asked both Ford and Carter what sacrifices they would call for in the next four years to accomplish their goals if elected. Ford answered the question directly by discussing the need for an increase in defense appropriations, by pointing to the need for leadership in solving foreign policy problems in the Middle East, Africa, and in the Pacific, and by restraining domestic budgetary increases. However, Carter connected the willingness of the American public to sacrifice to an argument he had made in the second debate: "The American people are ready to make sacrifices if they are part of the process, if they know that they will be helping to make decisions and won't be excluded from being an involved party to the national purpose." While Carter's statement did not directly indict Ford's trustworthiness, it reminded audience members to consider and compare their relationship with each candidate. Thus, Carter's themes of secrecy and exclusion on the part of the Ford administration worked to drive a wedge of doubt even further between Ford and the public, and the question of Ford's trustworthiness surfaced in the very first exchange of the debate.

Carter was limited in the ways in which he could press the issue, however. The public was growing weary of direct attacks on Ford's character. So in the second exchange of the debate, Carter announced that he would no longer be making any attacks on Ford's character. This development occurred in Carter's answer to Robert Maynard, who asked what responsibility Carter would accept for the low level of interest in the campaign, a campaign that Maynard argued had "digressed frequently from important issues into allegations of blunder and brainwashing and fixations on lust and *Playboy*." To sidestep the part of the question that related to his *Playboy* interview, Carter admitted that he had made a mistake in the heat of the campaign when he granted the interview. Turning back to the central issue in Maynard's question, Carter argued that previous disappointments stemming from the Nixon administration were the cause for the low interest. Carter stated: "Also, in the aftermath of Vietnam and Cambodia and Watergate and the CIA revelations, people have felt that they've been betrayed by public officials." Then Carter stated that in the remaining ten days of the campaign, the "American people will not see the Carter campaign running television advertisements or newspaper advertisements based on a personal attack on President Ford's character." Interestingly, Carter's character on this issue was tested in the next two exchanges of the debate. Immediately following Maynard's question, Nelson opened up the issue of Watergate and invited Ford to explain why he limited one of the original investigations of Watergate by the House Banking Committee.

This was an excellent opportunity for Carter to press his attack on Ford's character. However, when Nelson gave Carter the opportunity to refute Ford's claims of no involvement in Watergate, Carter remained consistent in this pledge to the audience and stated, "I don't have any response." Carter's character was tested once more in Kraft's follow-up question to Carter about his statements concerning how the United States would respond to the introduction of Soviet troops in Yugoslavia. In his first answer, Carter referred to reports he received from Averell Harriman and James Schlesinger to support the claim that the presence of Soviet troops in Yugoslavia posed no security threat to the United States. When Kraft asked Carter in follow-up if he had cleared the use of Harriman's and Schlesinger's reports for use in the debate, Carter told the truth: "No, I did not [clear my statements with them]."

By the third debate, Carter's attack on Ford's character had softened because Carter was attempting to embody the integrity he had been claiming Ford lacked. When Maynard asked Carter to explain why his lead in the polls had evaporated, Carter responded by arguing that he enjoyed the support of the people, not powerful political figures: "I campaign among people. I've never depended on powerful political figures to put me in office. I have a direct relationship with—hundreds of thousands of people around the country who actively campaign for me. . . . And my success in the primary season was, I think, notable for a newcomer, from someone who's outside of Washington, who never has been part of the Washington establishment." Carter's unique qualification for leadership, then, remained his identity as a candidate untainted by Washington politics. Although he did not state specifically how he was different from Ford, his claim that he had never depended on powerful political figures to place him in office suggested that he relied on the average citizen for support, and evoked an unsavory image of Nixon advancing Ford to the presidency with the implication that it was done so for the purpose of obtaining a pardon.

In these respects, Carter had successfully created doubts about Ford's sense of fairness in the first debate and had successfully characterized Ford's foreign policy as secretive, exclusive, and uncharacteristic of American community values in the second debate. In the third debate, Carter needed only to protect his image as an outsider untainted by Washington politics, because Ford was still unable to formulate an appealing presidential image with which to answer remaining questions about Watergate.

"But There Are Questions That Still Remain . . . "

Nelson's words in the fourth question of the final debate summarized Ford's rhetorical problem. Nelson provided Ford with one last opportunity to solve his problem, when he asked Ford if he would name the persons you talked to in connection with that investigation [an early investigation into Watergate by the House Banking Committee that Nelson asserted Ford limited], and since you say you have no recollection of talking to anyone from the White House, would you be willing to open for examination the White House tapes of conversations during that period?

Nelson's question placed Ford in a position of defending himself, illuminating the fact that Ford's integrity was still in doubt. This created a situation calling for a defense of character, an apologia.[16] Ford needed to vindicate himself to uphold his reputation and gain recognition of his greater worth as a candidate in relation to Carter. Ford also needed to gain recognition as a candidate who embodied the integrity of the community if he hoped to develop a desirable presidential image. All of this depended on his ability to erase doubts about this previous association with Richard Nixon. Here was Ford's answer:

Mr. Nelson, I testified before two committees, House and Senate, on precisely the questions that you have asked. And the testimony, under oath, was to the effect that I did not talk to Mr. Nixon, to Mr. Haldeman, to Mr. Erlichman, or to any of the people at the White House. I said I had no recollection whatsoever of talking with any of the White House legislative liaison people. I indicated under oath that the initiative that I took was at the request of the ranking members of the House Banking and Currency Committee on the Republican side, which was a legitimate request and a proper response by me. Now, that was gone into by two congressional committees, and following that investigation both committees overwhelmingly approved me, and both the House and the Senate did likewise. Now, in the meantime the special prosecutor—within the last few days after an investigation himself—said there was no reason for him to get involved, because he found nothing that would justify it. And then, just a day or two ago, the attorney general of the United States made a further investigation and came to precisely the same conclusion. Now, after all of those investigations by objective, responsible people, I think the matter is closed once and for all.

In each instance, Ford's character depended on some public official—congressional committees, the special prosecutor, and the attorney general. In this respect, Ford's argument was premised on the assumption that external authorities could clear away the doubts. What Ford did not understand, however, was that he needed to provide a personalized defense of himself, that he could not rely on the judgments of what he considered objective investigators because the legitimacy of government institutions was itself in question given the audience's memory of Watergate and of Ford's decision to pardon Nixon.

Ford failed a second test of personal integrity when he took the position that he did not control the tapes Nelson referred to in his question: "But to add one other feature: I don't control any of the tapes. Those tapes are in the jurisdiction of the courts, and I have no right to say yes or no. But all the committees, the attorney general, the special prosecutor—all of them have given me a clean bill of health. I think the matter is settled once and for all." Regardless of who controlled the tapes, as a prospective president, Ford needed to state his willingness to call for the tapes to be examined. But Ford's answer evoked memories of Nixon's reluctance to reveal the contents of his tapes and demonstrated that he was unwilling to advocate an open investigation. Despite his "clean bill of health," Ford's rhetorical response to the question failed to eliminate continuing doubts about his integrity. Now the audience had good reason to doubt Ford's character.

"I've Restored the Faith" Versus "I Can Bring a New Image to Washington"

Both candidates perceived public trust to be a significant issue in the closing statements of the third debate. Ford acknowledged that he took office at a time when the public had lost faith in the presidency: "I became president at the time that the United States was in a very troubled time. . . . The American people had lost faith and trust and confidence in the presidency itself." Ford then argued that he needed to put the nation on a steady course, which was potentially an effective strategy for dealing with questions about Watergate. But Ford's image of a steady course for the ship of state was undeveloped.

Ford tried to tell the people that much of the campaign discourse including television shows, bumper stickers, and slogans did not count because of the bicentennial: "But those are not the things that count. What counts is, that the United States celebrated its two hundredth birthday on July 4th. As a result of that experience all over the United States, there is a new spirit in America. The American people are healed, are working together. The American people are moving again, and moving in the right direction." Ford's assertion that the American people were healed depended on his credibility to recognize desirable community unity. But when Ford was asked to answer remaining questions about Watergate, he stated that the matter was closed, when it was not closed for the public. In these respects, then, Ford's assertion that the American people had been healed reflected an insensitivity to the lingering doubts about Watergate and the controversial decision to pardon Nixon.

When Ford discussed his accomplishments, he included the claim that "there has been a restoration of faith and confidence and trust in the presidency, because I've been open, candid, and forthright." This contention depended on Ford's image as a credible, trustworthy candidate, an image that Ford had not been able to enact in any of the key exchanges on this issue. By failing to offer substantive appeals, and by relying on appeals premised on his dubious character, Ford failed to solve his rhetorical problem in the closing statement, and highlighted the key issue for the audience to consider, his trustworthiness as a presidential candidate.

Carter's closing statement declared Ford's rhetorical shortcomings in terms of a very limited, general concept of the presidency: "The major purpose of an election for president is to choose a leader, someone who can analyze the depths of feeling in our country, to set a standard for our people to follow, to inspire people to reach for greatness, to correct our defects, to answer difficulties, to bind ourselves together in a spirit of unity. I don't believe the present administration has done that." Rhetorically, Ford could not answer difficult questions about Nixon and Watergate. This was clear from an examination of the three opportunities provided to Ford by the panelists in the first and third debates. From this failure sprang all other doubts about Ford's character. Ford could not justify a pardon for Nixon and yet treat draft evaders differently. Ford did not present himself as a noble person in answering questions about the character of American government. Ford could not respond satisfactorily to the charge that he limited the investigation of Watergate. Ford would not call for the tapes, the evidence that would prove he was unconnected to Nixon. In all of his answers on the issue of trust and integrity, Ford did not understand the need to respond to those doubts, did not inspire the public to put their doubts about public officials behind them, and did not provide good evidence that he had ended disunity in the nation. Here, in the closing statement, Carter underscored the nagging and often implicit doubts about Ford's character. But by this time in the campaign, those doubts were taking more definite form indicated by Nelson's question to Ford, which presumed Ford's involvement in Watergate, and asserted an unethical association with Nixon.

Having identified the issue between them, Carter argued that he embodied an untarnished image: "My own background is different from his ... and I believe we require someone who can work harmoniously with the Congress and can work closely with the people of this country, and who can bring a new image and a new spirit to Washington." Carter's statement defined the prerequisite qualification for office in 1976—basic integrity. Because Carter presented a new image, even though it was not necessarily well-grounded in the defense of his proposed policies for the nation, he met the basic qualification for office that Ford lacked. On these limited grounds, then, a vote for Carter seemed justified.

SUMMARY

The main question in the 1976 debates was whether the public wanted Ford, who was unable to polish an image tarnished by his association with Nixon, or Carter, who was able to remind the voters that he was untainted, an outsider to Washington politics, and who was willing to try to be president. The issues were fairness, openness, and trustworthiness. Because Ford could not present himself as fair, open, and trustworthy, and because Carter had no such rhetorical problem, Carter appeared to be, in the words of his campaign theme, as good as the people. Carter's humility in 1976 reinforced his image of a common person with common sense, who embodied the common character of the community he wished to represent as president. In this respect, Carter's vision of leadership reflected only the most minimal understanding of the requirements for office: Presidents must have integrity. Although competence and executive ability are important concerns for voters, the ability to embody values and moral character of a community was a prerequisite for leadership in the 1976 campaign. Despite the fact that the trust issue had been featured prominently in the three debates by Carter and the panelists, Ford neglected to respond to the doubts until the last few days of the campaign. The *New York Times* noted on October 31,1976, that Ford's appointment by Richard Nixon to the vice presidency and his subsequent pardon of Mr. Nixon had remained a major but largely unspoken issue in the campaign.[17] On October 28, 1976, James M. Naughton reported that on the basis of fresh opinion sampling in key states, Ford found it necessary to confront the issue of trust directly: "At a rally in the Villanova University field house this afternoon, a brief news conference in Atlantic City this morning and a television appearance last night in Chicago, Mr. Ford sought to distinguish his administration from that of his predecessor."[18] On November 1, 1976, the Ford campaign published a full page advertisement in the *New York Times* quoting Ford on the theme of trust.[19] Although all of these efforts contributed to a close race, they underscored the importance of the debates as vehicles for shaping the images of the candidates. Had Ford been able to respond to the growing doubts about his fairness and trustworthiness in the debates, he might not have needed to conduct the last minute attempts to win the trust of the voters.

NOTES

1. *New York Times*, September 19, 1976, IV, 1.

2. Kathleen Hall Jamieson, *Packaging the Presidency* (New York: Oxford University Press, 1984), chap. 8, 329–377.

3. Intelligence was a threshold issue for Ford. See Martin Schram, *Running for President 1976: The Carter Campaign* (New York: Stein and Day, 1977), 294; Peter Goldman and Tom Matthews, *The Quest for the Presidency 1988* (New York: Touchstone, 1988), 294.

4. Ford had been President for only a month before announcing that he had decided to pardon Nixon. This came as a shock to the American public. See

Clark R. Mollenhof, *The Man Who Pardoned Nixon* (New York: St. Martin's Press, 1976), chap. 8, "The Pardon Shock," 93–104; Jerald F. terHorst, *Gerald Ford and the Future of the Presidency* (New York: The Third Press, 1974), 216–217.

5. Robert T. Hartman, *Palace Politics: An Inside Account of the Ford Years* (New York: McGraw Hill, 1980), 267; terHorst, 217; Mollenhof, chap. 9, "Search for the Motive," 105–122.

6. *New York Times*, September 10, 1976, 19.

7. Ibid. See also, *New York Times*, October 13, 1976, A–20.

8. *New York Times*, October 15, 1976, B–4.

9. Warren Weaver, Jr., *New York Times*, November 6, 1976, 8.

10. Ford's rationale made some sense. See Hartman, *Palace Politics*, 259, 268–269. But Ford misanalyzed the way in which the public would react to the timing of the decision.

11. Ibid., 267. In passing, Hartman noted that "only the President himself could handle these suspicions" thus emphasizing Ford's need for a personalized defense.

12. Ibid., 266–267. Hartman noted how Jerald terHorst's resignation after the announcement of Nixon's pardon damaged the credibility of the Ford administration. terHorst had the confidence of the Washington press corps and was not a Nixon crony. When he resigned, his reason was that Ford did not treat the draft evaders and Watergate henchmen in equal terms with Nixon. This suggested that Ford embraced a double standard of justice. The question itself ultimately found its way into the debates.

13. Frederick T. Steeper, "Public Response to Gerald Ford's Statements on Eastern Europe in the Second Debate," in *The Presidential Debates: Media, Electoral and Policy Perspectives*, ed. George F. Bishop, Robert G. Meadow, and Marilyn Jackson-Beeck (New York: Praeger, 1978), 81–101. "The power of the news media to 'penalize bloopers severely' was amply demonstrated in the cases of Romney and Muskie. It was also the case with Gerald Ford's statement on eastern Europe's freedom from Soviet domination during the second presidential debate on foreign policy. The data to be presented in this chapter suggest that the general public did not know that the president had made an 'error' until they were told so by the news media the following day" (82).

14. See Dan Nimmo, Michael Mansfield, and James Curry, "Persistence and Change in Candidate Images," in *The Presidential Debates: Media, Electoral and Policy Perspectives*, 140–156. Using a Q-sort method, Nimmo et al. found interesting developments of candidate images over time. Carter's image in the sample for this study combined traits of moral leader and ambitious leader. Nimmo et al. found that moral leader was a positive trait while ambitious leader was a negative trait for Carter. After the first debate, Carter was perceived as more ambitious than moral. After the second debate, the sample began to perceive Carter as moral again. These findings are supported by the textual analysis. Carter focused on secrecy and integrity as issues during more than half of the second debate. The reason for the negative aspects of the ambitious leader image was probably due to the expectation that in 1976, the presidential candidates needed to appear as though they were motivated by noble concerns for the community, not selfish interests for personal gain. For a discussion of the polls, see John P. Robinson, "The Polls," in *The Great Debates: Carter vs. Ford, 1976*,

ed. Sidney Kraus (Bloomington, IN: Indiana University Press, 1979), 262–268. Robinson noted that according to the polls, Ford won the first debate, and Carter won the second and third debates. Despite the results that indicated that Carter won the second debate by a larger margin than any of the other victories, Robinson noted, "After the second debate, Harris noted increasing uneasiness about Carter's lack of experience and his avoidance of issues, as well as increasing confidence in Ford's leadership, especially in the area of foreign affairs" (265). The explanation of the Carter margin in the second debate, then, might have been in the public reaction to the media's claim that Ford misunderstood the relationship between Poland and the USSR.

15. Aristotle, *Rhetoric* (1358b20–1359a), trans. W. Rhys Roberts (New York: Modern Library, 1954), 32–33: "The political orator aims at establishing the expediency or the harmfulness of a proposed course of action; if he urges its acceptance, he does so on the ground that it will do good; if he urges its rejection, he does so on the ground that it will do harm; and all other points, such as whether the proposal is just or unjust, honourable or dishonourable, he brings in as subsidiary to this main consideration."

16. For a discussion of rhetorical strategies that can be used in situations calling for a personalized defense, see Jackson Harrell, B. L. Ware, and Wil A. Linkugel, "Failure of Apology in American Politics: Nixon on Watergate," *Speech Monographs* 42 (November 1975): 245–261.

17. *New York Times*, October 31, 1976, IV, 1.

18. *New York Times*, October 28, 1976, 48.

19. *New York Times*, November 1, 1976, 49.

Chapter Five

The 1980 Debates: Ronald Reagan Versus John Anderson and Ronald Reagan Versus Jimmy Carter

September 21, 1980, marked a historic moment in American politics because an independent candidate for the presidency was given an opportunity to debate a major party candidate, thereby challenging the idea that only Republican and Democratic candidates could be heard by national audiences. At the time, John Anderson did not enjoy widespread political support.[1] He had served as a Republican representative from Illinois, campaigned as a Republican in the presidential primaries, and then decided to continue his campaign for office as an independent in the hope that he would appeal to a national coalition dissatisfied with the Republican and Democratic alternatives.[2] When it was clear that Anderson would reach the 15 percent level of support established by the League of Women Voters for inclusion in the debate, he was invited to debate Ronald Reagan and Jimmy Carter.[3]

Uninterested in debating Anderson and Reagan, Carter held out until it became clear that his refusal to debate constituted a political issue in itself.[4] Late in the campaign, forced by public pressure to debate the Republican challenger, Carter accepted the Republican invitation to debate but performed poorly.

This chapter explains how, in the first debate, Reagan presented the audience with an image of a confident, sensitive, and able advocate who embodied what it meant to be an American, an image more desirable than Anderson's more cynical role as a critic of the candidate selection process and a prophet seeking to raise political consciousness of the American public.[5] Analysis of the second debate illustrated how Reagan's and Carter's performances in the exchange over arms control crystallized contrasting images that had been developing in less defined form throughout the other exchanges in the debate. In this exchange, Reagan was able to resolve doubts concerning his approach to foreign policy and the use of military force, whereas Carter's discourse confirmed doubts about his ability to respond competently to problems of leadership.[6] In this instance, specifically, Carter's failure to demonstrate rhetorical competence in solving problems was manifested in his limited ability to defend his position on arms control in response to Reagan's criticisms, in his inability to develop a persuasive attack on Reagan's opposition to prior arms control treaties and proposals, and in his decision to refer to his daughter's words on the problem of nuclear proliferation.

THE REAGAN-ANDERSON DEBATE

Three patterns emerged in the debate between John Anderson and Ronald Reagan. First, when attacked, Reagan defended himself on substantive grounds and through the use of humor. Second, Anderson could not sustain a substantive attack on Reagan. This was demonstrated in the exchange on Charles Corddry's question about the military draft when Reagan sidestepped Anderson's attack on his position supporting the MX missile program. Anderson's limitations could also be seen in the exchange over Daniel Greenberg's question concerning energy, conservation, and styles of living. Third, given Anderson's proclivity toward cynicism, Reagan was able to offer a more optimistic, sensitive, and compassionate image of leadership than Anderson, creating a favorable contrast for Reagan. These patterns were most evident in the answers to Greenberg's question on energy, Jane Bryant Quinn's question on economic forecasts, and in the closing statements; hence, these exchanges constituted the focal points for analysis.

Reagan Defends an Optimistic Outlook on Energy

When Greenberg asked, "What changes would you encourage in American lifestyles?" Reagan rejected Greenberg's assumption of scarcity, indicated his support for conservation, but warned, "I do not believe that conservation alone is the answer to the present energy problem, because all you're doing then is staving off, by a short time, the day when you would come to the end of the energy supply." Second, Reagan argued that we had a great deal of energy that had not been developed. Reagan cited oil, coal, nuclear, and solar energy as possible avenues for development and gave statistics to support his claims concerning oil and coal. Third, he was optimistic when he stated: "All of these things can be done. When you stop and think we are only drilling 2 percent—have leased only 2 percent of the possible—possibility for oil of the whole continental shelf around the United States." Fourth, in his conclusion, Reagan blamed "government" for the energy crisis: "When you stop to think that the government has taken over 100 million acres of land out of circulation in Alaska, alone, that is believed by geologists to contain much in the line of minerals and energy sources, then I think it is government, and the government with its own restrictions and regulations, that is creating the energy crisis. That we are indeed an energy-rich nation."

In response, Anderson began by asserting that Reagan misunderstood the energy crisis. He questioned Reagan's use of figures for the projected energy supplies but offered no evidence to refute Reagan's statistics. Second, unlike Reagan, Anderson chose to accept the premise of Greenberg's question—that it would be necessary to change American lifestyles dramatically. Again, he offered no evidence to refute Reagan's optimistic evaluation of the energy situation. Third, Anderson reviewed the need for his proposed excise tax on gasoline but failed to correct Reagan's interpretation of his proposal. Anderson asserted that unless the nation adopted his proposal and reduced gasoline consumption, it might be necessary to introduce U.S. troops into the Persian Gulf. Again, no evidence was offered to support this rather accurate prediction. Anderson's message seemed designed to appeal to a limited number of supporters who had the same understanding of these issues as did Anderson. Fourth, Anderson enumerated measures he saw necessary to reduce the amount of gasoline consumed in the nation: "We are going to have to resort to van pooling, to car pooling. We're going to have to develop better community transportation systems." Fifth, Anderson indicated that, compared to Germany's per capita rate of consumption, we consumed twice as much. Finally, Anderson cited the Harvard Business School study that revealed that in the commercial sector alone, 30 to 40 percent of the energy consumed could be saved. Anderson concluded by restating his stand—"Yes, we will have to change in a very appreciable way, some of the life-styles we now enjoy." Thus, Anderson's policy position was clearly developed, although the justification for the policy was predicated on Greenberg's assumptions of scarcity. No evidence was offered to refute Reagan's more optimistic outlook.

Reagan repeated that he was not opposed to conservation but added humor to his answer when he stated, "I wouldn't be called a conservative if I were," and then defended his figures by revealing they were those used by the Department of Energy. Reagan added that the Department of Energy was not known for its optimistic projection of future energy supplies. The evidence for this claim was "that is the same government that, in 1920, told us we only had enough oil left for thirteen years, and nineteen years later, told us we only had enough left for another fifteen

years." Second, Reagan argued that the American public had been conserving over the past decade:

As for saving energy and conserving, the American people haven't been doing
badly at that. Because in industry today, we're producing more, over the last
several years, and at 12 percent less use of energy than we were back in about
1973. And motorists are using 8 percent less than they were back at that time
of the oil embargo. So, I think we are proving that we can go forward with
conservation and benefit from that. But also, I think it is safe to say that we do
have sources of energy that have not yet been used or found.

This statement created an appealing image of the audience, one of
responsible citizens who had supported the cause of conservation.
Through his use of statistical comparisons of rates of energy consumption between 1973 and 1980, the statement suggested that Reagan understood the conservation issue. Furthermore, it gave Reagan the advantage
over Anderson because Reagan was appealing to those who supported
conservation and to those who preferred a more optimistic view of the
future.

Anderson's final rebuttal argued that the energy problem was not
only a national problem but also a worldwide problem. His criticism of
Reagan's stand was that Reagan overlooked upcoming scarcities in the
world oil market. Anderson referred to five studies but mentioned only
the American Petroleum Institute's study: "Somewhere along around
the end of the present decade, total world demand for oil is simply going
to exceed total available supplies." Anderson concluded his answer by
reasserting the need for conservation and a change in lifestyles now,
rather than later.

During this exchange, Anderson did not refute Reagan's more optimistic assumptions about the availability of energy resources. Since both
Reagan and Anderson were in favor of conservation, there was no clash
on the issue. In addition, Anderson's answer reflected a pessimistic
outlook whereas Reagan defended his optimism with more evidence
than did Anderson. Although Anderson had specific evidence on world
shortfalls in oil, he ignored Reagan's discussion of alternative energy
supplies. Thus, Reagan advocated conservation as Anderson did and
was more optimistic than Anderson, offered more evidence to support
that optimism, and defended his views of the energy situation more
ably than did Anderson. Although Anderson argued that Reagan misunderstood the energy situation, he did not make a compelling case to
prove this point. In these respects, Reagan's view of the energy situation
seemed coherent and defensible, whereas Anderson's best indictment
of Reagan was not well supported with evidence. In short, Anderson
did not defend effectively his pessimistic viewpoint in this exchange.

Anderson's Inability to Substantiate His Criticisms

Anderson used Quinn's question on economic forecasts as an opportunity to attack both Carter and Reagan, an important exchange because it showed Anderson attempting to prove himself more desirable than the alternatives of the major parties. Anderson began by criticizing politicians in general when he said that they often promise more than they can deliver. Anderson's evidence was Ford's advice to the voters that they should not vote for those who could not keep the promises they made. This set up Anderson's attack on Carter:

Well, we've seen what has happened. We haven't gotten either the economies in government that were promised; we haven't gotten the 4 percent inflation that we were supposed to get at the end of Mr. Carter's first term. Instead we had, I think, in the second quarter, a consumer price index registering around 12 percent. And nobody really knows, with the latest increase in the wholesale price index—that's about 18 percent on an annualized basis—what it's going to be.

The problem with this approach to the issue was that Anderson's use of Ford's advice as evidence put him back into the mainstream of the Republican party, reinforcing the fact that the choice was between two Republicans: Reagan or Anderson. Hence, his statement undercut his unique appeal as an independent candidate.

Anderson attacked Reagan by comparing programs. He used reluctant testimony from George Bush and the expert testimony of Paul McAvoy to prove that his program would be less inflationary than Reagan's: "His own running mate, when he was running for the presidency, said that they would cost 30 percent inflation inside of two years, and he cited his leading economic adviser, a very distinguished economist Paul McAvoy, as the source of that information. He went so far as to call it brutal economics." Anderson continued to promise a tax cut, as had Reagan, but argued that Reagan and Carter's rhetoric should have been characterized as a bidding process for the voters. The tone was denigrating. Anderson came across as condemning appeals to the voter's pocketbooks rather than as criticizing the demeaning quality of the appeals being made by Reagan and Carter. Whereas Anderson wanted the audience to think that Reagan and Carter were demeaning the American political process, he came across as cynical, and the cynicism overshadowed his appeal to prudence in his conclusion.

Reagan's response had four elements. First, he appeared to be one step ahead of Quinn's request for data when he stated:

Miss Quinn, I don't have to. I've done it. We have a back-up paper to my economic speech of a couple of weeks ago in Chicago, that gives all the figures.

And we used—yes, we used—the Senate Budget Committee's projections for five years, which are based on an average inflation rate of 7.5 percent, which I think, that under our plan, can be eliminated. And eliminated probably more quickly than our plan [*sic*], but we wanted to be so conservative with it, that the people could see how—how well it could be done.

Thus, Reagan appeared to be anticipating possible challenges to his leadership and demonstrating a conservative approach to developing policy by using the Senate Budget Committee's figures. Reagan then criticized Anderson on two grounds. First, he ridiculed Anderson's perspective on the budget issue by indicting Anderson's assumptions. Reagan used an analogy to make his point: "Now, John's been in Congress for twenty years. And John tells us that first, we've got to reduce spending before we can reduce taxes. Well if you've got a kid that's extravagant, you can lecture him all you want about his extravagance. Or you can cut his allowance and achieve the same end much quicker." Reagan appeared in the role of a father who would curtail the allowance of an extravagant child—government, exactly what the public was looking for in a prospective president. Then Reagan attacked Anderson on the grounds that his proposal called for increased government spending: "And when John talks about this non-inflationary plan, as far as I have been able to learn, there are eighty-eight proposals in it that call for additional government spending programs." Rhetorically, this was an effective move because it ignored the preliminary condition that Anderson had set up for any increase in government spending and called on Anderson to explain why he was advocating an increase when he claimed that he was against increased government spending. Then, basing a defense of his platform on his experience as governor of California, Reagan argued: "Now, I speak with some confidence of our plan, because I took over a state—California—10 percent of the population of this nation, a state that, if it were a nation, would be the seventh-ranking economic power in the world—in that state we controlled spending." Reagan's experience in California was presented as similar to that of a leading world power, and the situation in which he assumed leadership was presented as analogous to the situation that faced the American voter. Reagan continued:

We cut the rate of increase in spending in half. But at the same time, we gave back to the people of California—in tax rebates, tax credits, tax cuts—$5.7 billion. I vetoed 993 measures without having a veto overturned. And among those vetoes, I stopped $16 billion in additional spending. And the funny thing was that California, which is normally above the national average in inflation and unemployment, for those six years for the first time, was below the national average in both inflation and unemployment. We have considered inflation in our figures. We deliberately took figures that we, ourselves, believed were too conservative.

Reagan depicted himself as a leader on a more limited scale, then presented himself in the role of a national leader by stating in optimistic terms the belief that he could balance the budget by 1982 or 1983. He explained that he would do this by not spending the money that Carter had generated and by returning some of that money to the people. This final move was not as effective as Reagan's previous statements. His promise was optimistic, though, and if the audience accepted Reagan's version of his success as governor of California, then it might be willing to accept the notion that Reagan could balance the budget by 1982 or 1983. The burden of proof was now upon Anderson to show why Reagan would be unable to accomplish this feat.

Anderson began his answer by saying that he would not debate Reagan's record as governor of California. This would have been a mistake for Anderson because Reagan was running on the grounds that he had performed well as governor of California. However, Anderson went on to attack Reagan on these grounds by arguing that government spending had increased two-fold in the state of California. "Despite his [Reagan's] pledge to reduce state government spending . . . it rose from $4.6 billion when he took office in 1967, to $10.2 billion during his eight years in office." Anderson also challenged Reagan's optimistic view on balancing the budget and paying for huge increases in the nation's military budget:

That Senate Budget Committee report does not accommodate all of the Reagan defense plans. It doesn't accommodate the expenditures that he calls for [sic] for accelerated development and deployment of a new manned strategic bomber, for a permanent fleet in the Indian Ocean, for the restoration of the fleet to 600 ships, to the development and deployment of a dedicated modern aircraft interceptor. In other words, I have seen his program costed out to the point where it would amount to more than $300 million a year, just for military. And I think the figures that he has given are simply not going to stand up.

This was an excellent attack on Reagan's program. However, Reagan undermined Anderson's credibility with humor: "Well, some people look up figures, and some people make up figures. And John has just made up some very interesting figures." Reagan went on to say that he took the Senate Budget Committee report and factored in some of his own ideas "with regard to increases in the projected military spending that we believe would, over a period of time, do what is necessary." Again, Reagan used his own credibility as support for his policy proposals. No concrete evidence was offered to support the idea that the budget could be balanced while simultaneously increasing defense expenditures. And to the extent that the audience accepted Reagan as a credible source, it might be equally willing to accept Reagan's attack on Anderson's credibility. So Reagan's response had the dual effect of eroding Anderson's credibility and leaving the audience with the only credible candidate, himself. Reagan did more damage to Anderson's image as a strong executive by attacking Anderson on the grounds that he, unlike Reagan, had never held an executive position: "John doesn't quite realize—he's never held an executive position of that kind—and I think being governor of California is probably the closest thing to the presidency, if that's possible, of any executive job in America today— because it is the most populous state." Here, Reagan framed the issue in terms of who had had executive experience. Reagan compared the governorship of California to the office of the presidency and carefully qualified that claim so as to not overstate his case. Reagan also offered evidence of his effectiveness by saying that he "reduced, in proportion to other states, the per capita spending, the per capita size of government—we only increased the size of government one-twelfth what it had increased in the preceding eight years." All of this suggested that Reagan could function competently as an executive.

Several points can be drawn from this exchange. First, Anderson's performance during this exchange damaged his unique appeal as an independent candidate when he located himself in the mainstream of the Republican party. Also, Anderson appeared cynical when he attacked Carter and Reagan for appealing to the American public's pocketbook. Most Americans would rather have economy in government. And by criticizing the candidates who appealed to the public in this way, Anderson appeared to be demeaning the value of thrift rather than arguing that those candidates who make this kind of appeal are actually demeaning the American political process.

Despite these drawbacks, Anderson demonstrated an ability to attack Reagan's programs. He used reluctant testimony from Reagan's running mate George Bush, expert testimony on the economic issues from Paul McAvoy, and statistics when he attacked Reagan's record as governor of California. Anderson demonstrated his refutation skills when he pointed out that Reagan's use of the Senate Budget Committee's figures did not account for Reagan's program to increase military expenditures.

Reagan's performance in this exchange, however, could be considered more favorable. He appeared one step ahead of the panel when he stated that he already had published the figures dealing with economic forecasts; he disputed Anderson's assumptions about the budget through the use of an analogy that presented him as a strong father curtailing the bad behavior of government; he confidently defended his program based on his experience as an executive using statistics and analogies to support his case; his optimistic tone contrasted with Anderson's more cynical tone and served as a more appealing basis on which a favorable relationship with the audience might be constructed. When Anderson attacked Reagan's economic program and his promise to balance the budget, Reagan deflected the attack through the use of humor. Reagan relied on his credibility as a form of support for his policies while successfully calling into question Anderson's credibility as an executive. Reagan supported his claim to leadership by comparing his previous experience as governor to that of a leading world power, provided statistics to support his claim that he reduced government spending in California, and provided testimony from the *San Francisco Chronicle* that he prevented the state of California from going bankrupt.

In summary, Reagan provided more evidence of various forms to support his claim to be an effective leader whereas Anderson's statements diminished his appeal as an independent candidate. Reagan successfully challenged Anderson's credibility as a potential executive and in the course of doing so, disputed Anderson's credibility as a competent critic of Reagan's policies.

Closing Statements

Reagan made the first closing statement. Before launching into his prepared statement, he reminded the audience that Carter was absent from the debate and graciously thanked the League of Women Voters for allowing Anderson to participate. Reagan said:

Before beginning my closing remarks, here, I would just like to remark a concern that I have that we have criticized the failures of the Carter policy here rather considerably, both of us this evening. And there might be some feeling of unfairness about this because he was not here to respond. But I believe it would have been much more unfair to have had John Anderson denied the right to participate in this debate. And I want to express my appreciation to the League of Women Voters for adopting a course with which I believe the great majority of Americans are in agreement.

The statement reinforced criticisms of the Carter administration by treating them as though they were true and undeniable. In highlighting Carter's absence, Reagan drew attention to the fact that if a substantive defense could be made, then Carter should have participated in the debate. Also, Reagan's comment created a favorable relationship between himself and his audience by drawing attention to the fact that Anderson was a weak third party candidate, but applauding the fact that Anderson was given the opportunity to express his views. Reagan's statement placed him in the mainstream of the democratic tradition in which each person has the right to express his or her views. Carter's absence, then, was an example of a candidate's unwillingness to subject his actions to the scrutiny of the American public.

Reagan returned to his optimistic vision and tone in his closing statement. His comments reflected an understanding of the nation's history, drew on the myth of divine purpose for a chosen people, and created a favorable context for viewing the debate, the campaign, and the decision that Reagan was asking the audience to make. Initially, Reagan referred to his belief that "this land was placed here between the two great oceans by some divine plan. That it was placed here to be found by a special kind of people—people who had a special love for freedom and who had the courage to uproot themselves and leave hearth and homeland, and come to what, in the beginning, was the most undeveloped wilderness possible." Reagan's belief suggested a special role for audience members, that they were not an ordinary people but a special kind of people who demonstrated courage in the face of adversity. To the extent that Anderson had developed any expectation of imminent adversity, Reagan offered them an optimistic way to perceive the upcoming four years as a renewal of that national destiny, to find freedom and livelihood in a world fraught with doubts and uncertainties. Reagan continued: "We came from 100 different corners of the earth. We spoke a multitude of tongues—we landed on the eastern shore and then went over the mountains and the prairies and the deserts and the far western mountains to the Pacific, building cities and towns and farms, and schools and churches." Despite differences, then, Americans discovered unity in national purpose, overcame these differences of race, language, and culture, and created a nation where there once was wilderness. Reagan then connected the past with future in the image of what he described as a new breed of human: "If wind, water, or fire destroyed them [our cities], we built them again. And in so doing, at the same time, we built a new breed of human called an American—a proud, an independent, and a most compassionate individual for the most part. Two hundred years ago, Tom Paine, when the thirteen tiny colonies were trying to become a nation, said, we have it in our power to begin the world over again." Reagan's closing statement exemplified an individual who was proud, independent, and compassionate and shaped an image of his audience as a community of proud, independent, and compassionate individuals. To the extent that Reagan and the audience faced adversity together, he united his appeal for action with the nation's image of an active leader. The closing statement, then, presented Reagan in the image of a leader who understood how to develop bonds between different groups in the political community through the use of the nation's history, direct the nation's attention to the problems that might face the community in the future, and provide a sense of hope and confidence in the promise that by working together, these problems might be overcome.

To develop his image of the audience as competent Americans, Reagan reviewed the problems discussed in the debate and then recalled the problems that Americans had faced and overcome. Summarizing the debate, Reagan stated:

Today, we're confronted with the horrendous problems that we've discussed here tonight. And some people in high positions of leadership, tell us that the answer is to retreat. That the best is over. That we must cut back. That we must share in an ever-increasing scarcity. That we must—in the failure to be able to protect our national security as it is today—we must not be provocative to any possible adversary.

This statement acknowledged the existence of problems in the nation and attacked Anderson and Carter by characterizing their approaches as cynical. From here, Reagan could develop a more optimistic view of the future, completing the dialectical form of attack and defense. Reagan reviewed the darkest moments of our history to demonstrate that he understood the national history and the character of the community and then developed an optimistic vision of leadership in terms of previous success in overcoming adversity: "Well, we the living Americans, have gone through four wars. We've gone through a great depression in our lifetime that literally was worldwide and almost brought us to our knees. But we came through all of those things and we achieved even new heights and new greatness." Reagan made optimism a symbol of what it meant to be an American in this closing statement, and he was able to do this because he displayed an understanding of the nation's historical successes in overcoming difficult situations. By contrast, Anderson's rhetoric seemed un-American because it did not share Reagan's optimism. The power of Reagan's appeal could be found in the way he shaped the identity of the audience as a strong and active group of agents: "The living Americans today have fought harder, paid a higher price for freedom, and done more to advance the dignity of man than any people who have ever lived on this earth. For 200 years, we've lived in the future, believing that tomorrow would be better than today, and today would be better than yesterday. I still believe that." If the audience believed this about themselves, they would be predisposed to believe it about Reagan, because stylistically, Reagan's statement articulated the national identity better than the average citizen could. Reagan created his audience, then enacted the image of an optimistic agent of change, thus embodying what it meant to be an American in the face of adversity. Even if one assumed that Anderson's arguments about impending energy shortages were persuasive, Reagan's reassuring tone suggested that he would be more able to overcome these problems than Anderson. Reagan's image of leadership was characterized by optimism and confidence, whereas Anderson's was characterized by cynicism and impending crisis.

Reagan concluded with an appeal for action: "And together, we can begin the world over again. We can meet our destiny—and that destiny can build a land here that will be, for all mankind, a shining city on a hill. I think we ought to get at it." Reagan had refuted Anderson and, by implication, Carter's pessimistic outlooks by reliving the successes of the national community. Reagan's image was a reflection of his concept of what it meant to be an American.

Anderson's closing statement argued the case that a third choice existed for voters. He began by refuting Carter's claim that there were only two choices. His evidence for this claim was the debate, which he asserted revealed major differences between himself and Reagan: "I think you've seen tonight in this debate that Governor Reagan and I have agreed on exactly one thing: We are both against the reimposition of a peacetime draft. We have disagreed, I believe, on virtually every other issue." Anderson thanked the League of Women Voters for the opportunity to appear, then stated that he respected Reagan for appearing in the debate. The statement seemed awkward because it presumed that earning John Anderson's respect was an important endeavor for the other two candidates.

Anderson outlined the rationale for his candidacy when he stated: "I am running for president as an independent because I believe our country is in trouble. I believe that all of us are going to have to begin to work together to solve our problems." Again, he sounded pessimistic. Although he could point to potential difficulties facing the national community, the act of recognizing the existence of problems constituted insufficient evidence of leadership. Anderson needed to convince the audience that he was capable of solving those problems. On this issue, the closing statement revealed Anderson's major rhetorical problem. To demonstrate that the nation needed leadership, Anderson posed a series of rhetorical questions highlighting some of the problems that needed attention. It was the same tactic that Reagan would use in his closing statement in his debate with Carter. Anderson asked:

Do you really think that our economy is healthy? Do you really think that 8 million Americans being out of work and the 50 percent unemployment among the youth of our country are acceptable? Do you really think that our armed forces are really acceptably strong in those areas of conventional capability where they should be? Do you think that our political institutions are working the way they should when literally only half of our citizens votes?

These questions did not focus the audience's dissatisfaction in ways rhetorically suited to Anderson's purpose. Anderson's rhetorical questions might have created dissatisfaction with Carter, but they did not focus positive feelings or thoughts on Anderson's image because Anderson had not developed an image as a leader who embodied American ideals. Instead, he created an image of a nation that was on the verge of disaster. The problem with Anderson's candidacy was that he assumed that the capacity to articulate problems was sufficient to win national office. By not demonstrating an equally proficient understanding of the nation's history, and by not presenting a vision of leadership reflecting hope and optimism, Anderson gave the public no reason to vote for him, only a reason to vote against the incumbent, Jimmy Carter. Anderson continued in a pessimistic vein when he stated:

A generation of office seekers has tried to tell the American people that they could get something for nothing. It's been a time, therefore, of illusion and false hopes, and the longer it continues, the more dangerous it becomes. We've got to stop drifting. What I wish tonight so desperately is that we had more time to talk about some of the other issues that are so fundamentally important.

Here Anderson's closing statement was a call for political consciousness raising, not an attempt to embody national values or enact a specific concept of leadership.

The remainder of the closing statement demonstrated that Anderson saw his campaign as an attempt to raise the political consciousness of the public. Anderson cited Henry Steele Commager and argued that neither traditional party was looking beyond November, and that the really important issues, atomic warfare, use of our natural resources, and the issue of nationalism, still needed to be discussed. Anderson ended by notifying the audience that these were the issues that would be discussed in the final six weeks of the campaign.

Those are some of the great issues—atomic warfare, the use of our natural resources, and the issue of nationalism—that I intend to be talking about in the remaining six weeks of this campaign, and I dare hope that the American people will be listening and that they will see that an independent government of John Anderson and Patrick Lucey can give us the kind of coalition government that we need in 1980 to begin to solve our problems.

Anderson's closing statement, like his performance in the debate, did well in pointing out what problems faced the nation. However, his performance did not reflect a specific concept of presidential leadership, establish preferable values, or defend specific policies as necessarily more desirable than those of his opponent in the debate.

Summary of Findings in the Reagan-Anderson Debate

In his debate with Reagan, Anderson failed to demonstrate the Anderson difference. Anderson was unable to sustain his criticism of Reagan, could not answer Reagan's attacks on his candidacy, and presented himself as a pessimistic candidate. Reagan demonstrated superior advocacy skills, presented an optimistic outlook, and enacted a concept of presidential leadership that reflected a desirable image of what it meant to be an American. Anderson pointed to problems but gave no rhetorical evidence of his ability to solve them. In contrast, Reagan relived the American experience of overcoming adversity through unity and collective effort. On these grounds, one could conclude that Reagan would be more suited for the presidency.

THE REAGAN-CARTER DEBATE

The Reagan-Carter debate has already been examined in some detail by rhetorical scholars. Steven Brydon compared Jimmy Carter's 1976 debate with the 1980 debate to discover distinct differences in Carter's rhetoric.[7] According to Brydon, Carter's performance in 1976 featured more argumentative substance than his debate with Reagan in 1980. Robert C. Rowland has confirmed the absence of argumentative response to Reagan's challenge through a type of content-analytic research.[8] Both studies refute the widely accepted conclusion made by many media critics that Reagan "won" the 1980 debate with style whereas Carter's performance was better in terms of content.[9]

Carter's failure was due, in part, to his limited understanding of how to execute the strategy crafted for him by Pat Caddell, who advised him to reach out to his Democratic constituency along seven lines: four positive themes to portray Carter as a safe choice and three negative themes for Reagan suggesting that he was a risky option.[10] Research by Caddell identified the key rhetorical problems confronting both candidates but carefully noted that Carter had two rhetorical objectives: "Reagan can win if he solves his own problems. Carter cannot win by solving his own problems—he must deny Reagan as well."[11] In 1980, Carter did as he was advised—he stressed those themes identified by Caddell and reached out to various Democratic constituencies. But despite his attempt to perform according to plan, Carter could not win by simply stating what he wanted his audience to believe about him. Instead, he needed to enact the image of presidential character he was claiming for himself and hope that Reagan would play his part according to Caddell's script. But on October 28, 1980, Carter was not quite prepared for the part and Reagan chose a different role.

Of all the exchanges in the debate, the arms control issue contains the rhetorical actions that reflect most accurately Reagan's skills and Carter's rhetorical inabilities. This exchange provided a concise way to summarize how Reagan succeeded and Carter failed to enact an image of presidential competence in the debate. The closing statements were important to consider because in them Reagan reinforced the image of control that he had established in the debate. For these reasons, the analysis focuses on these two aspects of the debate.

Arms Control

The most significant exchange of the 1980 debate occurred over the question asked by Marvin Stone of *U.S. News and World Report* concerning the proliferation of nuclear arms:

President Carter, both of you have expressed the desire to end the nuclear arms race with Russia, but through vastly different methods. The governor suggests we scrap the Salt II treaty, which you . . . signed in Vienna, intensify the buildup of American power to induce the Soviets to sign a new treaty, one more favorable to us. You, on the other hand, say you will again try to convince a reluctant Congress to ratify the present treaty on the grounds it is the best we can hope to get from the Russians. You cannot both be right. Will you tell us why you think you are?

This question created the kind of rhetorical problem Caddell had referred to in his debate strategy. Carter needed to demonstrate presidential competence in the area of arms control while simultaneously reinforcing doubts about Reagan's judgment concerning the use of military force. Reagan needed only to reassure the audience that he was not prone to use military force at the slightest provocation.

Formulating the rhetorical situation in these terms makes it appear as though Reagan had the easier task, which was not necessarily the case. At this point in the campaign, Reagan's most serious rhetorical problem was that the public perceived him as a candidate who was much too willing to use military force as a solution to problems in foreign policy. Although it would be simplistic to argue that two or three minutes of responsible rhetoric could alter Reagan's image so drastically and change the course of the campaign, the exchange over arms control was symbolic of the larger confrontation taking place in the debate. Thus, Stone's question was a critical focal point for understanding how Reagan successfully enacted the image of a competent leader and for understanding how Carter failed to solve his rhetorical problem. Analysis of the arms control issue is divided between constructive and rebuttal speeches. Analyzing the patterns of response revealed Reagan's strengths and Carter's weaknesses.

Constructive Speeches

In his answer to Stone's question on arms control, Reagan specified his policy on the issue, attacked Carter's ability to negotiate with the

Soviets, and refuted Carter's claim that he had blocked SALT II. Reagan posited three specific goals as part of a general policy to increase "our margin of safety" while restraining the Soviet buildup: "a consistent foreign policy, a strong America, and a strong economy." Reagan then attacked Carter's handling of SALT II. He associated Carter with the negotiating team that linked Carter's competence to the negotiating team's competence and forced Carter to defend the actions of the committee. Reagan criticized the emissary's failure to spend more than twelve hours at the bargaining table but provided no specific evidence to support his claim. Reagan also attacked Carter's decision to cancel the B–1 bomber, delay the MX missile, and shut down the Minuteman invisible system. By listing these indictments, Reagan pushed Carter to defend his actions in these five cases, a difficult task given the limited time for response. Each of these examples functioned as evidence of Carter's incompetence on the defense issue. The five attacks also functioned as support for the claim that Carter had mishandled the SALT II negotiations. Reagan completed his argument by claiming that Carter's mishandling of the SALT II treaty was due to these unilateral concessions without any reciprocation from the Soviets whatsoever. Reagan also refuted Carter's claim that he had opposed SALT II. He said that SALT II was blocked by the Senate, which was Democratically controlled. Further support was offered by Reagan when he claimed that "the Senate Armed Services Committee voted 10 to 0, with seven abstentions, against the SALT II treaty, and declared that it was not in the national security interests of the United States." Reagan also claimed that the treaty was illegal on the grounds that (1) no treaty can be passed in which we are not equal and (2) we are not equal in this treaty because our bombers are considered strategic but their bombers are not. This final claim depended on the assumption that bombers must be considered similarly in the treaty. It was not supported by evidence and was only one way to consider the relative strength of the two countries. Carter had an opportunity to probe possible weaknesses in Reagan's answer on this aspect of the issue but failed to do so.

Initially, Carter elevated the issue of controlling nuclear weapons above other issues in the debate: "Inflation, unemployment, the cities— all very important issues, but they pale into insignificance in the life and duties of the President when compared with the control of nuclear weapons." Carter's move was an attempt to make one issue superordinate. Presumably, if he were perceived as superior in his analysis of this issue, in his use of evidence to support his claims about the dangers of proliferation, and in his ability to explain and defend his handling of the treaty, then Carter was superior to Reagan in his ability to lead the nation because this was the most important issue in the debate and the most important test of national leadership.

Selecting proliferation as the most important issue was strategic. For many observers during the campaign, Reagan's willingness to use military force and, if necessary, nuclear weapons to maintain America's strategic interests was alarming. This was popularly known as the "button" issue, and Reagan's earlier statements constituted a significant rhetorical obstacle.[12] However, elevating one issue above the others was also risky. Carter needed to perform favorably on this issue or fail his own test for presidential leadership.

Carter's strategy was to reinforce doubts about Reagan. To develop his attack on Reagan's willingness to use force, Carter tried to characterize Reagan's approach to the issue as a pattern: "To negotiate with the Soviet Union—balanced, controlled, observable, and then reducing levels of atomic weaponry. There is a disturbing pattern in the attitude of Governor Reagan." Evidence for this pattern came in Carter's references to Reagan's opposition to the limited test ban treaty, the SALT I treaty, the antiballistic missile treaty, and the Vladivostock treaty. However, although Carter labeled the opposition to the treaties a "pattern," he failed to explain why Reagan's political position on these policies demonstrated opposition to the broader issue of arms control. In one respect, the test ban treaty, the ABM treaty, SALT I, and the Vladivostock treaty can all serve as tests of a candidate's commitment to stopping proliferation of nuclear weapons but only if these treaties are suggested in some way to be in the best interests of the nation. This was the part of Carter's argument that he failed to provide for the audience. Carter assumed the audience perceived each of these treaties as desirable and without making the case that Reagan opposed very desirable treaties that would have been in the best interests of all parties concerned, Carter's criticism of Reagan rested on an incomplete objection to Reagan's position in the debate.

Carter developed his attack on Reagan's position on SALT II by claiming that Reagan wanted to "throw into the wastebasket a treaty to control nuclear weapons on a balanced and equal basis between ourselves and the Soviet Union, negotiated over a seven-year period, by myself and my two Republican predecessors." This statement implied that the treaty created balance between equals, but no support was offered, and thus Reagan's criticism that Carter had made unilateral concessions that weakened our bargaining position went unanswered.

Next, Carter shifted responsibility for the treaty by indicating that it was the result of negotiations undertaken by two Republican presidents. In one respect, this functioned as refutation of Reagan's claim that Carter and his negotiating team mishandled the negotiation. But Reagan's attack was more specific: He attacked a specific emissary, specific periods of negotiation, and specific concessions made unilaterally by the Carter administration. Carter did not answer Reagan on these points.

Carter then attempted to refute Reagan's claim that the Senate, controlled by the Democrats, did not support the treaty by stating that the Senate had not yet voted on the SALT II treaty. Carter acknowledged preliminary skirmishing in committee, thus answering Reagan's statement about the vote in the Armed Services Committee. Carter advised, however, that the Senate, in floor debate, might "correct" irresponsible, ill-advised" statements that may have been made by some senators. This could have been a veiled defense against the inconsistency in the Democratic party noted by Reagan, but, again, Carter did not provide sufficient explanation to clarify his argument.

Carter's final move was to suggest that Reagan was a dangerous and disturbing candidate. He claimed that Reagan wanted to discard the treaty without a serious debate and exploration of issues and that such action would be a failure to capitalize on "this long negotiation." However, the attack was not effective because Reagan was not claiming that we should reject the treaty without debate, but that the treaty was not in our best interests and was illegal. These claims went unrefuted by Carter. Carter's response, then, misrepresented Reagan's position, failed to deal with Reagan's evidence, and failed to demonstrate that Reagan was dangerous and disturbing.

Rebuttal Speeches

In Reagan's first rebuttal to Carter, he made three points. First, he defended his opposition to previous arms limitations treaties by indicating that we had been out-negotiated in those instances. His support for this claim was that, although we had been working toward arms reduction, the Soviets had gone forward with arms increases. The evidence was not specific, however.

Second, Reagan defended Republican leadership and placed responsibility for the SALT II treaty back to Carter. He indicated that Ford had been within 90 percent of an acceptable treaty but now Ford was against Carter's version of the treaty. This turned Carter's evidence into support for Reagan's position, suggesting that Republican leadership was consistent with the best interests of the United States.

Third, Reagan clarified his position on SALT II: "I am not talking of scrapping; I am talking of taking the treaty back, and going into negotiations." This highlighted Carter's misrepresentation of his position and allowed Reagan to explain how he might renegotiate the treaty: "And I would say to the Soviet Union, we will sit and negotiate with you so long as it takes, to have not only legitimate arms limitations, but to have a reduction of these nuclear weapons to the point that neither one of us represents a threat to the other." This passage also suggested Reagan's firmness in contrast to Carter's willingness to grant unilateral concessions. Finally, Reagan repeated that this position was not one of "throwing away a treaty and being opposed to arms limitations." The comment highlighted Carter's misrepresentation of Reagan as dangerous and instead suggested that Reagan was sensible and firm about the negotiation of nuclear arms limitation.

In Carter's first answer to Reagan's rebuttal, he reemphasized his earlier claim that Reagan was making misleading and disturbing statements. Carter repeated his claim that Reagan's position on SALT II was to scrap the treaty. Carter added the claim that Reagan had advocated nuclear superiority as a condition for future negotiations with the Soviets. Carter expanded this last criticism in a number of interesting ways. He presented a scenario of what might happen if one of the superpowers suddenly scrapped the SALT II treaty. Carter suggested that if the Soviets took an action similar to what he claimed Reagan proposed, the United States would reject it as untenable. He claimed that such an action would cause a resumption of a nuclear arms race because it changed the basic commitment to nuclear arms control that had been our policy since World War II. Three effects of this alleged reversal were noted: (1) the American people would be "disturbed"; (2) our allies, all of whom support this nuclear arms treaty, would be "disturbed"; (3) our adversarial relationship with the Soviets would be aggravated. All of these effects depended on whether Carter was correctly stating Reagan's position on SALT II. In two previous exchanges, Reagan repeated that he did not advocate the scrapping of SALT II but advocated renegotiation. If Carter's representation of Reagan's position were incorrect, the charges that Reagan was dangerous and disturbing would not be substantiated because the dangerous and disturbing effects would not follow from a sensible policy as it had been defended by Reagan in this debate. What is important to note here is that Reagan's position of renegotiation would have constituted a de facto scrapping of SALT II, but Carter never explained why "renegotiation" and "scrapping" reflected the same action. Since "renegotiation" sounded different and reasonable, and since Carter never explained why the two terms were equivalent, Reagan's rhetoric appeared to embody a plausibly prudent course of action. Moreover, Reagan's defense of renegotiation appeared sensible, firm, and pragmatic in contrast to Carter's position in the debate that Reagan had criticized. Carter's choice of the adjective "disturbing" to describe the effects of Reagan's policy was not vivid enough to create an image of potential disaster because Carter failed to demonstrate why the American people should be disturbed about Reagan's stand on nuclear proliferation. In these ways, Reagan appeared sensible, firm, and pragmatic.

Carter concluded his response by repeating his contention that Reagan was "extremely" dangerous. Further, he claimed that Reagan's tone was belligerent, although Reagan spoke with a quiet voice. But because belligerence had not been evident in Reagan's responses thus far, Carter needed to provide evidence to support his claim.

Reagan attacked Carter's ability to represent his policy positions: "I know the president's supposed to be replying to me, but sometimes, I have a hard time in connecting what he's saying with what I have said or what my positions are. I sometimes think he's like the witch doctor that gets mad when a good doctor comes along with a cure that'll work." Although this comment did not develop a defense of Reagan's policy, it highlighted Carter's inability to represent Reagan's position accurately, swept aside indictments of Reagan's policy by suggesting that Carter had ignored alternative solutions to the problem, and implicitly underscored Carter's ineffectiveness in limiting nuclear arms.

Reagan clarified his position for the second time and refuted Carter's claim that his policy required nuclear superiority as a condition for future arms reduction negotiations: "And to suggest that the SALT II treaty that your negotiators negotiated was just a continuation, and based on all of the preceding efforts by two previous presidents is just not true. It was a new negotiation, because, as I say, President Ford, was within about 10% of having a solution that would be acceptable." Finally, Reagan answered Carter's claim that our allies would be disturbed about his approach to SALT II: "And I think that our allies would be very happy to go along with a fair and verifiable SALT agreement."

Carter's final response on the arms limitation issue was particularly disappointing. He attempted to do three things: put the issue into perspective, describe the potential destructiveness of nuclear war, and reemphasize the responsibility of the President to control nuclear arms.

None of these moves advanced the debate on the SALT treaty or the debate about the best way to control nuclear proliferation. Not one of these responses answered the indictments Reagan had advanced in the exchange thus far: (1) that Carter's unilateral concession to cancel the B-1 bomber, delay the MX, the Trident submarine, and the cruise missile, and shut down the Minuteman invisible system have weakened our bargaining position; (2) that we are unequal in the present version of the SALT treaty because our bombers are considered strategic; (3) that Reagan's opposition to previous arms limitations agreements was justified due to their unbalanced nature; (4) that Republican leadership was responsible for an acceptable balanced treaty while Democratic leadership was responsible for an unacceptably unbalanced treaty; (5) that Reagan's policy position was not to scrap the SALT treaty, but rather to renegotiate a more balanced treaty that would be in the best interests of the United States; (6) that Carter was misrepresenting Reagan's policy position on strategic arms limitation talks; (7) that our allies would be pleased with a treaty that Reagan would negotiate.

All of these charges demanded some kind of answer. Instead, Carter attempted to put the issue into perspective by telling a story in which he asked his daughter Amy what was the most important issue of the campaign. Amy's answer: "nuclear weaponry and the control of nuclear arms." The anecdote did not address the list of indictments Reagan had made against Carter's ability to deal effectively with the most important responsibility of a president. Carter's choice to turn to his daughter's opinion highlighted his own incapacity to muster an adequate defense for his positions, and was inept, rhetorically, because it showed a President speaking in the persona of a child. The "Amy line" concluded Carter's weakest performance in a fitting way by confirming doubts about his competence. Carter's image as an inept leader had coalesced.

In summary, Reagan set a pattern of supporting his claims with evidence, commented on Carter's pattern of misrepresenting his positions, and seemed to be making sense. Carter, by comparison, would raise an issue, then drop it after Reagan answered his claims. When Carter spoke, it was to raise another question, to which Reagan again responded, at which point Carter again retreated. Although Reagan spoke sensibly on the nuclear proliferation issue, Carter claimed that Reagan was dangerous without providing evidence. On the most important issue in the debate and in the campaign, then, Carter ignored Reagan's arguments and evidence, could not substantiate his claims, and misrepresented Reagan's positions.

The Closing Statements

Carter's closing statement began by thanking the League of Women Voters, said that the debate had been constructive and useful, and thanked the people of Cleveland and Ohio for being hospitable hosts. After indicating his gratitude for the opportunity to speak, Carter then shifted roles from that of candidate to president. He spoke of his four years of experience and referred to the number of decisions he had had to make, indicated that he had learned from each decision, implying that he knew more than someone who had not had his experience in office, and reviewed the events he had witnessed in the term of his office, suggesting that no other individual could have made better decisions.

Carter attempted to draw sharp distinctions between himself and Reagan by locating himself in the mainstream of his party and in the mainstream of bipartisan presidents who had served before him. In doing so, he identified himself with positive aspects of both Democratic and Republican leadership.

Carter then shifted abruptly to a series of claims: the nation must be strong, secure, just, fair, and peaceful at home and abroad. He portrayed himself in the lonely role of the president determining the "interests of my country and the degree of involvement of my country." He said that experts divide evenly over controversial issues and that he alone must determine what the correct course of action should be. Carter then said that the "final judgment about the future of our nation—war, peace, involvement, reticence, thoughtfulness, care, consideration, concern— has to be made by the man in the Oval Office." These elements of the closing statement reflected Carter's strategy to stress the differences between himself and Reagan in the hope of making Reagan appear to be an unacceptable choice.

Carter's error in the closing statement was stylistic in nature. He asked the American public to share with him the responsibility of governing: "It's a lonely job, but with the involvement of the American people in the process, with an open government, the job is a very gratifying one." Carter asked the American people to join him in a partnership "to stay strong, to stay at peace, to raise high the banner of human rights, to set an example for the rest of the world, to let our deep beliefs and com- mitments be felt by others in all other nations." But Carter's notion of a partnership was inappropriate because the separation between the president and the people was blurred. The American people cannot perform the function of the president. To ask them to be partners in governing the nation is to ask them to share in the decision-making processes of the Executive Office. Because candidates campaign on the grounds that they can perform as national leaders better than other candidates running for office, Carter's pleas for a partnership could have been read as a request for assistance, suggesting implicitly that the job was too big for him. Although in previous presidential campaigns the theme of partnership had been effective in giving the electorate a sense of participation, especially in the 1976 campaign, in the 1980 campaign, Carter's plea for partnership reinforced doubts about his ability to fulfill the duties of office.

Reagan's closing statement began with a gracious thanks to the League of Women Voters. Then he added a note of regret that Anderson could not participate in this event, although he noted that Anderson had been heard at least once. This was an implicit attack on Carter's unwillingness to debate and his intransigence about not including Anderson. Reagan then proposed a series of rhetorical questions:

I think when you make that decision, it might be well if you would ask yourself, are you better off than you were four years ago? Is it easier for you to go and buy things in stores than it was four years ago? Is there more or less unem- ployment in the country than there was four years ago? Is America as respected throughout the world as it was? Do you feel that our security is as safe, that we're as strong as we were four years ago? And if you answer all of those questions "yes," why then, I think your choice is very obvious as to who you'll vote for. If you don't agree, if you don't think that this course that we've been on for the last four years is what you would like to see us follow for the next four, then I could suggest another choice that you have.

The questions provided criteria for a balanced assessment of Carter's term and made Carter's abilities the focus of the debate. Reagan did not need to demonstrate himself superior to Carter if Carter could not meet the minimal standard of preventing things from becoming worse. Reagan's questions, however, suggested that things had worsened. Hence, the burden of proving who was the better leader was on Carter, not Reagan, and this passage closed the debate nicely on Carter's weakest grounds.

Reagan's device also revealed that he had gained control of the debate. Instead of asking the audience for its support as Carter did, Reagan gave the audience the grounds for making the decision. Implicitly, Carter's request for support suggests that he had lost control whereas Reagan's question implied that he had taken control from Carter and returned it to the people. This action fit with the pattern of control developed in the exchange on arms control. Because the closing statement was a way of creating a context for the previous transactions, Reagan's question underscored the competing images of leadership that had crystallized for the audience.

Reagan then suggested himself as a competent leader stating that "this country doesn't have to be in the shape it is in. We do not have to go on sharing in scarcity, with the country getting worse off, with unemployment growing. . . . All of this can be cured, and all of it can be solved." Again, the element of optimism was evident in Reagan's performance, suggesting that the audience could gain hope at the prospect of Reagan's leadership. Again, as he did in the debate with Anderson, Reagan portrayed himself in the role of an effective leader by comparing his governorship of California to the leadership of a small nation—the seventh-ranking economic power in the world. Additionally, Reagan noted that he, too, had some lonely moments when making decisions. His decisions, he argued, were effective, however. "We cut the cost— the increased cost of government—the increase in half over the eight years. We returned $5.7 billion in tax rebates, credits, and cuts to our people. We . . . fell below the national average in inflation . . . we did give back authority and autonomy to the people." In short, Reagan portrayed himself as effective in every way that Carter had not been. It was a sharp contrast, well supported, and well executed by Reagan.

Finally, in direct contrast to Carter's invitation to a partnership, Reagan asserted his desire to lead. "I would like to have a crusade. I would like to have a crusade today, and I would like to lead that crusade with your help." Here, the role of the people and the role of the president were clear. Reagan would lead the crusade while the people supported him. There was no suggestion of cooperative decision making. Reagan wanted to release the people from the binds of government: "And it would be one [a crusade] to take government off the backs of the great people of this country and turn you loose again to do those things that I know you can do so well, because you did them and made this country great." It was clear that Reagan wanted only the political support necessary to legitimize his leadership and that the decision to support Reagan would not bind the electorate to a fictitious partnership. In this respect, Reagan appeared more willing than Carter to assume responsibility for decision making at the executive level.

SUMMARY

In his first debate with John Anderson, Ronald Reagan successfully presented an image of an optimistic and competent leader by reliving the community's triumphs over adversity. Because Anderson did not provide rhetorical evidence of his ability to solve problems, he failed to display the "Anderson difference" and presented himself as a cynical candidate who could only point to problems without offering solutions.

In the debate between Reagan and Carter, the arms control issue was important because it summarized the contest between the two candidates in terms of presidential competence. Because the proliferation of nuclear weapons constituted a serious threat to peace, both candidates needed to show the audience their potential ability to control nuclear weapons wisely. On a symbolic level, Carter's decision to elevate this issue above others suggested that it was a key test of who could control the grounds of the debate. If Carter had performed well on this issue, it would have implied that he could respond favorably to other serious issues. The act of controlling the most important issue of the debate would have been a way of controlling the debate. And because debates, by their very nature, create threatening rhetorical situations, a successful performance by Carter on this issue would have demonstrated his ability to control threatening situations, a kind of competence that many doubted he had.[13]

Carter's failure to solve his rhetorical problem had enormous repercussions for the images of presidential leadership being shaped in the debate. The pattern of argumentative response that has been noted by others was most evident in this exchange: Reagan argued his case but Carter did not. This pattern of action had significance on two levels. First, within this transaction, Reagan's image as a warmonger was refuted and Carter's image of a weak leader, unable to control threatening situations, was confirmed. But because Carter chose this issue as the most important one, and because these patterns of response were evident throughout the rest of the debate, this exchange encompassed the essential images of character that had been developing in less dramatic ways at other points in the debate. In short, the arms control exchange contained the dramatic enactment of each candidate's character, reinforced the larger pattern taking shape throughout the debate, and crystallized the differences in character between the two candidates.

The closing statements confirmed the developments that had occurred in the debate. Carter's closing statement contained numerous claims about his ability but in no way demonstrated that he had sufficient leadership potential to justify another term. Although Reagan's closing statement framed the question for the voters on Carter's weakest grounds, it was significant rhetorically as a symbolic act of leadership. By controlling the question before the voters, Reagan gained control over the rhetorical situation and reinforced his image as a strong candidate while simultaneously diminishing Carter's image as a candidate who could exercise control over events. Thus, Reagan demonstrated his potential for leadership through his use of argument. And in failing to respond effectively to Reagan's arguments, Carter gave evidence of his limited ability to perform the role of a leader.

NOTES

1. Anderson did not enjoy widespread support of a major party nomination. His strategy was to appeal to a coalition of members of both parties. See Elizabeth Drew, *Portrait of an Election* (New York: Simon and Schuster, 1981), 152–153.

2. Ibid., 152–153.

3. The League of Women voters established 15 percent of popular support as the criterion for a major candidate for the presidency.

4. Carter waited until the polls indicated that his reluctance to debate was constituting an issue in itself.

5. See Kathleen Hall Jamieson, *Packaging the Presidency* (New York: Oxford University Press, 1984), 378–445.

6. Drew, *Portrait of an Election*, 312, 314.

7. Steven R. Brydon, "The Two Faces of Jimmy Carter: The Transformation of a Presidential Debater, 1976 and 1980," *Central States Speech* 36 (Fall 1985): 138–151.

8. Robert C. Rowland, "The Substance of the 1980 Carter-Reagan Debate," *Southern Speech Communication* (Winter 1986): 142–165.

9. See Goodwin F. Berquist and James L. Golden, "Media Rhetoric Criticism, and the Public Perception of the 1980 Presidential Debates," *Quarterly Journal of Speech Communication* 67 (May 1981): 125–137.

10. See Drew, *Portrait of an Election*, 410–439.

11. Ibid., 421.

12. See "The Battle of the Button," *Newsweek*, September 1, 1980, 8. The Reagan camp knew that this issue was critical to the campaign and wanted a debate to get national exposure for Reagan to demonstrate that he was a sensible

candidate who would not start a nuclear war. See also Jack Germond and Jules Witcover, *Blue Smoke and Mirrors* (New York: Viking, 1981), 267; Drew, *Portrait of an Election*, 374–377.

13. Originally, there had been discussion of the possibility of more than one debate. Hedrick Smith quoted a Carter aide in the *New York Times*, August 11, 1980, A–1: "Reagan's greatest vulnerability is Ronald Reagan himself. . . . Those debates are going to be terribly important in the fall. We want as many of them as we can get. The President does well in debates. Reagan will make his bobbles and we'll make him the issue." Morton Kondracke quoted Elaine Komarck of the Democratic National Committee in *The New Republic*, September 20, 1980, 5, thinking that the debates would show Carter "more knowledgeable, more Presidential, than Reagan. Reagan will project a nice lovable image, but Carter will know what he is talking about." *Newsweek*, August 25, 1980, 22, reported that the Carter camp was "counting even more on the debates to cut Reagan down to size and showcase what they consider the President's superior virtues—his experience, his restraint, his mastery of complexity."

Chapter Six

The 1984 Presidential Debates: Ronald Reagan Versus Walter Mondale

According to Robert Friedenberg's work concerning why candidates agree to debate their opponents, the 1984 debates should not have occurred.[1] Throughout the campaign, Ronald Reagan held a substantial lead in the polls.[2] Although there was little reason for him to risk confrontation with Walter Mondale, Reagan agreed to two debates.[3] Although the debates gave Mondale an opportunity to criticize Reagan's leadership for the previous four years, Mondale also needed to overcome perceptions of himself as a whining, stylistically unexciting candidate.[4] As the challenger, Mondale had the burden to prove that Reagan was not in control of the office and to challenge any rational justification for rewarding Reagan with a second term.[5] Had Mondale been able to accomplish this in both debates instead of only one, the election might have been much closer.[6]

In the first debate, Mondale proved that he understood the nature of presidential leadership by successfully defending his strategy for dealing with the deficit. Also, Mondale challenged Reagan's polished image of a compassionate and consistent candidate in the rebuttals on tax policy proving that Reagan was vulnerable to a clever, well-developed, substantive attack. But most importantly, analysis of the first debate revealed Mondale's grasp of the facts and Reagan's limited ability to defend his administration on factual grounds.[7] In these ways, the first debate showed that Reagan was not a reliable source of facts, making reliability the salient issue of presidential competence in 1984.

Mondale's performance in the first debate was so effective that it led to speculation about how Reagan's age affected his abilities and these impressions created minimal expectations for Reagan in the second debate. Reagan needed to appear only less than senile to dismiss doubts created by Mondale in the first debate. Because the audience had already chosen Reagan by a significant margin, Mondale needed two dramatic victories just to stay in the race.[8] Because Reagan's defense in the second debate was more skillful, Mondale was unable to muster sufficient evidence to support his claim that Reagan was not qualified for a second term. This chapter focuses primarily on the first debate, which was the only real threat to Reagan's campaign,[9] and discusses the second debate only in terms of Reagan's ability to dismiss doubts about his age.

THE FIRST DEBATE

According to Barbara Walters, the first debate concerned the "economy and other domestic issues," but Mondale changed the focus to bear primarily on the budget deficit. To develop this argument, I explain first how the three exchanges not specifically tied to the deficit issue were inappropriate focal points for analyzing each candidate's image and then examine the ways in which Mondale developed the charge that Reagan refused to confront the facts as he saw them in the exchanges over the deficit, leadership qualities, relief to the poor, the changing electorate, and view of opponent.

Excluding Religion, Abortion, and Taxes

The third, fifth, and sixth questions concerning religion, abortion, and taxes, respectively, were not exchanges that defined essential contrasts in the images of presidential character for Reagan and Mondale. On the issue of separation of church and state, the differences between Reagan and Mondale could be reflected in their attempts to appeal to their constituencies. For example, Reagan stated in his rebuttal, "It's very difficult to rebut, because I find myself in so much agreement with Mr. Mondale. I, too, want that wall that is in the Constitution of separation of church and state to remain there." However, Mondale and Reagan disagreed over how the separation of church and state was to be maintained. Reagan's interpretation of the separation of church and state meant that government should allow prayer on school, and presumably, state property; that any action by federal courts prohibiting prayer on school property was an example of state action interfering with religious practice. Mondale constructed his interpretation of the church and state doctrine more narrowly, arguing that Reagan's proposed constitutional amendment would require local politicians to select official prayers for recital in schools. Given this view, Mondale argued that the policy would be unworkable by posing three rhetorical questions: Who would write the prayer? What would it say? How would it be resolved when those disputes occurred? Although both candidates agreed on the principle of separation of church and state, each candidate appealed to his constituencies by defining that separation in different ways and appealing from distinctly different views of the Constitution. Because the appeals seemed directed at partisan audiences, were not developed in sufficient detail to determine which view of the issue was substantively preferable, and called for evaluation on the basis of whether one agreed or disagreed with a particular viewpoint, the religion issue was an inappropriate focus for analyzing the first debate.

The abortion issue could have been a key issue in the first debate. Both of the candidates had, in Diane Sawyer's words, positions that were "clearly different and lead to very different policy consequences." Despite the potential for clash, the candidates developed their positions without much criticism of their opposition's argument. Reagan constructed a case for treating the fetus as a human being; Mondale contended that Reagan's proposed constitutional amendment making abortion illegal should be rejected on the grounds that it was an inappropriate intrusion by government into the rights of the individual. For the purposes of direct clash, these two arguments could have been aligned more clearly in the rebuttals, but the discussion turned to the problem of pregnancy induced by rape. Reagan's final position was that, in our society, under the unfortunate circumstances when an infant is conceived through rape, we should be able to provide for the unborn infant rather than doing away with a living being. In his final rebuttal, Mondale agreed with this particular portion of Reagan's stand, then argued that he had followed this course of action by sponsoring legislation to provide for abortions. But Mondale maintained that Reagan's other option, making abortion illegal, should not be pursued. Rather than developing this argument in further detail, Mondale used the remaining time to answer a previous issue concerning agriculture. As a result of the rebuttal exchanges on the issue of abortion, Mondale and Reagan ended up in agreement on the sanctity of life but disagreed on what to do about unwanted pregnancy. Because the debate over unwanted pregnancies was not developed in the rebuttals and because both candidates appeared to be in agreement on the sanctity of life, the abortion exchange blurred important differences between the candidates and failed to provide a clear contrast for their ability to defend their respective positions. For these reasons, the abortion exchange did not constitute an appropriate focus for analyzing the first debate.

Finally, before turning to a specific consideration of the deficit issue, the rebuttals in the exchange over tax policy for middle income families requires brief consideration. In the first four exchanges, two interesting moments occurred: Mondale predicted that Reagan would increase taxes, and Reagan used his now famous "There you go again" line, implying that Mondale was repeating a tired, if not unsubstantiated theme. In the 1980 debate with Jimmy Carter, Reagan's use of lines like, "There you go again" highlighted Carter's inability to sustain his arguments against Reagan's stylistic use of humor. Rhetorically, this line implied a pattern of unsubstantiated statements; it functioned enthymematically, suggesting to the audience that one's opponent can only repeat claims but not substantiate them. For Carter, the obvious counterattack should have been to prove his point with supporting evidence, thus forcing Reagan to respond to a substantive issue. But Carter's refutative performance in the 1980 debate was simply not as strong as Reagan's.

In the 1984 debate, Mondale turned the rhetorical ploy against Reagan by reminding the audience that Carter had been correct, and then extended the attack to a series of Reagan's actions:

Mondale: Now, Mr. President, you said: "There you go again." Right? You remember the last time you said that?

Reagan: Um hmmm.

Mondale: You said it when President Carter said that you were hoping to cut Medicare, and you said: "Oh no, there you go again, Mr. President." And what did you do right after the election? You went out and tried to cut $20 billion out of Medicare. And so when you say, "There you go again," people remember this, you know. And people will remember that you signed the biggest tax increase in the history of California and the biggest tax increase in the history of the United States and what are you going to do? You've got [*sic*] a $260 billion deficit. You can't wish it away. You won't slow defense spending; you refuse to do that.

This was one of the few instances when a political candidate directly addressed his opponent in the debate.[10] When Mondale directly asked Reagan if he remembered the last time he had used this line and Reagan answered Mondale's question, he acknowledged the direct nature of the dialogue. This suggested that both candidates shared a similar understanding of the public record on this issue. In one respect, Mondale's question was a test of Reagan's memory, in another respect it was a rhetorical trap. Reagan could not state that he was unable to recall one of his finest moments against Carter without appearing as though his memory had faded in his first term. By answering the question directly, though, Reagan participated in Mondale's ploy, placing him outside the protective constraints of the format and enjoining him to a dialectic controlled by Mondale. Reagan's answer implicitly revealed Mondale's ability to shape Reagan's role in the debate, to suggest him in the role of an interrogatee; and in accepting the role prescribed for him by Mondale, Reagan's actions suggested that he had lost control of the rhetorical situation.

Mondale would have been happy to continue the attack had Walters not interrupted to preserve the integrity of the format. Reagan's answer was disappointing. He denied the charge that he had proposed a $20 billion cut, but could not explain what he did, in fact, propose: "And, no, I never proposed any $20 billion should come out of Medicare. I have proposed that the program—we must treat with that particular problem. And maybe part of that problem is because during the four years of the Carter-Mondale administration medical costs in this country went up 87 percent." The attack on the Carter-Mondale administration was not apparently relevant. The issue was whether Reagan's actions were consistent with his statements on public record, not whether his administration had lowered medical costs. More importantly, even if Reagan were correct, his statement suggested the need for maintaining or increasing Medicare support, not decreasing it as Mondale had charged.

By itself, this exchange did not constitute sufficient evidence to support the claim that Mondale's performance was better than Reagan's. However, on this particular issue, and in these rebuttals, Mondale demonstrated his ability to sustain a desirable image. Through his use of humor, evidence, and dialectical enjoinment, Mondale turned Reagan's tactics against him, proving that Reagan was vulnerable and that he was a viable candidate. Had Mondale continued this level of performance, there would be need for more attention to the stylistic elements of the discourse. But this was Mondale's best and Reagan's weakest moment, and the exchange was uncharacteristic of their performances during the 1984 debates.

The Deficit

It would be difficult to dispute the fact that the deficit was the most important issue in the first debate. James Wieghart opened the debate with a question on this issue, suggesting that it was, by itself, an important issue in the campaign. In the seven following exchanges, Mondale strategically connected the deficit to four other issues: leadership qualities, the changing electorate, relief for the poor, and each candidates' view of his opponent. In the last exchange, Mondale stated that the deficit was the most important issue of our time. He used the deficit to challenge Reagan's credibility as a candidate in control of the facts, to define leadership in terms of a candidate's ability to understand the facts, and then to focus the debate on this key issue in the final exchange. Reagan never refuted Mondale's charge that the deficit was a test of leadership or that the debt was the dominant domestic issue. When

Reagan denied Mondale's claims concerning the budget, Mondale appealed to the public record of Reagan's statements and proposals. Because the first exchange of the debate concerned the deficit and because the factual basis of Mondale's argument was established in this exchange, the analysis begins with Wieghart's opening question on the budget deficit.

Wieghart asked Reagan if he had a "secret plan to balance the budget some time in the second term, and if so, would [he] lay out that plan for us tonight." Reagan's answer contained a straightforward description of his policy and a prediction for success. Stating that he had "a plan that is based on growth in the economy, recovery without inflation, and reducing the share that the government is taking from the gross national product, which has become a drag on the economy," Reagan concluded his answer by stating that these actions would lead to a balanced budget. Wieghart's follow-up offered refutation of Reagan's projections from the Congressional Budget Office and asked if Reagan would have to raise taxes or take other fiscal measures to reduce the deficit. Reagan's strategy in the follow-up answer was to reject the use of the CBO figures: "I do not . . . take seriously the Congressional Budget Office projections, because they have been wrong on virtually all of them, including the fact that our recovery wasn't going to take place to begin with." Reagan concluded his follow-up answer by restating the conditions under which he thought his administration could balance the budget:

If the rate of increase in government spending can be held at 5 percent—we're not far from there—by 1989 that would have reduced the budget deficits down to a $30 billion or $40 billion level. At the same time, if we can have a 4 percent recovery continue through that same period of time, that will mean—without an increase in tax rates—that will mean $400 billion more in government revenue. And so, I think the lines can meet.

After reminding the audience of Carter's unfulfilled promise to balance the budget, and criticizing the Democratic platform for maintaining an $89 billion deficit after increasing taxes and reducing outlays, Wieghart then pressed the question to Mondale: "What other steps do you think should be taken to reduce this deficit and position the country for economic growth?"

Mondale's strategy deferred a direct answer to Wieghart's question until the conclusion of his statement. Instead, Mondale attacked Reagan's credibility as a leader by defining leadership in terms of the ability to see clearly the nature of the problem facing the nation and then suggesting that the deficit was the dominant domestic issue: "One of the key tests of leadership is whether one sees clearly the nature of the problem confronted by our nation. And perhaps the dominant domestic issue of our times is what we do about these enormous deficits." Before criticizing Reagan, however, Mondale distinguished the man from the institution he represented: "I respect the president; I respect the presidency, and I think he [Reagan] knows that." In stating his respect for the office, Mondale suggested that his motive in criticizing Reagan was not to denigrate the president or the office but rather to demonstrate the limited appeal of Reagan as a candidate.

Once Mondale made it clear that he respected the office, he separated Reagan, the candidate, from Reagan, the president.[11] This move allowed him to criticize Reagan's policies without appearing unpatriotic. Even Mondale's attack avoided Reagan's name. Referring to the Reagan administration as "this administration," Mondale stated:

But the fact of it is, every estimate by this administration about the size of the deficit has been off by billions and billions of dollars. As a matter of fact, over four years, they've missed the mark by nearly $600 billion. We were told we would have a balanced budget in 1983. It was $200 billion deficit instead. And now we have a major question facing the American people as to whether we'll deal with this deficit and get it down for the sake of a healthy recovery. Virtually every economic analysis that I've heard of, including the distinguished Congressional Budget Office, which is respected by, I think, almost everyone, says that even with historically high levels of economic growth, we will suffer a $263 billion deficit. In other words, it doesn't converge, as the president suggests. It gets larger, even with growth.

Mondale went on to state the undesirable impact of the deficit measured in terms of foreign and domestic trade problems, then stated briefly that his policy would decrease the deficit to 2 percent of the gross national product. But Mondale's conclusion emphasized the point that the deficit was a key test of leadership, and that he had fulfilled that test when he stated: "I've stood up and told the American people that I think it's [the deficit] a real problem, that it can destroy long-term economic growth, and I've told you what I think should be done. I think this is a test of leadership, and I think the American people know the difference." Mondale had defined leadership in terms of a realistic approach to the deficit, presented facts suggesting that Reagan's perception of the budget crisis was unrealistic and then suggested that he had successfully enacted that role by acknowledging the nature of the problem but that Reagan had not.

Also, Mondale had defended the credibility of the Congressional Budget Office by asserting that it was respected by everyone. Rhetorically, the defense of the CBO projections underscored the fact that the issue depended on which source had more credibility for the audience, the CBO or the president. Although Mondale's credibility depended on the audience's perception of the CBO as a reliable source for economic projections, Reagan's credibility rested on the audience's perception of his ability to represent the facts accurately. Reagan usually needed no expert testimony to bolster his arguments. He was regarded highly by the public as a credible source in his own right. However, by predicating his substantive appeals on his own view of facts, Reagan's credibility as a knowledgeable candidate became connected to his credibility as a reliable candidate, one who could be trusted to report the facts accurately. When Mondale used the public record to reveal Reagan's inconsistency on Social Security and failure to comprehend the seriousness of the deficit, Reagan's image as a credible and competent candidate began to erode. These two problems developed in this first exchange. Having established the problem, Mondale continued to extend his attack on Reagan's credibility in the other exchanges.

Wieghart's follow-up attempted to trap Mondale in an inconsistency by claiming that controlling Democrats in Congress had blocked Reagan's attempts to reduce spending. But Mondale demonstrated his ability to distinguish between desirable and undesirable reductions in spending by accepting the principle of responsible reductions, then arguing that Reagan's proposed reductions had been in the areas of Social Security, Medicare, and student assistance—programs that assisted the most vulnerable groups in society. Mondale suggested that there were other ways of reducing the deficit than "picking on our senior citizens and the most vulnerable in American life." As a last jab, Mondale offered an example of reluctant testimony by indicating that even Republicans in Congress resisted the president's recommended reductions.

Reagan's response to Mondale's attack was vulnerable. Reagan argued that Mondale had no plan to balance the budget—which was not accurate given the brief description presented by Wieghart and Mondale in the previous comments; that Mondale planned to increase taxes—which was not at issue since Mondale had not denied Wieghart's statement that he would increase taxes; and that Carter and Mondale had raised taxes in 1977—which was a weak argument because Mondale was not directly responsible for the Carter administration's policy. Reagan concluded by stating that he would never stand for a reduction in Social Security benefits. In all of this, Reagan did not respond to Mondale's claim that the deficit was a key test of leadership and the dominant domestic issue in the campaign. In fact, throughout the rest of the debate, Reagan never answered Mondale's argument that the budget crisis was the key issue. From this point, Mondale controlled the most important issue in the debate and, presumably, the key issue in the campaign: leadership ability defined in terms of a candidate's mastery of the facts.

In the last rebuttal, Mondale offered direct refutation of Reagan's promise by appealing to the audience's memory of Reagan's first term:

That's exactly the commitment that was made to the American people in 1980: He would never reduce benefits. And, of course, what happened right after the election is they proposed to cut Social Security benefits by 25 percent—reducing the adjustment for inflation, cutting out minimum benefits for the poorest on Social Security, removing educational benefits for dependents whose widows were trying—with widows trying to get them through college. Everybody remembers that: people know what happened.

Mondale concludes with the claim that his actions had been consistent with his promise to fight for those most vulnerable in society. Although Reagan challenged Mondale's consistency on the deficit issue in the last exchange, Mondale defended his previous support of deficits. Also, Reagan later admitted that he had proposed a reduction in Social Security benefits. The factual basis of Mondale's position on the deficit and Social Security were reinforced in subsequent exchanges. Thus, as the debate progressed, Mondale's answers suggested that he was in control of the facts; Reagan's did not.

Leadership Qualities

In political debates, the opportunity for immediate response creates a dramatic tension by exposing both candidates to the danger of opposing arguments. Sawyer's question about leadership qualities was a good example of a threatening rhetorical situation. After reviewing earlier campaign statements, Sawyer asked each candidate to "substantiate your claims—Mr. Mondale first. Give us specifics to support your claim that President Reagan is a showman, not a leader; has not mastered what he must know to be president after four years, and then, second, tell us what personal leadership characteristics you have that he does not." This was an excellent opportunity for Mondale to press the attack; Sawyer could not have phrased the issue more favorably for Mondale when she asked him to prove that Reagan had "not mastered what he must know to be president after four years." In this question, Sawyer, like Mondale in the prior exchange, characterized leadership as mastering the facts. In the previous question, Mondale had established a factual basis as his approach to the issue. By appealing to the audience's understanding of the public record to refute Reagan's interpretation of the Social Security issue, and then to the audience's respect for the Congressional Budget Office's projections to refute Reagan's optimistic outlook for the budget, Mondale was challenging Reagan's mastery of the facts.

On the leadership issue, Mondale pushed the strategy one step further by arguing that Reagan's stance was out of step with consensus opinion: "There is no question that we face this massive deficit, and almost everybody agrees unless we get it down, the changes for long-term healthy growth are nil. . . . The president says it will disappear overnight because of some reason. No one else believes that's the case." By characterizing his perception of the issue as one shared by everyone except Reagan, Mondale placed Reagan on the defensive. Reagan needed to prove that his perspective on the deficit was consistent with the audience's or appeal to experts who supported his position. Mondale concluded this point by reemphasizing that candid discussion of the deficit issue was a characteristic of leadership. Unless Reagan could defend his perception of the deficit in terms of a similar consensus to which Mondale was appealing, or substantiate his view of the issue with expert testimony, Reagan appeared less than candid about this problem, and hence not fulfilling the expectations for leadership as defined by Mondale.

Mondale could have developed the attack even further when he criticized Reagan for not responding to signs indicating imminent terrorist attacks in Lebanon. But Mondale softened the criticism by accepting the first two attacks as part of the complex problem in Lebanon and not stating directly that Reagan ignored those facts pointing to a third attack. Though Mondale said there was a warning preceding the third terrorist attack, he did not develop this criticism in explicit terms of Reagan's failure to comprehend the problem and act accordingly. Mondale concluded his answer by stating that a president must master facts, and then asserted that he was doing this by participating in the debate process.

Sawyer's follow-up question created a special rhetorical problem for Mondale by calling on him to explain why the polls gave him lower ratings on leadership than Reagan. Although this was not related to the deficit issue, it was important to the issue of leadership. Mondale needed a rhetorical stance that would acknowledge the factual basis of Sawyer's statement but suggest potential grounds for shifting one's opinion, and presumably, vote. Mondale's solution was to cast the issue not in terms of the present position each candidate held but in terms of his ability to sustain his case in the debates: "Tonight, as we contrast for the first time our different approach to government, to values, to the leadership in this country, I think as this debate goes forward, the American people will have for the first time a chance to weigh the two of us against each other." By implicitly accepting the terms of Sawyer's follow-up question—that he lacked support in the polls—Mondale remained consistent with his concept of leadership by candidly confronting the facts. More importantly, Mondale's answer emphasized the importance of the debates. For Mondale, the key to leadership was one's ability to stand up under fire from the opposition. Here, Mondale defined leadership in terms of characteristics Reagan was unable to offer—command of the facts and a perception of the issues shared by others: "And I think, as a part of that process, what I am trying to say will come across, and that is that we must lead, we must command, we must direct, and a president must see it like it is." The key to Mondale's candidacy, then, was his ability to make his argument. Because he pressed the deficit issue and because Reagan could not defend his policy on the budget or his proposed reductions in Social Security during the second exchange on the leadership, Mondale's claim that Reagan was not in command of the facts appeared true. Reagan appeared unable to "see things as they were."

When Sawyer put the question to Reagan, he defined leadership in terms of three broad ideas. First, he indicated that leaders must have some principles. Underlying his philosophy was that "people are supposed to be dominant in our society—that they, not government, are to have control of their own affairs to the greatest extent possible, with an orderly society." Second, he described his approach to leadership as finding people who have the talent and abilities to get a job done, putting them in positions of responsibility, and letting them go to work with an understanding of his overall policy. Third, he asserted that he approached policy decisions in a nonpolitical way, with the desire to "hear only arguments as to whether it [the policy in question] is good or bad for the people—is it morally right?"

In closing, Reagan indicted Mondale's record in the Carter administration by quoting Mondale in praise of deficits. For the moment, Mondale let this criticism pass, although later he would defend his previous statements. In fairness to Mondale, Sawyer asked Reagan an equally tough follow-up question: "Recently you showed up at the opening ceremony of a Buffalo old age housing project, when in fact, your policy was to cut federal housing subsidies for the elderly. Yet you were there to have your picture taken with them." Sawyer's question presumed a factual basis. Reagan's answer denied it: "Our policy was not to cut subsidies." Reagan went on to defend his administration's record on housing but did not address Sawyer's specific example. The important thing to note here was Reagan's flat denial. Two different views of the "facts" were developing. Even though Reagan's answer presented an optimistic assessment of the housing issue, he did not defend the factual basis of his answer. In contrast, Mondale defended the factual basis of his position in the rebuttals. For example, his rebuttal highlighted the factual basis of his stance on Social Security: "The fact of it is: The president's budget sought to cut Social Security by 25 percent. It's not an opinion; it's a fact." Following up Sawyer's example, Mondale emphasized that Reagan sought to terminate federal housing subsidies, not maintain them as Reagan had asserted:

The second fact is that the housing unit for senior citizens that the president dedicated in Buffalo was only made possible through a federal assistance program for senior citizens that the president's budget sought to terminate. So, if he'd had his way, there wouldn't have been any housing project at all. This administration has taken a meat cleaver out, in terms of federal-assisted housing, and the record is there. We have to see the facts before we can draw conclusions.

On both points Mondale pointed to facts, thus fulfilling the burden of proof. To maintain his image as a candidate in control of "the" facts, Reagan needed to refute those "facts" as Mondale had characterized them, or appear out of touch with political reality.

In his final rebuttal on the leadership exchange, Reagan chose to respond only to the Social Security issue. But Reagan shifted his ground. Instead of answering Mondale by explaining why his proposed reduction was desirable, Reagan defended his administration in terms of its success in preventing Social Security from going bankrupt. Although the statement revealed that the Reagan administration had solved the Social Security problem with bipartisan legislation, it did not address the issue of who had control of the facts, and ignored the problem created by Sawyer and Mondale concerning his attempt to take credit for a program his budget sought to terminate.

After this exchange, it appeared as though Reagan was no longer in control of the "facts"; his answers had not appealed to a consensus of public opinion as had Mondale's, nor had they the support of experts sharing Reagan's perception of the problem. If mastering the facts was a key test of leadership, Reagan had failed where Mondale had succeeded and there was good reason to doubt that Reagan had mastered what he needed to know to be president for four more years.

Relief for the Poor

The first exchange on the deficit was an attempt to discover how each candidate proposed to deal with the problem. Although Mondale's performance on this issue suggested that his approach was more realistic and thus more defensible because of the quality of data supporting his claims, the exchange on leadership spotlighted Reagan's inability to refute Mondale's evidence concerning proposed reductions in programs. The exchange over relief for the poor deserves brief mention because it illustrated Mondale's strategy of focusing the debate on Reagan's weakest grounds, the budget.

Wieghart asked Reagan to respond to the claim that the rich were getting richer and the poor getting poorer. Reagan's answer was an excellent defense of his administration's record for his point of view. In contrast, Mondale's proposals for relieving the poor began with getting the debt down and concluded by arguing that the nation's foreign trade was harmed by the deficit. Mondale implicitly suggested that the president lived in his own world, away from the facts of the real world, when he stated:

There is no question that the poor are worse off. I think the president genuinely believes that they're better off. But the figures show that about 8 million more people are below the poverty line than four years ago. How can you cut school lunches, how can you cut student assistance, how can you cut housing, how can you cut disability benefits, how can you do all of these things . . . I don't know. Now, we need a tight budget, but there's no question that this administration has singled out things that affect the most vulnerable in American life, and they're hurting.

In this excerpt, Mondale underscored the fact that Reagan operated from a particular belief structure, one that was not informed by the facts. And Mondale used more than one example. Mondale had established a pattern of substantiating his claims with continued appeals to a "consensus" in the audience. In response, Reagan had either admitted Mondale was right or ignored the attack, and failed to respond with supporting evidence or an appeal to a similar consensus. Although Reagan could argue that the rate of increase in poverty had slowed, he could not refute the factual basis of the question. In comparison, Mondale's answer seemed more consistent with the facts presumed in the question and exploited the credibility gap opened up in the exchanges on the deficit and leadership. In 1980, Reagan had used a similar strategy of enumerating defense projects that Jimmy Carter had canceled. In 1984, Mondale turned the strategy against Reagan by calling on him to justify reductions in school lunches, student assistance, housing, and disability benefits for the most vulnerable in American society.

In his rebuttal, Reagan ignored Mondale's criticism concerning specific programs and, instead, disputed the connection between the deficit and interest rates. Again, the refutation was developed from Reagan's personal perspective:

The interest rates are based on inflation. And right now, I have to tell you I don't think there is any excuse for the interest rates being as high as they are because we have brought inflation down so low. I think it can only be that they're anticipating or hope—expecting, not hoping—that maybe we don't have a control of inflation and it's going to go back up again. Well, it isn't going to go back up. We're going to see that it doesn't.

There was no supporting testimony in this answer except for Reagan's own words: "I have to tell you; I don't think; I think it can be." To persuade the audience that his administration would prevent further problems and preserve present gains, Reagan relied on a strategy of personal reassurance: "Well, it isn't going to go back up. We're going to see that it doesn't.'' Thus, Reagan's defense rested on his perception of "the" facts, a world view that Mondale's use of the "facts" had been challenging.

In his rebuttal, Mondale tied the issue of relief for the poor more directly to the problem of the deficit. After explaining why Reagan's refutation concerning the connection between the deficit and interest rates was wrong, Mondale argued that Reagan was without support on the deficit issue:

But when these huge deficits went into place in 1981, what's called the real interest rates—the spread between inflation and what a loan costs you doubled— and that's still the case today. And the result is interest costs that have never been seen before in terms of real charges, and it's attributable to the deficit. Everybody—every economist, every businessman—believes that. Your own Council of Economic Advisers—Mr. Feldstein in his report told you that. Every chairman of the Finance and Ways and Means committees, Republican leaders in the Senate and the House, are telling you that. That deficit is ruining the long-term hopes for this economy.

Mondale identified several potential sources for the president's perception of the issue, but found no one supporting his view. Through the use of reluctant testimony and an appeal to consensus, Mondale placed Reagan outside the mainstream understanding of this issue. More important, Mondale's evidence suggested that any economic gains by the Reagan administration would be only temporary and ultimately offset by the harmful effects of the deficit. The long-term health of the economy was dependent on solving the deficit and Reagan had done poorly in defending the factual basis of his projections on this issue.

The Changing Electorate

In the fourth exchange, Wieghart asked Mondale to explain why the Republicans were enjoying so much political support. The question put Mondale in the same position Sawyer had earlier: Mondale needed to acknowledge the fact that the Democrats were behind but argue that the present positions were not as important as the political dialogue that tested them, revealing which was more preferable.

Mondale stated that the campaign was not over yet and predicted that the American people would prefer the Democratic solution to the Republican one on a series of problems, one of which was the deficit. Mondale's statement was basically a list of positions endorsed by the Democratic platform. What was important about Mondale's answer was that he concluded by saying that "I think as you make the case, the American people will increasingly come to our cause." Mondale was arguing that the debate, not the polls, revealed the quality of the candidates.

Wieghart's follow-up question challenged Mondale's initial position: "Mr. Mondale, isn't it possible that the American people have heard your message—and they are listening—but they are rejecting it?" Mondale chose to feature the deficit and Social Security cuts in his response to Wieghart's follow-up, two issues that had been cutting away at Reagan's credibility earlier in the debate:

Well, tonight we had the first debate over the deficit. The president says it will disappear automatically. I've said it's going to take some work. I think the American people will draw their own conclusions. Secondly, I've said that I will not support the cuts in Social Security and Medicare and the rest that the president proposed. The president answers that it didn't happen or, if it did, it was resolved later in a commission.

Mondale's statement clearly reemphasized Reagan's inability to deal with the facts. If the audience accepted Mondale's premise, that they should decide on the basis of the case that each candidate made for his positions, then Mondale would have appeared more preferable than Reagan on the grounds that he could make his case but Reagan could not.

The remainder of the exchange was tangential to this issue. After Mondale repeated his criticisms of Reagan, Wieghart asked a different question of Reagan: "What is your program for America for the next decade, with some specificity?" This question allowed Reagan to defend his record with some specific examples; however, none related to the deficit or Social Security cuts. Wieghart's follow-up pursued another tangent concerning the environment. Finally, the rebuttals wandered further away from the deficit issue when both candidates chose to argue about when Reagan really left the Democratic party.

View of Opponent

In this exchange, Mondale's strategy of focusing attention on Reagan's budget policies and attacking his command of the facts was most evident. Sawyer's question asked each candidate to identify the most outrageous thing his opponent had said and in following up asked what remaining questions each would like his opponent to answer. These questions gave the candidates the opportunity to choose important statements and issues to focus on in the last exchange.

Mondale chose not to identify an outrageous statement and instead gave the president some credit: "I think the president has done some things to raise the sense of spirit, and morale, good feeling, in this country, and he's entitled to credit for that." After giving the president credit for raising the national spirit, Mondale stated simply that we needed to do more than congratulate ourselves. His decision to give the president credit suggested that Mondale's criticisms of Reagan were not motivated by personal ambition, but by genuine interest in the welfare of the nation. This was important because Mondale needed to set aside popular sentiment for Reagan as a person and focus the audience's attention on Reagan as a leader. To do this, Mondale borrowed some of the popular appeal of Reagan by stating that he liked Reagan as a person, but disagreed with his policies: "I like President Reagan and—this is not personal—there are deep differences about our future, and that's the basis of my campaign." By identifying with Reagan as a person, and congratulating him on raising the morale of the nation, Mondale prepared the audience for a decision based on substantive, rather than personal, grounds.

Sawyer's follow-up question set up the argument that Mondale had been making throughout the debate: "What remaining question would you most like to see your opponent forced to answer?" Mondale returned to his contention that the deficit needed to be solved: "Without any doubt, I have stood up and told the American people that the $263 billion deficit must come down. And I've done what no other candidate for president's ever done, I told you before the election what I'd do." In his next move, Mondale asked Reagan to acknowledge that what he had argued was recognized by everyone else in the country, the fact that the deficit would not be solved by present policies:

Mr. Reagan, as you saw tonight—President Reagan takes the position it will disappear by magic. It was once called voodoo economics. I wish the president would say: Yes, the CBO is right. Yes, we have a $263 billion deficit. This is how I'm going to get it done. Don't talk about growth, because even though we need growth, that's not helping. It's going to go in the other direction, as they've estimated. And give us a plan. What will you cut? Whose taxes will you raise? Will you finally touch that defense budget? Are you going to go after Social Security and Medicare and student assistance and the handicapped again, as you did the last time?

Mondale was suggesting that Reagan was not in command of the facts because he ignored the deficit problem. By asking a series of rhetorical questions concerning what Reagan would do, Mondale implied that Reagan had no solution to this problem, and thus was not in control of the situation.

For Reagan, the most outrageous claim Mondale had made was that the Reagan administration proposed reductions in Social Security benefits. The first part of Reagan's answer denied the truth of the claim without offering any evidence. Reagan criticized Mondale on the grounds that his statements scared millions of senior citizens. Again, Reagan presented no evidence to refute Mondale's claim concerning Social Security. After interrupting his answer to make sure that he had more time, Reagan stated that he would lay the Social Security issue to rest. Again, Reagan denied that he would "do such a thing" without providing any evidence to support his position. Then Reagan argued that Social Security was not tied to the deficit in any way, answering one of Mondale's questions from his answer to Sawyer's follow-up question. Reagan concluded his answer by responding to the charge that he was relying on magic to solve the deficit. But here Reagan's defense relied on his approach to the problem: "Now, again, to get to whether I have—am depending on magic—I think I have talked in straight economic terms about a program of recovery that was—I was told wouldn't work. And then, after it worked, I was told that lowering taxes would increase inflation. And none of these things happened. It is working, and we're going to continue on that same line." Whether Reagan's program was "working" depended on the nature of the problem and how someone defined the term. Mondale's argument—that the deficit would not be solved under Reagan's policy—had been supported with evidence from experts, by reference to reluctant testimony from Republicans, and with an appeal to consensus opinion. However, when Reagan chose to answer Mondale's attacks, his refutation consisted simply of denials that relied on his credibility for their persuasive appeal.

By this point in the debate, the audience could choose between Reagan's world view or Mondale's. In Reagan's view, things were fine as long as you ignored the facts that Mondale was presenting. From Mondale's perspective, Reagan had ignored the most serious issue facing the nation for the last four years and in this debate was demonstrating that he did not comprehend the need to develop a viable policy to solve that problem in the next four.

Despite these problems, Reagan responded with a strong attack in his follow-up answer in which he criticized Mondale for being in favor of budget deficits in 1976 and 1979:

The deficits are so much of a problem for him now, but that in 1976, when the deficit was $52 billion and everyone was panicking about that, he said, no, that he thought it ought to be bigger, because a bigger deficit would stimulate the economy and would help do away with unemployment. In 1979 he made similar statements, the same effect, that the deficits—there was nothing wrong with having deficits.

This was a strong challenge to Mondale because it relied on the public record to show how Mondale was in favor of deficits, something Reagan had not been able to do in previous exchanges on this issue. Reagan reminded the audience that he found a trillion-dollar debt upon arrival in office, implying that he was not responsible for the problem and then stated that he hoped to make some payments on the debt in the next four years.

To substantiate his case and sustain his image, Mondale needed to respond to Reagan's indictment in the last rebuttal. First, Mondale pointed out that despite Reagan's concern about the deficit, Reagan's policy had still not been revealed: "Well, we've just finished almost the whole debate. And the American people don't have the slightest clue about what president Reagan will do about these deficits." Second, Mondale reemphasized that the deficit was the most important issue of the campaign: "And yet, that's the most important single issue of our time." Third, Mondale defended his statements on record by arguing that deficits were necessary in 1976, only minimal in 1979, and creating a disaster for the nation in 1984: "I did support the '76 measure that he told about, because we were in a deep recession and we need some stimulation. But I will say, as a Democrat, I was a real piker, Mr. President. In 1979 we ran a $29 billion deficit, all year. This administration seems to run that every morning." Again, Mondale accepted the facts on record but used them to contrast his image as a candidate, controlling a $29 billion deficit in 1979, with Reagan's inability to control a $263 billion deficit in 1984.

Summary of Findings in the First Debate

In three exchanges, Mondale argued that the deficit was the most important issue. Also, Mondale defined leadership in terms of the ability to see the facts clearly. Reagan did not dispute these claims. On the deficit and Social Security issues, Mondale demonstrated that Reagan's understanding of the facts was suspect. Reagan's response to Mondale's attack on his proposed cuts in Social Security was inconsistent and unsupported. After Mondale had argued that the cuts held the status of a fact, not an opinion, Reagan was unable to explain why the proposed cuts were desirable. Mondale appealed to expert opinion, reluctant testimony, consensus opinion, and the public record to establish the factual basis of his claims. Reagan argued from his own view of the issues. On the deficit, Social Security, and housing exchanges, Mondale's statements appeared to be grounded in a more reliable estimate of the facts, whereas Reagan's statements appeared to be based on his particular perception of the issues, a perception not based on the facts as Mondale had established them. Because Reagan accepted Mondale's measure of leadership and then failed to meet it, Reagan did not enact leadership as Mondale had defined it for this debate. Mondale's use of evidence suggested that he saw the facts more clearly than Reagan did and thus presented himself in the image of a leader capable of recognizing national problems and moving to correct them.

Also, Mondale's answers were consistent with his concept of leadership, that a president must see the facts clearly. When asked to explain why he was behind in the polls, Mondale accepted the facts, then argued that the audience should decide on the basis of the case that he and Reagan made for their respective positions.

Finally, the analysis of the first debate also revealed how a reliable use of facts constituted an important dimension of presidential character. In the first debate, Mondale's capacity to base his criticisms of the Reagan administration on a sound factual basis and Reagan's corresponding inability to defend his programs on that basis revealed that Reagan was not a reliable source for information. In the 1984 debates, then, the salient dimension of presidential character was reliability as it related to competence, not sincerity and fairness, as in 1976 or competent action as in 1980.

THE SECOND DEBATE

The second debate was largely irrelevant to the outcome of the campaign. Although Mondale had narrowed Reagan's lead to within six points immediately after the first debate, these gains were not sustained,[12] and Reagan added nine points for a fifteen-point lead in the two weeks between the first and second debates.[13] It is doubtful that even a Mondale victory like that of the first debate would have caused a dramatic conversion of many Reagan supporters. In 1984, the second debate was not a crucial campaign event. Reagan was too far ahead in the polls and there was not an important group of undecided voters to whom both candidates needed to appeal.

The second debate is interesting, however, as a study of Reagan's ability to present himself to the audience in familiar terms. Analysis of the second debate reveals that Reagan regained his ability to answer criticism. In each of the exchanges, Reagan defended his administration against Mondale's attacks. Mondale, instead of refuting Reagan's arguments, repeated his charges. In different ways and in different degrees, this pattern developed throughout the exchanges on Central America, arms control, resorting to force, immigration reform, Armageddon, and friendly dictators. The first part of the analysis establishes the presence of this general pattern. The second part of the analysis focuses on the "age issue." Mondale's performance in the first debate was so effective that the *Wall Street Journal* published an article after the debate questioning Reagan's health and vigor.[14] Despite the implication that Reagan appeared senile in the first debate, the article recast the issue from one of leadership ability—measured in terms of a reliable command of facts on a given issue—to a question of whether Reagan was too old to continue as president. Framing the question in this way affected the expectations for both candidates. Reagan needed to appear only coherent to dismiss doubts about his age while Mondale needed another dramatic victory if he hoped to narrow an ever-widening gap in the polls.[15]

Although the exchange over the age issue was relatively brief and occurred in the middle of the debate, it was a very concise way of summarizing Reagan's ability as a rhetor. Examining the age issue revealed the ways in which Reagan's one-liners communicated a sense of control over a threatening rhetorical situation.[16] Thus, the exchange over the age issue functioned in a way similar to the exchange over arms control in the 1980 debate between Reagan and Carter. In 1980, the arms control exchange summarized the essence of each candidate's image by confirming doubts about Carter's ability and revealing Reagan's competence and reinforced a larger pattern in the debate by giving the audience a vivid way of understanding the implicit image of each candidate developing in other exchanges. In 1984, Reagan's one-liners on the age issue reaffirmed his image as a candidate in control of the situation and reinforced this image as it developed in other exchanges throughout the debate.

Reagan Defends His Administration against Mondale's Attacks

In the exchange over Central America, Mondale argued that Reagan was not aware of the instructions booklet for terrorists and he listed several examples of Reagan's factual errors. Reagan explained how the "terrorist manual" came into existence and defended CIA actions in editing the manual so that it was consistent with Reagan's 1981 policies. Mondale argued in his rebuttal that Reagan had violated his oath of office by allowing this manual to be published, but Mondale failed to attack Reagan's explanation of how the manual came into being. Thus, Reagan ignored Mondale's rebuttal and answered instead the charge that he thought nuclear weapons could be fired and then recalled. Mondale's claim that Reagan violated his oath of office was not developed substantively, but Reagan's defense was.

On arms control, Mondale pressed the indictment of Reagan's knowledge by repeating the alleged error: "Three years into this administration he said he just discovered that most Soviet missiles are on land, and that's why his proposal didn't work." But because Mondale could not locate the president's statements in the public record, he invited the public to tune in the following day when he would issue the statement quoting Reagan. Mondale asserted again that Reagan "said what he said he said" but was unable to indicate where in the public record. What was lacking in this attack was Mondale's ability to use the public record against his opponent as he had in the first debate.

Reagan pitted his credibility against Mondale's by characterizing Mondale's attack on his knowledge of nuclear weaponry as "falsehoods." Then Reagan attacked Mondale's campaign ad in which he stood on the deck of the *Nimitz*:

If he had had his way when the *Nimitz* was being planned, he would have been deep in the water out there because there wouldn't have been any *Nimitz* to stand on—he was against it. He was against the F–14 fighter, he was against the M–1 tank, he was against the B–1 bomber, he wanted to cut the salary of all of the military, he wanted to bring home half of the American forces in Europe. And he has a record of weakness with regard to our national defense that is second to none.

The criticism was forceful because it enumerated several examples to prove the case and created in ironic image similar to that of Reagan showing up for pictures at a housing project he had sought to terminate.

Mondale began his rebuttal by asking Reagan to accept his commitment to a strong national defense. But the act of asking for support from one's opponent was reminiscent of Nixon's appeal to Kennedy and reflected Mondale's defensive posture. Mondale was asking Reagan to accept the position Reagan was attacking. When Mondale answered Reagan, he refuted only one of the four examples, that dealing with the F–14. Finally, Mondale argued that Reagan's definition of national defense was to throw money at the Defense Department and that his own definition was to spend money wisely. This distinction would have been more persuasive had Mondale answered Reagan's other examples; Mondale would have appeared to have been defending the wisdom of his opposition to undesirable programs. Instead, given Reagan's rebuttal, Mondale's definition of national defense could have been interpreted as not spending enough. Mondale needed to distinguish between desirable and undesirable defense policies more effectively.

On the topic of resorting to force, Morton Kondracke asked the candidates different questions, hence the first set of answers featured little clash and the emphasis shifted in rebuttals. In the follow-up question to Reagan, Kondracke asked why Reagan had ignored warnings of terrorist attack in Lebanon and why he had been unable to retaliate. Reagan distinguished between the Iran and Beirut situations to defend his actions and argued that retaliation was appropriate only if we could put our hands on the responsible parties.

Mondale's rebuttal was strong because he appealed to the public's knowledge of the issue, recounted the warnings from the Joint Chiefs of Staff, reviewed the facts that had been established by the secretary of state, and noted the repetition of the bombings despite warnings. In these ways, it looked as though Reagan had ignored warnings from various sources.

Reagan refuted Mondale's attack by arguing that the commander in the field, not he, had ordered the marines into the barracks. Then Reagan turned the tables on Mondale by asking him what he would do in the same situation. Reagan noted that the terrorists were suicidal, making retaliation on the perpetrators difficult. Reagan questioned Mondale's motives when he stated his opposition to "simply kill[ing] some people to say, oh look, we got even." Reagan's answer revealed the complexity of the problem and indicated that he was trying to locate those who were guilty and that he wanted to avoid retaliating against innocent people. It was a fitting response to Mondale's criticism and provided a plausible justification for his policy on terrorism.

On the issue of immigration reform, both candidates indicated agreement with the need for legislation but both had reservations about the proposed Simpson-Mazzoli bill. The nuclear Armageddon and nuclear freeze issues focused on Reagan's strategic defense initiative. Potentially, these could have been important exchanges, but Mondale was unable to criticize the hypothetical nature of the program. Reagan argued that if it were possible to build an effective space-based weapons defense system, then we should do it. Thus, Reagan seemed optimistic while Mondale appeared to oppose a potential solution to nuclear war.

Finally, in the discussion of friendly dictators, the debate moved quickly from foreign policy back to the strategic defense initiative (SDI). The same positions were taken by each candidate: Reagan suggested that SDI would be a great step forward, Mondale argued it would start an arms race. Neither position was developed in sufficient detail to warrant a decision on substantive grounds. The audience was left to choose between Mondale's view and Reagan's.

Reagan's Age

Although the discussion of terrorism featured Mondale's strongest attack on Reagan, the age issue was perhaps the key moment in the second debate. In response to Henry Trewhitt's question, Reagan stated that "I will not make age an issue of this campaign. I am not going to exploit for political purposes, my opponent's youth and inexperience." With this quip, Reagan showed some cleverness and lightly dismissed questions about his competence.

The age issue was not pursued by either candidate in this exchange. If it had been a rhetorical problem for Reagan, he had laid it to rest and the remainder of the exchange focused on Reagan's judgment in Lebanon, on arms control, and in providing effective leadership for the country. But even on these issues Mondale could not sustain his case. At several points in the debate, Mondale had charged that Reagan was not fulfilling the duties of office since he had not mastered the facts. Yet, Mondale had not been providing the kind of support for his claims that he had during the first debate. Thus, when Mondale repeated these criticisms without additional support, Reagan was able to cast Mondale's claims as seemingly extreme in nature through the use of another one-liner when he opened his rebuttal: "Yes, I know it'll come as a surprise to Mr. Mondale, but I am in charge." Mondale's strategy had been effective in the first debate because Reagan could not demonstrate a command of the facts. But in this debate, Reagan had been offering explanations to justify his actions. Mondale never directed his attacks to these justifications, and as a result seemed to be repeating unsubstantiated claims. Now Mondale seemed out of touch with the situation in which Reagan was in control, and the one-liner was not only an economical way to express the contrast between the candidates but also demonstrated Reagan's control of the rhetorical situation.

SUMMARY

In the first debate, Mondale developed a concept of leadership based on a candidate's command of the facts. Mondale fulfilled that image by using evidence in such a way as to prove that Reagan did not have control of the facts and that Reagan was unable to measure up to Mondale's definition of leadership.

Mondale extended his concept of leadership in the second debate by arguing that Reagan was not in control of foreign policy. However, in the second debate, Reagan defended his actions with explanations. In response to Reagan, Mondale repeated his claims without answering these explanations or analyzing the justifications for his actions.[17] From the standpoint of the media and much campaign commentary, the key exchange was on the age issue. Reagan showed that he was in control of the situation when he responded with a one-liner that implied that Mondale was inexperienced. In the rebuttals on this issue, Reagan used another one-liner to emphasize that he was in charge despite Mondale's claims and implied that Mondale was overstating his case.

In the end, the one-liners were effective because they were economical ways for Reagan to show that he was in control of the situation, that he understood the nature of the circumstances and could, through the use of humor, set aside any threat to his image. In the face of a twenty-point deficit, Mondale's performance was insufficient to justify a shift in voter intentions. In the second debate, Reagan showed himself to be in command of the situation, and Mondale failed to justify new leadership.

NOTES

1. Robert Friedenberg, "We Are Present Here Today for the Purpose of Having a Joint Discussion: The Conditions Requisite for Political Debates," *Journal of the American Forensic Association* 16 (Summer 1979): 1–9; " 'Selfish Interests,' or the Prerequisites for Political Debate: An Analysis of the 1980 Presidential Debate and Its Implications for Future Campaigns," *Journal of the American Forensic Association* 18 (Fall 1981): 91–98.

2. Jack W. Germond and Jules Witcover, *Wake Us When It's Over: Presidential Politics of 1984* (New York: Macmillan, 1985), 1. The authors noted that Reagan had led the campaign for months until his poor performance in the first debate.

3. Stu Spencer, a close Reagan aide, believed that Reagan could not refuse a debate without being hurt in the polls. See Peter Goldman and Tony Fuller, *The Quest for the Presidency 1984* (New York: Bantam, 1985), 307.

4. William A. Henry, *Visions of America: How We Saw the 1984 Election* (Boston, MA: Atlantic Monthly Press, 1984), 67–68, 119–20, 242, 254; Germond and Witcover, *Wake Us When It's Over*, 58–59.

5. Germond and Witcover, *Wake Us When It's Over*, 494. See also Keith Blume, *The Presidential Election Show: Campaign '84 and Beyond the Nightly News* (South Hadley, MA: Bergin and Garvey, 1985), 121.

6. Germond and Witcover, *Wake Us When It's Over*, 3.

7. In *The Presidential Election Show*, p. 128, Blume quotes Leslie Stahl's report on the Republican debate preparation strategy, indicating that Reagan's advisers wanted the debates to show that Reagan was in command of the facts.

8. Ibid., 15. Blume argues that the only time the media gave Mondale a chance to win was after his first debate with Reagan.

9. See Germond and Witcover, *Wake Us When It's Over*, chap. 21, "A Real Bump in the Road," 492–537. In *The Presidential Election Show*, p. 147, Blume says that Mondale's performance in the first debate created "volatility" in the electorate.

10. This was described by Caddell as a "pivot" and was designed for Mondale to dominate Reagan physically. See Goldman and Fuller, *The Quest for the Presidency*, 432–434.

11. Germond and Witcover indicated that this was Caddell's strategy for Mondale, to surprise Reagan with a more respectful and deferential image. See Chapter 21 in *Wake Us When It's Over*, 492–537. For excerpts of the Caddell memorandum outlining the strategy for the first debate, see Goldman and Fuller, *The Quest for the Presidency*, 432–434.

12. Austin Ranney, *The American Elections of 1984* (Durham, NC: Duke University Press, 1985), 153.

13. Germond and Witcover noted that Gallop had Reagan leading by 20 points just prior to the second debate, *Wake Us When It's Over*, 3. See also Ranney, *The American Elections of 1984*, 158.

14. Reagan staffers were worried that any debates would raise the age issue.

See Goldman and Fuller, *The Quest for the Presidency*, 306–307. However, this actually worked to Reagan's advantage. According to Henry, in *Visions of America*, p. 250, a *Wall Street Journal* article published after the debate legitimized discussion of the age issue. This recast the issue from one of leadership ability to health and vigor. Henry also noted that the first debate changed the expectations for the second debate. Theoretically, Reagan needed to appear only coherent while Mondale needed to score another dramatic victory. See also Blume, *The Presidential Election Show*, 147.

15. In *The Presidential Election Show*, p. 147, Blume argued that despite the low showing in the polls, the potential for an upset remained, depending on how the second debate turned out.

16. Sidney Blumenthal, *Pledging Allegiance: The Last Campaign of the Cold War* (New York: Harper Collins, 1990), 257. Blumenthal argues that the age issue was the one moment of insecurity during the 1984 campaign and it passed when Reagan delivered his one-liner.

17. It is interesting to note that Mondale was determined by the media to have won the second debate on points and issues. See Blume, *The Presidential Election Show*, 162. Goldman and Fuller reported that Mondale thought he was winning on issues, *The Quest for the Presidency*, 340. The analysis of the text suggests a different conclusion.

Chapter Seven

The 1988 Presidential Debates: George Bush Versus Michael Dukakis

At the time of the first debate, George Bush had a substantial lead over Michael Dukakis but after the first debate, Dukakis closed to within a few percentage points of Bush.[1] One reason for Dukakis' gain can be seen in the way that the first debate shaped doubts about Bush's ability to present his ideas in a manner consistently clear enough to suggest that he was satisfactorily qualified to assume office.[2] The analysis of the debates also explains why Dukakis, having narrowed Bush's lead to a small margin, was unable to overcome Bush's lead in the polls during the final weeks of the campaign. In the second debate, Bush was able to project a more coherent vision of leadership and appear more personable than Dukakis.[3] More important, Bush was able to eliminate doubts about his ability to respond spontaneously, genuinely, and coherently to important questions about his candidacy whereas Dukakis was unable to communicate an equally genuine, personal appeal for his leadership ability.

THE FIRST DEBATE

The impact of the first debate can be seen in the way that it crystallized doubts about each candidate's abilities. Although the first debate raised doubts about Bush's ability to provide coherent leadership for the country, it simultaneously provided the audience with little evidence to believe that Dukakis knew where he wanted to take the country, knew what difficult choices he would make, or knew in what way he might inspire undecided voters to cast their ballots for him.[4] The analysis first identifies the ways in which Bush's performance shaped doubts about his thinking processes and then illustrates the ways in which Dukakis' answers failed to provide important details about the kind of leadership he offered the nation.

Coherence as a Rhetorical Problem for Bush

There are two ways in which Bush's rhetorical limitations were manifested in his language choices in the first debate. First, in six of the first seven exchanges, his answers featured interruptions in his train of thought. Although some of these interruptions seemed minor, taken together, they constituted a stylistic pattern that reflected a certain weakness of presidential character under fire—the fact that Bush's thinking process was subject to self-disruption. For Bush to convince his audience that he was better qualified for office, his answers needed to feature a more smoothly flowing style in response to the strain of the debate. Second, on the issue of penalties for women who obtain abortions illegally, Bush appeared unprepared to specify what those penalties should be. Together, these two aspects of Bush's actions in the debate gave form to the doubt that Bush's thinking processes were as yet unready for presidential office.[5] The analysis begins with the identification of a pattern of nonfluencies in Bush's train of thought and then focuses on the issue of penalties for women seeking abortions.

In the second question of the debate, after Dukakis answered John Mashek's question about what three programs he would cut to reduce the deficit, Bush's rebuttal went quite well except for his concluding sentences: "And I have made a specific proposal for what I call a flexible freeze. And it permits—economists on the East Coast and West think it's good—it permits the president to sort the priorities, and we continue to grow because I will not raise taxes." Here, Bush interrupted his analysis of what his program would permit him to do as president to interject expert support of his program. Then he returned to explaining what the program would permit him to do as president but interjected at the end of the answer an irrelevancy concerning whether he would raise taxes.

In the next question from Mashek, Bush's answer featured another shift in thought. In answering Mashek's question, "Is the deficit no longer really a concern of yours, the Republican Party, or the taxpayers?" Bush's lapse came in the middle of his answer: "And if we—and the actually—this year Congress is doing a little better in controlling the growth of spending." Two false starts were featured here before he completed his original line of thought.

In the next question on health insurance from Anne Groer, Bush's lapse occurred in the middle of his answer:

I do not want to see us mandate across-the-board that every company has to do this, because I really think that marginal operators are going to say, "We can't make it." And I think then you're going to see that people are put out of work. All of these programs—and this costs on his is—was—I saw an estimate—I'd love to know what he thinks—35–40 billion dollars—and it seems to me that somebody pays that.

In the last sentence of this excerpt, Bush shifted from health insurance programs in general, to Dukakis' cost estimates, to a shift in tense from the present to the past, to the fact that he saw an estimate of the costs of Dukakis' program, to a desire to know what Dukakis thinks about something—presumably the cost of his health insurance proposal—to an inserted cost estimate that was not connected specifically to Dukakis' program, and then finally, to an undeveloped criticism that somebody would have to pay for the program.

In the very next exchange over access to AIDS drugs, Bush's rebuttal to Dukakis' answer featured another lapse in concentration: "And we are working with the FDA and they have sped up bringing drugs to market that can help. And you've got to be careful here, because there is a safety factor, but I think these things—and then also I am one who believed we've got to go an extra mile in clean—being sure that that blood supply is pure." Here, Bush shifted directions from a general discussion of safety factors to qualifying his answer with the interruption of another set of implied topics—"but these things"—then moved in a different direction to the topic of clean blood supply completing his statement with the broken syntax: "Go an extra mile in clean—being sure that that blood supply is pure."

In the very next question concerning Dukakis' style of leadership, Bush began his rebuttal with another set of shifting trains of thought: "Well, I don't question his passion. I question—and I don't question his concern about the war in Vietnam." And in the middle of the rebuttal, Bush changed the direction of thought: "He—We have a big difference on issues." This rebuttal set up a question from Peter Jennings concerning Bush's use of the phrase "card-carrying liberal." When asked what is wrong with being liberal, Bush answered awkwardly: "Nothing's wrong with it. But just take a look at the positions of the—just take a look at the positions of the ACLU. But, Peter, please understand—the liberals do not like me talking about liberal." In the last part of his answer, Bush replied that nothing was wrong with the criticism of Dukakis' membership in the ACLU, shifted to an implied criticism of the ACLU's political point of view, and then shifted to another train of thought that was irrelevant to the first two parts of the answer.

The last example comes from Mashek's question concerning which weapons systems Bush would be willing to eliminate given tight budgetary constraints. Bush's lapse came in the middle of the answer:

We are going to have to make some changes and tough choices before we go to deployment on the Midgetman missile, or on the Minuteman, or whatever it is. We're going to have to—the MX—we're going to have to do that. It's Christmas. It's Christmas. Wouldn't it be nice to be perfect? Wouldn't it be nice to be the iceman so you never make a mistake? These are the—these are the—these are the—my answer is do not make these unilateral cuts.

This was the most obvious of Bush's gaffes. When it became clear that his memory had failed him on whether he was discussing the Midgetman, Minuteman, or MX, the audience laughed. Even though this excerpt revealed a significant lapse, it also showed that Bush was able to laugh at himself and the lines about it being "Christmas" and "wouldn't it be nice to be the iceman" suggested a sense of endearing playfulness, an ability to recognize and laugh at his own mistakes, which was the kind of personal quality that Dukakis was unable to convey in the first debate.[6] The stress of the campaign showed in the last line when Bush repeated three attempts to finish his answer before he finally realized he was repeating himself and then closed abruptly with "my answer is do not make these unilateral cuts."

All of these examples suggest that Bush's ability to provide coherent leadership was limited at this point in the campaign. Because his thought processes were reflected in his interruptions, false starts, shifts in trains of thought, and awkward syntactical structures, an appropriate inference for the audience would be that the quality of his leadership suffered from the same drawbacks. Thus, Bush's pattern of interruptions created doubts about his ability to provide coherent and decisive leadership.

A critical exchange that reinforced doubts about Bush's ability to provide coherent and decisive leadership was in Groer's follow-up question on abortion after she queried Dukakis about the inconsistency between opposing the death penalty but favoring abortion on demand. When Groer asked Bush if women who obtain abortions illegally should go to jail, he answered: "I haven't sorted out the penalties." Dukakis' rebuttal seized on Bush's failure to state his position.

Well, I think what the vice president is saying is that he's prepared to brand a woman a criminal for making this decision. It's as simple as that. I don't think it's enough to come before the American people who are watching us tonight and say, "Well, I haven't sorted it out." This is a very, very difficult and fundamental decision that all of us have to make. And what he is saying, if I understand him correctly, is that he's prepared to brand a woman a criminal for making this choice. . . . Let me simply say that I think it has to be the woman in the exercise of her own conscience and religious beliefs that makes the decision, and I think that's the right approach, the right decision, and I would hope by this time that Mr. Bush had sorted out this issue and come to terms with it as I have. I respect his right to disagree with me. But I think it's important that we have a position, that we take it, and we state it to the American people.

Bush's failure to specify the penalty and Dukakis' criticism of this failure spotlighted the only real question about Bush's political image, that in a difficult situation, despite all of his credentials, George Bush might freeze up and fail to make a satisfactory decision. The lapses in concentration in the first part of the debate and in this particular failure to provide a defensible substantive answer on a major campaign issue gave shape to the nagging doubt that George Bush was unready for the Presidency.

Dukakis' Failure to Reveal his Decisions, Directions, and Inspiration

Dukakis faced a paradox in both debates. When his answers featured a well-formed argument with concise syntax, good evidence, and appealing forms of reasoning, his language choices reinforced an image of a technocratic passionless leader. When at his best, then, while answering Bush's attacks on his positions or while attacking Bush, the rational tone and argumentative substance of his answer contributed to his rhetorical problem.

The issue was brought into sharp focus by Jennings when he asked Dukakis: "Given the fact that a president must sometimes lead by sheer inspiration and passion. We need to know if this is a fair portrait of your governing or is it a stereotype? And if it isn't fair, to give us an example of where you have had that passion and leadership that sometimes a president needs." Dukakis' answer, however, fell far short of inspiration. He began by saying that he cared

deeply about people, all people, working people, working families, people all over this country who in some cases are living from paycheck to paycheck, in other cases are having a hard time opening the door of college opportunity to their children, in other cases don't have basic health insurance which for most of us we accept as a matter of course and assume we're going to have in order to pay the bills we incur when we get sick. I'm someone who believes in genuine opportunity for every single citizen in this country and that's the kind of passion I brought to my state.

Even though this answer asserted a deep concern for the people of the country, it did not demonstrate that concern. There is an important difference between claiming to be concerned and demonstrating concern through language. Even in listing those groups that he cared about, Dukakis' concern remained unspecific and distant. There were no anecdotes to convey a vivid sense of passion or examples that could bring to life an intense desire for change due to some enormous injustice, oversight, or neglect on the part of the present administration. Further, the syntax of the answer communicated a sense of distance. When Dukakis said that "I am somebody who believes deeply in genuine opportunity for every single citizen in this country," he spoke about his own feelings as though they were objects for analysis. If he possessed an inspiring passion for leadership, his use of language distanced him from that passion and suggested that it is yet another resource one uses in the course of governing rather than an intuitive, spontaneous response to an immediate problem. Instead of communicating a uniquely personal vision of himself for the audience, Dukakis' answer reinforced the image of a passionless technocrat.

Nor did Dukakis' conclusion on this answer provide a glimpse of a more personable candidate. After indicating that he had learned from his experience as a defeated candidate for governor, and then defending his record in Massachusetts, he summarized by saying:

These are things that I believe in very very deeply. I may be a little calmer than some about it. I may be a greater consensus builder these days than I used to be and I think that's a good thing. But I'm running for presidency of the United States. I've been in public service for twenty-five years because I believe deeply in American goals and values and the people of this country and that's the kind of president I want to be.

Although this excerpt asserted his deep belief in American goals and values, Dukakis failed to indicate what those benefits, goals, and values were. Thus, the kind of president that Dukakis wanted to be was still unclear from his answers in the debate. In this respect, Dukakis' vision of leadership lacked a coherent content and if he hoped to offer a vision of leadership that could compete with Bush's, he needed to give the audience a more specific sense of where he intended to lead the country.

Dukakis was not at a loss for opportunities to reveal a more detailed vision of leadership. On at least five occasions during the first third of the debate, he was asked to offer examples of action he proposed to take as president. Yet he failed to give the audience any sense of what to expect. For example, in the second exchange, Mashek asked Dukakis to identify three specific programs that he would be willing to cut to bring down the deficit. Dukakis said that he had been very specific about those programs but did not identify them, argued that there were certain weapons systems we did not need but failed to specify which ones, stated that we needed to invest in economic growth but did not reveal how, and claimed that we needed to decrease interest rates and come up with a solid plan to decrease the deficit but failed to reveal his plan for doing so.

In his rebuttal to Bush's answer to Mashek's question concerning the homeless, Dukakis argued his case in terms of commitment to lead, not in terms of a specific policy: "And while I'm all for the McKinney bill, that, by itself simply won't do. We've got to have a president that can lead on this issue, that can work with the Congress and I'm prepared to do so." Again, Dukakis provided no hint of what policy he would pursue in working with Congress, only that he was willing to lead.

When Mashek asked Dukakis what realistic hope he could hold out for Americans seeking to own their own homes in a time of tight economic pressures, Dukakis argued that bankers, builders, developers, and housing advocates were seeking leadership from Washington but never defined the nature of the leadership needed, thus leaving it up to the audience to figure out how he could best provide for the homeless. When Dukakis closed his answer on the housing question, the audience was still left with an incomplete picture of the policy Dukakis favored:

Washington, by itself, can't do it all. We shouldn't expect that. But governors are ready; mayors are ready. Builders and community leaders are ready. It will require some funds, John. And we ought to be prepared to provide those funds. But that, too,—will require some choices. Mr. Bush wants to spend billions and trillions on "Star Wars." Well, that's a choice we have to make, isn't it? Do we spend money on that weapons system in the billions and trillions, or is providing some decent and affordable housing for families of this country something that is at least as important—and probably more so—because it's so essential to our economic strength and to our future. Now, that's the kind of presidency I believe in. And simply to say, well, the McKinney bill will do it, just doesn't do. We need a president who will lead on this issue, who has had experience on this issue. It's the kind of priority that will be at the top of our list beginning in January of 1989.

Dukakis' answer stopped short of specifying which policy he would pursue. The closest that he came to identifying his policy was when he phrased the issue in terms of a trade-off between financing "Star Wars" and spending money on housing. But here it was presented as a choice "we" have to make, not one that he had made. This position was vulnerable to great misunderstanding: Those who favored "Star Wars" could read into Dukakis' answer the implication that he would cut it to finance housing programs for the poor, those who favored government housing programs could not conclude that Dukakis had decided to cut "Star Wars" because he treated the problem as a choice yet to be made. In short, Dukakis seemed reluctant to outline in greater detail his solution for the housing problem. Since it was unclear at this point in the campaign what policy he would pursue—other than the McKinney bill— we have no clear referent for what Dukakis characterized as the "kind of presidency" he believed in.

Even though the issue of the homeless was not central to the campaign, Dukakis' answer was characteristic of his appeal in the first debate. Instead of describing his policies and developing a rationale for his programs, Dukakis' goal was to diminish the appeal of Bush's proposals. If he could create doubts about Bush's policies, he would not necessarily be required to outline his policies in the course of the debates. This approach would have minimized the potential for criticism on substantive issues while allowing Dukakis to develop a rationale for his leadership in terms of his willingness to lead.

The strategy was most evident in the first exchange on foreign and national security policy. When Mashek asked Dukakis if he would respond to Bush's assertions that he lacked experience, was weak, and was naive in the area of foreign policy, Dukakis defended himself by attacking Bush and asserting his willingness to lead:

It's not the amount of time you spend in Washington. It's not the length of your resume. It's your strength, it's your values, it's the quality of the people you pick. It's your understanding of the forces of change that are sweeping the world, and whether or not you're in a position to provide leadership to make those forces of change work for us and not against us. . . . So I don't believe that the fact that you've got that long resume or had that experience is the real question. The question is values; the question is strength, the question is your willingness to provide the kind of leadership that must be provided. I'm ready to provide that leadership. I want to be commander in chief of this country. I think it takes fresh leadership now, and an understanding of those forces of change to provide the kind of strength that we need.

The problem with this approach, however, was that Dukakis' willingness to lead constituted insufficient grounds for favoring him over Bush. Before an audience would grant its support to an enthusiastic candidate, it would want some assurance of the candidate's ability. Essentially, willingness to serve cannot be equated with capability. Thus, Dukakis' strategy depended on an artistic use of language that conveyed a more complete vision of his leadership for the country. Because that was not forthcoming in the first debate, Dukakis gave the audience grounds for doubting his ability to make satisfactory choices. In short, we did not know what kind of leadership he was willing to provide and we had no way of evaluating his substantive choices in the debate because he avoided those choices when the panelists called upon him to make them.

THE SECOND DEBATE

The second debate started off on a weak note for Dukakis. Bernard Shaw began by asking Dukakis if he would still oppose the death penalty if his wife Kitty were raped and murdered. Dukakis showed little emotion in justifying his opposition to the death penalty, arguing that research showed it served no deterrent value. Germond and Witcover have argued that this answer in particular defined the emotional vacuum in Dukakis' appeal as a leader.[7] Instead of responding with some personal reaction to the hypothetical brutality, Dukakis spoke rationally but coldly as though the scenario left him unaffected. Although the lack of a personal reaction to the illustration reinforced Dukakis' image of an unemotional technocratic leader, there were other opportunities for Dukakis to reveal a more personalized side to himself in the second debate. However, what developed in this first question was a characteristic pattern for Dukakis in the second debate: an inability to respond to the panelists' questions with anything resembling a personalized appeal to the audience.

Shaw's question called for Dukakis to distinguish between his personal and public response to the situation in much the same way that Kennedy distinguished between his role as a member of the Catholic church and his prospective role as a president sworn to uphold the Constitution in the 1960 campaign; or, as Geraldine Ferraro did when she distinguished between her role as member of the Catholic church and as a public official elected to represent her constituency, or that despite the fact that she was a female candidate seeking office, her femininity would not preclude her from acting responsibly if she were challenged by the Soviet Union. In all of these examples, there was a potential conflict between personal values and public responsibility. Although Kennedy and Ferraro successfully noted the importance of fulfilling their covenant with the public to serve the community's values first, their answers also revealed something of the personal character behind the candidate. Because Dukakis failed to acknowledge the potential conflict between personal values and public responsibility and failed to provide a glimpse of how he would personally respond to such conflicts, the audience had no way to gauge the inner character of Dukakis as a candidate.

In a sense, Margaret Warner did Dukakis a favor by defining Dukakis' problem as likability when she noted that he won the first debate on intellect but lost it on heart. This provided an opportunity for Dukakis to solve his rhetorical problem when she invited him to respond in a personalized way to the charge that he was "unlikable" in the first debate. Defining Dukakis' problem, Warner asked: "The American public admired your performance, but didn't seem to like you much. Now, Ronald Reagan has found his personal warmth to be a tremendous political asset. Do you think that a president has to be likable to be an effective leader?" Dukakis had two choices: He could have refuted the assumption that likability was an essential element of leadership and shift the focus of the comparison to competence concerning the issues, or he could have chosen to respond in a personalized way in an attempt to measure up to the likability criterion that Warner was suggesting was so necessary to effective presidential leadership. However, Dukakis chose to accept this measure of leadership and then failed to answer in a personalized way when he stated:

I won the Democratic nomination in 51 separate contests. I think I'm a reasonably likable guy. I'm serious—though I think I'm a little more lovable these days than I used to be back in my youth when I began in my state legislature. But I'm also a serious guy. I think the presidency of the United States is a very serious office, and I think we have to address the issues in a very serious way. So I hope and expect that I will be liked by the people of this country as president of the United States; I certainly hope I will be liked by them on the eighth of November.

In this excerpt, Dukakis revealed an incompatible desire to be serious yet reasonably likable and more lovable. He offered no personal statement except that he hoped and expected the people would like him on election day. Also, his portrayal of himself as a serious guy did little to develop the kind of rapport that Warner asserted was so critical to leadership. No one was describing George Bush as giddy, silly, or flippant. So describing himself as serious did not help to distinguish him from Bush's seriousness. Thus, in this answer, Dukakis painted an inconsistent picture of himself as serious yet likable and lovable, failed to refute Warner's assumption that an effective leader must be personally appealing to the audience, failed to develop that personal rapport with the audience by sharing with the audience an anecdote that portrayed him as likable or lovable, and reinforced an image of himself as serious, and thus somewhat distant and aloof from what Bush would describe in his rebuttal to this answer as the "heartbeat" of the country.

In his rebuttal, Bush defined the issue in terms of sharing the broad dreams of the American people. Even though Bush did not describe what those broad dreams were, he had the advantage of inheriting the Reagan administration's conservative rhetoric. The patriotic appeal had been couched in terms of antiliberal policies and values inside and out of the debates. When he stated that "you've got to understand that it is only the United States that can stand for freedom and democracy around the world," he invoked the patriotic appeal utilized effectively by his campaign. In this respect, Bush provided a slightly more coherent vision of leadership, but certainly one that drew largely on the conservative vision of the Reagan administration.[8]

In Warner's follow-up question to Bush concerning his performance in the campaign, Dukakis had another opportunity to present a more detailed description of his vision for the country. However, Dukakis used the strategy of attacking Bush without detailing his positions. In his rebuttal to Bush's attempt to defend ideology and labels as legitimate issues for the campaign, Dukakis stated:

It's not labels. It's our vision of America. And we have two fundamentally different visions of America. The vice president is complacent, thinks we ought to stick with the status quo, doesn't think we ought to move ahead, thinking things are okay as they are. I don't. I think this is a great country because we've always wanted to do better, to make our country better, to make our lives better. We've always been a nation which was ambitious for America and we move forward. And that's the kind of America I want. That's the kind of leadership I want to provide. But I don't think these labels mean a thing.

The argument was reminiscent of Kennedy's strategy for the 1960 debates. The difference, however, was that Kennedy was able to identify specific problems to be solved and was able to defend specific policies as solutions. A similar degree of substance was missing from Dukakis' answer.

We do not know what Dukakis' vision of America was except that we were to move forward. From where we move and to where we move were left for the audience to figure out; this ambiguity constituted the source of doubts about Dukakis' leadership. Moreover, by not being specific about where he wanted to lead the country, Dukakis' strategy of attacking Bush's "vision thing" would be insufficient by itself to constitute good reason to reject Bush's claim to the office. Even if we accepted Dukakis' claim that Bush was complacent, that things were not OK, we had no notion of what Dukakis wanted in place of the status quo, except perhaps, Michael Dukakis. Absent a more coherent understanding of Dukakis' policies, the audience was forced to consider Dukakis' style of leadership as a basis for deciding between the candidates, and this measure of leadership was unfavorable for Dukakis given his uninspired responses to the panelists.

There was a final opportunity for Dukakis to reveal an inner spark of charismatic appeal in Ann Compton's question about heroes. However, when asked if he would point out heroes to young Americans today who should inspire this country, Dukakis could think only of Jonas Salk, an example that failed to satisfy Compton's criterion of a contemporary hero. Although Dukakis was able to identify groups of people he believed were heroes—public office holders, Olympic athletes, doctors and scientists, teachers, members of the clergy, drug counselors, and law enforcement officers—there was not a single example to illustrate in a vivid and dramatic way Dukakis' understanding of contemporary heroism. In each instance, Dukakis identified the abstract category of a potentially heroic career but in none of the examples did he provide a specific example of a contemporary hero that the audience could relate to and in doing so, gauge his ability to comprehend and express the qualities of heroism.

In contrast, Bush was able to provide four specific examples of what he considered contemporary heroism:

I think of a teacher right here, largely Hispanic school, Jaime Escalante, teaching calculus to your kids, 80 percent of them going to college. I think of a young man now in this country named Valladares, who was released from a Cuban jail. Came out and told the truth in this brilliant book *Against All Hope* about what is actually happening in, in Cuba. I think of those people that took us back into space again, Rick Hauck, and that crew, as people that are worthy of this. . . . I think of Dr. Fauci. Probably never heard of him. You did, Ann heard of him. He's a very fine research—top doctor at National Institute of Health—working hard doing something about research on this disease of AIDS.

Bush's examples were much more appealing than Dukakis'. Bush identified a teacher fighting successfully against an educational system that writes many inner city youths off as incapable of college education, praised an individual for his fight against oppression in Cuba, reminded us of our greatest national adventure in space exploration, and spotlighted one doctor's crusade against AIDS. These examples portrayed Bush as a candidate who had a clearer notion of what constituted contemporary heroism and compared to Dukakis, Bush appeared more sensitive to these struggles and more knowledgeable of what constituted an appropriate role model for Americans.

A final exchange for consideration concerned Warner's question to Bush asking him to justify his position on abortion. Bush's answer was very personal, possessing the capacity to elicit feelings of sympathy for Bush's family as well as his position on the issue. After relating his personal loss of a child to leukemia, he argued that medical knowledge evolved and that we should maintain the sanctity of life in the hope that we can solve some of the diseases that Warner had specified in her question as appropriate justifications for abortion. The crucial part of the answer, though, was his conclusion in which he stated:

And, look, this hasn't been an easy decision for me to work—meet. I know others disagree with it. But when I was in that little church across the river from Washington and saw our grandchild christened in our faith, I was very pleased indeed that the mother had not aborted that child, and put the child up for adoption. And so I just feel this is where I'm coming from. And it is personal. And I don't assail him on that issue, or others on that issue. But that's the way I, George Bush, feel about it.

The answer created sympathy for his personal loss and sidestepped the issue posed by Warner's question. More importantly, through the personal anecdote of his grandchild's christening, he implicitly suggested a transformation of the issue. Had the mother aborted her baby, he would have lost his grandchild. Thus, those who support abortion deny others the opportunity to adopt and love the unwanted children. Bush's seemingly spontaneous sincerity suggested that he took this position not on the basis of political expediency, but on the grounds that it was consistent with his values, appealing to the audience on personal grounds. Bush also communicated a sense of charity when he stated that he did not "assail" Dukakis or others on this issue as the more conservative elements of his party had done, but rather that he had arrived at this point on the issue as a result of his very personal loss.

Dukakis tried to relate a similar personal loss in his rebuttal, but it was undeveloped and lacked the same degree of pathos generated by Bush's answer. After this statement, Dukakis turned to the issue of who makes the decision. Even though I think the substance of Dukakis' answer was superior to Bush's response, the important element in this exchange seemed to be Bush's ability to speak personally to the audience when Dukakis could not. And that was the key difference between the two candidates. Throughout both debates, Dukakis never achieved the kind of rapport that Bush was able to establish as a more moderate representative of the Reagan administration.

SUMMARY

Although this analysis has focused less on substantive issues and more on stylistic considerations of the candidate's language choices, the approach seems well justified.[9] On October 13, 1988, the *New York Times* reported that Bush needed "to be competent on substantive questions, and more importantly, appear warmer and more personable than Dukakis" in the second debate.[10] The Dukakis camp was aware that its candidate "was considered skilled but rather chilly by many reviewers" in the first debate and tried to "schedule folksy, regular-guy kind of events" in the last few days prior to the debate, but it was unable to prepare him adequately for Warner's question concerning likability as a measure of presidential character.[11] The difference between the candidates then became more a distinction of style than argumentative substance. But given the way that style is related to rhetorical substance, the debates constituted an important opportunity to see how well each candidate's language choices shaped his images of presidential character. More important, for the Dukakis campaign, it is interesting to note that the strategy of attacking Bush was inadequate to win undecided voters unless Dukakis could have provided that audience with a more definite vision of his leadership in the debate. Although Dukakis may have been more specific in describing his programs outside the debates, he needed to be specific about his programs in the debates. Although the very nature of the forum creates risks for candidates who are specific in describing policy positions, a candidate who takes risks, especially in circumstances in which the polls indicate that the audience is unsure of what the candidate stands for, and can emerge from the debate having withstood the attacks of the opposing candidate, greatly enhances the changes of improving his standings among the voters. But this was not the case for Michael Dukakis in 1988.[12] Comparatively, Bush's performance in the debates suggested a clearer sense of direction for the country, and the public seemed more willing to vote for a continuation of the Republican order than take a chance on an undeveloped vision of leadership under the Democratic candidate.

NOTES

1. *New York Times*, Oct. 5, 1988, A–1, A–30.

2. Texts for analysis come from the *New York Times*, Sept. 26, A–16–A–19; Oct. 14, 1988, A–14–A–17. All quotations are from the *New York Times* transcripts.

3. E. J. Dionne of the *New York Times* attributed Dukakis' failure to win the election to his performance in the second debate. See Daniel R. Runkel, ed., *Campaign for President: The Managers Look at 88* (Dover, MA: Auburn House, 1989), 252; also, Susan Estrich noted that Dukakis was ill the morning of the second debate; *Campaign for the President*, 253.

4. Dukakis never was able to articulate a rationale for his candidacy. See Peter Goldman and Tom Matthews, *The Quest for the Presidency 1988* (New York: Touchstone, 1989), 60, 62–63, 75, 119, 336. Nor was there a message for the debates, according to Goldman and Matthews (375–376, 393). See also Sidney Blumenthal, *Pledging Allegiance: The Last Campaign of the Cold War* (New York: Harper Collins, 1990), 302, 312.

5. Goldman and Matthews, *The Quest for the Presidency*, 193.

6. Ibid., 378; Blumenthal, *Pledging Allegiance*, 303. This was a tactic that had been discussed by Bush and Roger Ailes. Bush had made the mistake of referring to September 7 as the date of the Japanese attack on Pearl Harbor. In joking about the debates, Bush asked why he had to debate on "Christmas" day, September 25.

7. Jack W. Germond and Jules Witcover, *Whose Broad Stripes and Bright Stars: The Trivial Pursuit of the Presidency 1988* (New York: Warner, 1989), 446.

8. *New York Times*, October 13, 1988, p. B–10: "A stunning 60 percent of all Americans now approve Mr. Reagan's job performance and only 30 percent disapprove, his best rating since October 1986, just before the Iran-contra scandal became public."

9. The 1988 debates have received a substantial amount of attention from rhetorical scholars. For an examination of values in the second 1988 debate, see Duane Fish, "Image and Issue in the Second Bush-Dukakis Debate: The Mediating Role of Values," in *Spheres of Argument: Proceedings of the Sixth SCA/AFA Conference on Argumentation*, ed. Bruce Gronbeck (Annandale, VA: SCA, 1989), 151–157; for a study of argumentation over Bush's charge that Dukakis was liberal, see Donn W. Parson, "Congregation by Segregation: An Analysis of Argument Strategies in the First 1988 Presidential Debates," in *Spheres of Argument: Proceedings of the Sixth SCA/AFA Conference on Argumentation*, 136–139. In addition, two special issues of *Argumentation and Advocacy* have been devoted to the 1988 debates: 25(Spring 1989) and 27(Winter 1991).

10. *New York Times*, October 13, 1988, A–1.

11. Ibid., B–10.

12. Parson comes to a similar conclusion based on his analysis of Dukakis' ability to respond to Bush's charge that he was liberal; see "Congregation by Segregation," 139. See also Blumenthal, *Pledging Allegiance*, 303 and 312.

Chapter Eight

The Vice Presidential Debates of 1976, 1984, and 1988

Vice presidential debates serve four purposes in a presidential campaign. First, they provide us with an opportunity to see how well the vice presidential candidate can defend himself or herself because they force a candidate to take positions and explain reasons, revealing something about the character of the person who might become president. Even when the questions from the panelists focus on the presidential candidates' previous records and on the policies they intend to pursue if elected, the arguments can shift to a direct comparison of the vice presidential candidates' ability to represent the values and policies of the front runner. Second, vice presidential debates are also opportunities to compare candidates on the basis of their ability to defend their presidential ticket in a clash over party, policies, and presidential character. Since there is some chance that a vice presidential candidate will be called upon to assume the office of the presidency, the debates give the public a chance to see how well the second person on the ticket can present himself or herself as a potential presidential office holder by defending the party's values and platform. Third, vice presidential debates are opportunities to gauge the judgment of the presidential candidate—choosing the vice presidential candidate is the first decision the presidential candidate gets to make and the debates help us to see how well each candidate chose. Thus, the vice presidential candidate's performance can affect perceptions of the presidential candidate. Finally, vice presidential debates reassure us that the system can survive if the vice presidential candidate is called upon to assume the office of the presidency. The debates give us a chance to scrutinize the persons seeking to be next in line for the presidency so that we can evaluate their ability to enact democratic values through rational dialogue. Despite the fact that vice presidential debates are overshadowed by the more critical presidential debates, vice presidential debates can affect the development of political images of vice presidential candidates, the presidential candidates, and subsequent events in the presidential campaign. Any of these four purposes can become important focal points for analyzing the debates, depending on the campaign and the candidate. And sometimes what is important for one candidate may not be important for another, so that in the 1984 campaign, for example, Geraldine Ferraro was under close examination to see how she would stand up under fire, but George Bush's primary objective was to defend Ronald Reagan after his poor showing in the first presidential debate with Walter Mondale. In 1988, many people thought that Bush made an error in selecting Dan Quayle but that could be determined only by how well Quayle responded to attacks on his character, his party, and his ticket. This chapter examines the ways in which the vice presidential candidates' language choices reflected these rhetorical purposes in the vice presidential debates of 1976, 1984, and 1988.

THE 1976 VICE PRESIDENTIAL DEBATE: ROBERT DOLE VERSUS WALTER MONDALE

In the 1976 vice presidential debate, Robert Dole's dry humor reinforced the public's dark image of him as a political "hatchet-man."[1] Although Dole claimed that the current administration had maintained peace and prosperity, his responses in the ten exchanges that composed the debate failed to defend the last eight years of Republican leadership. Also, by employing standard partisan attacks on the Democratic ticket, Dole could not expand his appeal beyond conservative Republicans to include undecided voters.[2] In contrast to Dole, Walter Mondale's opening and closing statements established a framework for evaluating the last eight years of Republican control of the White House and argued that eight years of Republican leadership had been ineffective in solving the nation's problems.[3] By asking the audience to reflect on how well Ford and Nixon had responded to the nation's ills during the last eight years, Mondale's rhetoric constituted a broader appeal based on a rational evaluation of Ford's record and effectively questioned Ford's ability to provide effective leadership in the next four years. Also important to explaining Mondale's appeal was the way in which he demonstrated a superior understanding of his prospective role as vice president in the first exchange and in his rebuttal to Dole's attack in the second exchange.[4] Mondale's answer not only suggested that he had a better sense of how he could contribute to the Carter administration but also that he had a more definite sense of the obligations of the office.[5]

The analysis begins with the opening statements about which I argue that Dole's attempt to define the campaign in terms of a conflict between conservative and liberal ideologies was unresponsive to Mondale's charge that the last eight years of Republican leadership proved that change was needed. Next, I develop the claim that Dole's language choices suggested a dark side to his political character. This argument is constructed in two ways: first, by considering the many places in the text of the debate in which Dole's sense of humor seemed to violate expectations of a more noble political character particularly suited for high office, and second, by illustrating how, in a single exchange, a candidate's performance can crystallize an implicit image of character developing throughout the debate in less defined form.[6] Finally, I consider the ways in which the closing statements served both candidates' strategies in the debate, specifically, how Dole's attempt to cast the debate in a conservative versus liberal frame to respond to the problems identified by Mondale and how well Mondale reinforced his argument that things had not improved over the past eight years of Republican leadership.[7]

The Opening Statements

Dole's opening statement consisted of five basic parts: thanking the League of Women Voters, establishing a tone of friendly debate with his friend Walter Mondale, making a statement of praise for Ford, attacking Carter, and attacking Mondale. The two most important parts of the opening statement concerned the attacks on Carter and Mondale. In his attack on Carter, Dole defined the key issue in the debate as liberalism when he said:

Now I don't know much about Governor Carter. I've tried to find out. I know he's very ambitious. I know he wants to be president—he's been running for three years. But I know he's said at least one thing—that he does agree with my opponent, my friend Walter Mondale, probably the most liberal senator in the United States Senate. And that's really what this debate is all about.

Also, in the conclusion of the opening statement, Dole echoed the liberal characterization of Carter: "My opponent [Mondale] has a record of voting for every—every inflationary spending program, except in defense, when he votes for every cut. And we'll explore that as this debate goes on." Thus, Dole asked the audience to understand the debate in terms of a contest between a liberal and a conservative ideology.

Although the liberal versus conservative conflict is almost always an important dimension of presidential campaigns, Dole's decision to frame the debate this way neglected the more important need to defend the actions of the Ford administration. Since the value of an ideology depends on how well its principles serve a political community, Dole needed to defend the conservative orientation in terms of desirable actions taken by the Ford administration. In failing to defend the Republican record, Dole relinquished control of the way the audience would understand his party's conservative approach to the problems faced by the nation. Also, framing the debate in terms of a liberal versus conservative contest would turn out to be problematic for Dole because the campaign was not only about ideology but also about political character. Mondale's strategy of framing the decision in terms of political character placed the focus of the debate on Dole's ability to defend the conservative ideology in the separate exchanges, a risky venture since he had no control over the questions that would be asked and thus had no way of knowing how well he could press his attack on Mondale's liberal record. Finally, Dole's failure to offer a more specific defense of the Ford administration or a more detailed attack on the Carter-Mondale platform left the debate over policy issues unfocused. Dole's opening did not force Mondale to defend the claim that he and Carter could improve on the Republican record over the past eight years. In this sense, Dole made a critical error in allowing Mondale to define the nature of leadership being offered by the Republican ticket. How one viewed the Republican record over the past eight years would become important later in the debate as the means by which one determined whether Ford deserved four more years.

Mondale's opening statement listed the problems that the country faced and argued that the problems had gotten worse, not better, under the Republican administration. Mondale summarized the case for change in the conclusion of his opening statement:

The Republican administration, the Republican party, has had eight years to solve these problems. All of them have gotten worse. The Republican ticket does not offer new plans for their solution, but is engaged in a frantic effort to defend the past. This nation desperately needs new leadership. The Carter-Mondale ticket would offer a new generation of leadership dedicated to solving the problems which I have listed, and that is the basis of our appeal.

The difference between the two opening statements was in the degree of support each offered for his claims. Dole had asserted only that Carter and Mondale were too liberal for the nation. By failing to offer examples to support his claim, Dole's opening statement appealed only to those who already supported the Republican ticket. But by listing specific problems that had remained unsolved under Republican leadership, Mondale's opening statement constituted a compelling reason to change for those members of the audience who were undecided. The decision for the audience, then, became framed in terms of effectiveness at solving those problems that had confronted the nation over the past eight years. Unless Dole could defend the administration on those charges, Mondale's argument for change would seem valid.

The Dark Side of Robert Dole

Candidates who seek high office must behave in ways that suggest they possess noble character, that is, that they possess the best possible character to represent and defend the values of the political community. Since debates allow audiences to compare candidates' language choices, they are opportunities for candidates to choose words that best reflect an image of excellence in political leadership. But in the 1976 vice presidential debate, Dole's dry sense of humor suggested that streaks of cynicism and mean spiritedness lay within his character, and his language choices failed to reveal the noble qualities more discerning of presidential or vice-presidential character.

As a rhetorical strategy, humor can be very effective at disarming an opponent. Throughout his career, Ronald Reagan was particularly masterful at the use of the one-liner to defuse attacks on his character. But Dole's use of dry humor throughout the debate reinforced doubts about his character. In any other election, the electorate might not have been so sensitive. However, in the wake of Watergate, Carter and Mondale were arguing that the Republicans did not represent mainstream American values of decency and integrity in government. Consequently, Dole's humorous barbs only reinforced doubts about the Republican party's ability to choose candidates who would conduct themselves "decently" in the course of their duties.

Dole's attempts at humor were evident throughout the debate. In the opening statement, Dole presumptuously claimed victory before his opening statement had even been concluded when he stated: "I think tonight may be sort of a fun evening. It's a very important evening, it's a very historic evening. But I've known my counterpart for some time, and we've been friends, and we'll be friends when this debate is over, and we'll be friends when this election is over and he'll still be in the Senate."

In the first exchange of the debate when Hal Bruno asked him what his view of the office was, Dole's humor contradicted his substantive message. First, Dole responded humorously by saying: "Well, I've said as I've traveled around the country in, mostly in jest, that is 'Why are you running for vice president?' I said, "Well, it's indoor work and no heavy lifting.' " Dole attempted to return to a more serious vision of the office when he continued by saying that he had thought very seriously about it and that he thought it was a great opportunity and a great responsibility, but then immediately qualified his assertions about the importance of the office by stating that "I can't stand here tonight in Houston, Texas, and say that come January, when I'll be sworn in as vice president, that I'm going to do anything in the first hundred days." At this point in Dole's response, the audience was left with an inconsistent message: The office is a great responsibility but Dole could not describe what those responsibilities would entail. Dole concluded his answer by identifying two responsibilities—increasing agricultural exports and continuing to seek some accounting for the missing in action in Southeast Asia, but these responsibilities seemed rather limited compared to Mondale's vision of the office.

Mondale defined his role as being responsible for the restructuring and reorganization of the federal government. In his rebuttal to Mondale's answer, Dole used humor to attack Carter's plan for reorganization when he stated, "I'm happy that you are going to be responsible for reorganization. I hope you don't pattern it after Governor Carter's efforts in Georgia." In this answer, Dole implicitly acknowledged Mondale's role and ability in the proposed Carter administration and even though he pressed the attack on Carter, Mondale's vision of the vice presidency seemed intact.

Dole's use of sarcasm was also evident in his rebuttal to Mondales' in the first exchange. Criticizing Carter for his proposal to do away with the Department of Agriculture, Dole stated dryly, "I know the farmers who may be viewing will be pleased to know that." Later, in the fourth exchange concerning the economy and the priorities of the Carter administration, Dole stated that, "In fact I've been suggesting that George Meany was probably Senator Mondale's makeup man—he may or may not have been, they did a good job."

In addition to suggesting sarcastically that Mondale's makeup man was George Meany, Dole was condescending in his refutation of Mondale's implicit assertion of friendship with Alexander Solzhenitsyn: "Well, I'm glad you mentioned Solzhenitsyn. I checked with his interpreter and I understand you've never met Mr. Solzhenitsyn—neither has Mr. Carter. Now I've had the privilege of meeting Mr. Solzhenitsyn—maybe you shook his hand somewhere." Later, in the same answer and in the same condescending tone, Dole commented on Carter's *Playboy* interview, "I couldn't understand frankly why he was in *Playboy* magazine—but he was, and we'll give him the bunny vote."

In addition to his poor humor, sarcastic tone, and condescending attitude, Dole's conclusion to his final rebuttal in the seventh exchange suggested an image of an unpolished, unrefined candidate clumsily striking back with a feeble attack on Mondale's voting record on national security issues. Although Mondale's voting record on national security issues was an important aspect in evaluating his candidacy, Dole did not set up the criticism effectively. After Dole responded to Bruno's question about the influence of lobby groups in Washington, Mondale presented a well-developed defense of his voting record. Mondale began by listing the various groups that rated him highly and then argued that he and Carter represented the mainstream of public life because of the ratings he received from the League of Women Voters. Characterizing the League of Women Voters as "an independent, dispassionate organization that represents the views of all Americans—conservative, liberal, moderate, and so on," Mondale stated that,

For five years the League has prepared the list of the most crucial issues that they believe affects governmental effectiveness, that affects governmental honesty, that affects dealing with America's real problems. And I'm proud of the fact that in each of those five years, the League of Women Voters has rated me 100 percent in favor of every one of those issues that they on an independent and bipartisan basis, have believed to be the most important to this country. And I note in that same record, that my opponent was wrong half the time. He only was there 50 percent of the time. And I noted that the president of the United States, Mr. Ford, when he was in Congress, was right only 35 percent of the time. And I think that says something about balance. We are in the mainstream of public life.

Although Dole responded by suggesting that the League of Women Voters was wrong half the time because it "tend[s] to be a little bit liberal," he did not develop any support for this claim. Despite the fact that an objective standard does not exist for evaluating how liberal or conservative the League of Women Voters was, Mondale's characterization of the League was probably closer to the way in which the majority of Americans viewed the organization. Mondale also was careful to indicate that the League represented the views of all Americans—conservative, liberal, and moderate. Thus, to suggest that the League was a little bit liberal did not explain why Dole's voting record was off the mark 50 percent of the time. Also, given Mondale's assertion that the League's ratings were developed on an independent and bipartisan basis, Dole's conservativism appeared to be slightly to the right of what Mondale described as the mainstream of public life. Finally, Mondale's use of the League of Women Voters as a standard for measuring the desirability of his candidacy was strategic. By sponsoring the debates, the League seemed genuinely committed to rational, dispassionate dialogue on the issues. Dole could not criticize the League, the host for the debate, beyond being a little bit liberal without overstating his claim and appearing as an ungracious guest. In these respects, Mondale's use of voting records placed Dole outside the mainstream of public life and constrained Dole's rhetorical options for refutation.

After characterizing the League of Women Voters as liberal, Dole attacked Carter and Mondale for their attempts to repeal right-to-work laws and for their support for California's Proposition 14, which would allow farm union organizers three hours a day to organize farm workers on private property. Then, as if it were an afterthought, Dole concluded his answer with this attack: "What about your national security voting record where you get a zero every year, when you talk about our defense." This conclusion, while a legitimate topic for discussion, came off as a kind of poorly aimed parting shot. Because Dole never presented any evidence to indicate that the League of Women Voters rated Mondale a zero in national security, the impression created by Dole's concluding comment is that this was an entirely partisan view of Mondale's voting record. Also, because of its brevity, the fact that it was placed as a parting shot in conclusion, and because it had only marginal relevance to the greater substance of the argument that Dole was developing in his answer, Dole's demand that Mondale "talk about our defense" seemed to suggest a certain awkwardness in Dole's counterattack.

In the eighth exchange, the tone of Dole's rebuttal implied a disdainful attitude toward Mondale for having missed opportunities to vote on congressional issues. Dole stated, "Well, Watergate is a Republican problem, and I voted for the Watergate investigation. My opponent was absent. We're all absent sometime, but he's absent more than others." The problem with this criticism was that it reached too far. Although Dole's first claim that Mondale missed the vote could be verified, Dole's second charge that Mondale had been absent more than others took on a relative standard. Without knowing whom to compare Mondale's attendance record to, the audience lacked a clear standard against which to measure Mondale's attendance, reflecting a partisan attitude. And such an approach to the issue, despite Dole's statement of friendship toward Mondale, suggested an overly competitive and uncharitable attitude toward the contest for the vice presidency. In short, the audience might be compelled to ask if Dole is Mondale's friend, why would he imply that Mondale was irresponsible in his voting record? And if Mondale had been absent more than others, why hadn't Dole presented any evidence to justify this claim?

Finally, in the conclusion of his rebuttal in the eighth exchange, Dole asserted that Carter "has three positions on everything—that's why they're having three TV debates." Again, Dole relied on humor rather than supporting his claim with evidence to prove Carter's lack of consistency. For Republican supporters, the humor might have seemed appropriate but by neglecting to present any evidence to support his claim, Dole's argument might have been unappealing for undecided voters.

None of these instances individually portrayed undesirable character, but together they suggested certain limitations in the appeal of Robert

Dole's political image. The element of presumptuousness veiled by humor in the opening statement, the cynical and inconsistent attitude toward the nature of the office suggested in the first exchange, the sarcastic humor best exemplified by proposing that George Meany had been Mondale's makeup man, the condescending tone evident in the fourth exchange, and the partisan, unrefined, and uncharitable image as an advocate who might lash out clumsily revealed in the seventh and eighth exchanges all contributed to a pattern of mean spiritedness. In contrast, Mondale's attitude and tone toward the nature of the office, the debate, and his opponent carried no such negative qualities.

The Ninth Exchange: Dole's Image as a "Hatchet Man" Coalesces

Up to this point in the analysis, each of the instances identified as contributing to an undesirable image for Dole constituted only short extracts from the debate, and, in a sense, the argument that these short excerpts constituted a pattern of language choices that reflected undesirable aspects of political character might seem controversial. But in the 1976 vice presidential debate, like the 1980 presidential debate between Carter and Reagan, one particular exchange reinforced the larger pattern evident in the rest of the debate. And, like the 1980 debate, that crucial exchange occurred late in the debate, allowing it to function as a lens through which an audience might see each candidate's political image take on a more definite form.

In the ninth exchange, Walter Mears asked Dole if he thought that Watergate was an appropriate topic for the campaign. Dole indicated that it was an appropriate topic but not a good issue. Comparing a discussion of Watergate to discussing the Vietnam War, the Korean War, and World War I and World War II, Dole attempted to equate the two topics as partisan issues. Although the remainder of Dole's answer developed the argument that we should put Watergate behind us, an altogether appropriate and appealing position to take on the issue, equivocating Watergate with the idea that all of the wars in this century had been caused by the Democratic party reflected a narrow, partisan view of the issues. When Mondale was given the opportunity to respond, he attacked Dole for his partisan attitude:

I think Senator Dole has richly earned his reputation as a hatchet man tonight, by implying and stating that World War II and the Korean War were Democratic wars. Does he really mean to suggest to the American people, that there was a partisan difference over our involvement in the war to fight Nazi Germany? I don't think any reasonable American would accept that. Does he really mean to suggest that it was only partisanship, that got us into the war in Korea? Does he really mean to forget that part of the record, where Mr. Nixon and the Republican party wanted us to get involved earlier in the war in Vietnam?

Until this point in the debate, Dole had had the entire debate to demonstrate that his prior image as a "hatchet man" was undeserved or that in some way his character had been refined; however, in blaming all wars on the Democrats, Dole remained true to his image as a partisan politician.

Closing Statements

Dole closed the debate with three claims: (1) the Republicans were concerned about the American people; (2) the Republicans had faith in the American people; and (3) the Democrats wanted bigger and more expensive government, but the Republicans did not. None of these three claims were developed effectively.

Dole implicitly refuted the second claim of his closing statement when he suggested in the introduction that the role of the panel and the audience was to "indulge" the candidates. Here his choice of words implied that those members of the audience who had remained for the entire debate were merely indulging the candidates rather than participating in a serious political event inviting judgments of competence: "Well, first I wish to thank the panel for their indulgence and of course all those in the viewing audience who may still be with us." Although it might have been true that some members of the audience had discontinued viewing the debate, Dole's statement implicitly questioned the importance of the debate by viewing it as an "indulgence" and one that many viewers might discontinue because they, like him, saw it as an indulgence rather than a serious performance of leadership skills. This contradicted the claim that he represented the party that had faith in the American people. The lack of faith is communicated more directly in the next immediate sentence when Dole stated that "I really hope you were listening, and we were able to tell you who's concerned about the American people, which party has faith in the American people, which party and which candidates want bigger and bigger and bigger government." Although the "I really hope you were listening" line might be heard as Dole's concern for the importance of the message and the hope that the audience was deliberating carefully, the rest of Dole's performance in the debate seemed to contradict a consistently genuine concern for the audience and the office. In this respect, the "I really hope you were listening" line could also be heard as an impatient teacher or parent scolding the audience for not paying attention to the lesson. In the introduction of the closing statement, then, Dole's cynical tone, his unflattering image of the audience, and his assertion of a superior-subordinate relationship to the audience contradicted Dole's professed faith in the American people.

Dole combined the first and third claims in an attack on the Democratic platform when he argued that the Democrats did not care about the American people and that the Democrats wanted bigger government and increased spending. There are two weaknesses in this argument. First, although the argument of increased cost from government spending was plausible, Dole did not explain how increased taxes required by an increase in social spending resulted in inflation. Although many Americans might have been familiar with the economic effects of increased spending, Dole's objection to the Democratic platform rested on an unarticulated causal relationship. Thus, the charge that the Democrats did not care about inflation was incompletely developed. Second, Dole did not defend the incumbent administration by arguing that the Democratic programs were unnecessary. Presumably, if the programs were necessary, then some benefits could have been realized from Democratic spending despite the increase in taxes. Having chosen to attack the Democratic platform on the grounds that it would cause inflation, Dole needed to develop the relationship between increased taxes and inflation more clearly. At this point, Dole had conceded that new programs might be justified and his claim that the Democratic platform would cause inflation was insufficiently developed to function persuasively for his nonpartisan audience.

Nor did Dole's style communicate a genuine concern for the American people. Consider the way in which Dole expressed his concern: "We're concerned about the poor. We're concerned about the sick. We're concerned about the disabled. We're concerned about those on Social Security. And we have programs for that. We're concerned about housing—Carla Hills announced one today, to reduce the interest payments, from 8½ to 8 percent for FHA and VA homes." The first thing that stands out about this passage is the use of the collective *we*. Dole communicated no personal feeling here in the sense of a single individual representing the collective pathos of the Republican party. Additionally, the lack of specific examples to demonstrate how Republicans care as a collective group left these statements as unsupported claims. The audience would be required to accept these statements on the credibility of the speaker. And in this respect, Dole's syntactic structure does not serve his purpose well. Each sentence declared concern without support and, together, as a list of unsupported declarations of concern, one gets a sense of a bureaucrat using categories in a distant, uninvolved way rather than a candidate championing the needs of the human beings represented by these groups. Dole's only example of support related to housing, and it was a report of an announcement of a decrease in interest rates for FHA and VA homes. Again, there is no dynamic sense of involvement in this instance; Dole's language suggested him in the role of a bureaucrat reporting an action taken by someone else in the administration. Also, how this particular decrease in FHA and VA interest rates reflected concern on the part of the Republicans was left unexplained. We have no sense of Dole's personal involvement or responsibility for the plight of the poor, the sick, the disabled, and those on Social Security. On these grounds, Dole's concern seemed inevident.

Two additional moves in the final minute of the closing statement merit consideration. The first is Dole's personal testimony to Ford's character when he stated: "It's an honor and a privilege to have known President Ford for sixteen years—sixteen years, as I said at the outset. He's a man of unparalleled decency and honesty and courage. He's a man we can be proud of."As I argued in Chapter 4, Carter's strategy was to use the debates to focus attention on the ways in which Ford's character was shaped by the Nixon pardon. The fact that Dole felt it necessary to bolster Ford's character with his own personal testimony lends additional support for the claim that doubts about Ford's integrity constituted a serious problem for the Republican campaign.

Second, Dole closed the debate by claiming that Ford would deliver more effective leadership. At the end of his personal testimony to Ford's character, Dole stated: "He's gonna give us that leadership that America needs." In this excerpt, Dole seemed to be predicting that Ford would deliver strong leadership in the future. Given the fact that Ford was the incumbent, the absence of some compelling example of leadership might cause the audience to ask why it should believe that Ford would provide effective leadership in the future. The prediction, then, seemed an odd way of demonstrating what should clearly be more apparent in the administration's track record. Here, the problem that developed was Dole's inability to present a more specific defense of the incumbent administration. Dole's last request to the audience was to "Just take a look at the leadership. Take a look at President Ford, and thank President Ford for the fact that we live in peace, and freedom, and your sons and your husbands and your relatives are home and they're safe." But Dole's claim that Ford's leadership skills had allowed us to live in peace and freedom lacked examples of specific actions or policies that have maintained peace and freedom. The audience was left to determine for itself what Ford had accomplished in office, and the most significant action for which Ford was known was his pardon of Nixon.

In summary, Dole's closing statement was ineffective in substantiating his three claims that (1) the Republicans were concerned about the American people, (2) the Republicans had faith in the American people, and (3) the Democrats wanted bigger and more expensive government while the Republicans did not. Dole's view of the debate as an "indulgence" did little to bridge the distance between himself and the audience and contradicted his "faith in the American people." Betraying a bureaucratic outlook, his verbal style failed to demonstrate a personal concern for the poor, the sick, the disabled, and those on Social Security. He did not offer a defense of the incumbent administration's record. His attack on the Democratic platform rested on an unexplained causal relationship between government spending and inflation. More importantly, he explicitly acknowledged doubts about Ford's character and then asked the audience to measure Ford's leadership but failed to supply the audience with a more favorable standard of measurement other than that action for which Ford was most known and most vulnerable, Nixon's pardon.

Mondale attempted to set aside partisan debating as the standard for evaluating the debate and in its place suggested that the candidates and their ticket should be evaluated according to their capacity for problem solving. The success of this approach depended on whether Mondale could establish the existence of problems and indicate that the Ford administration had failed and would continue to fail unless new policies were offered. To develop this argument, Mondale made four points in the closing: (1) the Ford administration had failed to reduce unemployment, inflation, and the deficit; (2) the nation needed a government that cared about health care, housing, senior citizens, the environment, and energy resources; (3) the Democrats believed in a strong defense; and (4) the country needed new leadership. With the exception of the comment on needing a strong defense, this statement closely resembled his opening argument and asked the audience to reflect on the Republican record for the last eight years:

For eight years now, the Republicans have controlled government. For eight years they've controlled the White House, and every one of those problems has gotten worse. They are not now proposing new policies and new directions. Tonight, you heard what they are doing. They are defending the past—"Everything is all right"; "The problems are not as bad as the statistics or the people believe, and therefore they might go away." That is not enough. This country cries out for new leadership. We need a fresh start. And the Carter-Mondale ticket promises that start.

At this point, Mondale had successfully focused the decision on an assessment of the Republicans' last eight years in office. Because Dole's defense of the Ford administration was indirect, unspecific, and developed in a partisan tone, his appeal never extended beyond a conservative audience. Mondale's argument, then, suggested that the Democrats did care about the people and were more willing to solve the problems facing the nation than the Republicans. In these ways, Mondale's performance reflected a less partisan, more appealing vision of leadership for the national community.

Summary of Findings in the 1976 Vice Presidential Debate

Analysis of the 1976 vice presidential debate demonstrated how Mondale developed a rationale for change, how Dole failed to develop a rational defense of the Republican ticket that would transcend partisan conservative values and appeal to a broader national audience, and how Dole's partisan image, although evident in many of his answers, ultimately came into sharp focus in the ninth exchange of the debate.[8] The analysis of the first vice presidential debate also suggested that Mondale had developed a sensitive understanding of how he would contribute to a presidential administration as vice president, but Dole had not. Finally, examination of the closing statements revealed that Dole's claim of believing in the people was implicitly contradicted by his tone, syntactic structure, and relationship with the audience.

THE 1984 VICE PRESIDENTIAL DEBATE: GEORGE BUSH VERSUS GERALDINE FERRARO

Several factors make the Bush-Ferraro debate interesting for analysis. The most important concern for the Reagan camp was the fact that Ronald Reagan had performed poorly in his first debate with Walter Mondale.[9] Even though Barbara Walters had claimed that the first debate concerned "the economy and other domestic issues," Mondale focused the debate primarily on the budget deficit. On this issue, Mondale challenged Reagan's credibility as a candidate in control of the facts. Mondale defined leadership in terms of a candidate's ability to understand the facts and to draw appropriate conclusions regarding those facts. Reagan never refuted Mondale's charge that the deficit was a test of leadership or that the debt was the dominant domestic issue. When Reagan denied Mondale's claims concerning the budget deficit, Mondale appealed to the public record of Reagan's statements and proposals. Reagan's inability to control the facts in the first debate created significant doubt about his ability to understand and use the facts of an important political matter to make decisions, develop policy, or solve problems. Thus, Republicans were interested in the vice presidential debate to see whether Bush could restore Reagan's image as an effective leader.[10]

The vice presidential debate was also important for Bush and Geraldine Ferraro.[11] For Bush, who had had limited experience in winning elective office but held aspirations for future presidential campaigns, the debate was an opportunity to display his advocacy skills as a representative of the Republican party.[12] As the first female vice presidential candidate in the nation's history, Ferraro was under close scrutiny to see, first, how a woman would perform in the stressful situation of a public debate and, second, how well she could defend the Democratic vision of leadership and enlarge the critical opening that Mondale had established in his first debate with Reagan.[13]

Finally, the 1984 vice presidential debate underscored the significance of vice presidential candidates in the presidential campaign. Together, the assassination attempt on Reagan in his first term and Ferraro's historic opportunity to demonstrate that women were capable of serving competently in a high political office reinforced the expectation that vice presidential candidates needed to display their abilities to represent and defend desirable community values as well as explain, analyze, and defend viable policies designed to implement and maintain those values.[14]

The analysis of the debate is developed in three segments.[15] The first considers Bush's performance as a cheerleader for Reagan, as an effective rebuttalist, and as a partisan advocate capable of characterizing the Democratic ticket in negative terms. The second segment evaluates Ferraro's performance, first by identifying her strongest moments in the debate, which included her rebuttal of Bush's patronizing tone on the issue of terrorism and her ability to demonstrate that she was qualified for high office, and then by focusing on her shortcomings as a rebuttalist in the debate. The final section compares the merits of each candidate's closing statement.

Bush as a Cheerleader for Reagan

One of the most consistent impressions left by the vice presidential debate was that Bush took several opportunities to praise Reagan.[16] This was true in the first exchange when Bush stated that "one of the reasons I think we're an effective team is that I firmly believe in his leadership. He's really turned this country around." In the second exchange, Bush argued that the Reagan administration had not been hostile to minorities and defended Reagan on the grounds that he had extended the Voting Rights Act for the longest period of time. Over the issue of separation of church and state, Bush characterized Reagan's appointment of Sandra Day O'Connor as outstanding. On the problem of how to cope with terrorism, Bush praised Reagan for his willingness to take responsibility for the effects of his policy in the Middle East: "I don't think you can go assigning blame. The president, of course, is the best I've ever seen of accepting that. He's been wonderful about it in absolutely everything that happens." Perhaps the most effusive praise came in answer to Norma Quarles' follow-up question on the topic of arms control when Bush said:

Let's encourage the Soviets to come to table, as we did at the Gromyko meeting. I wish everyone could have seen that one. The president, giving the facts to Gromyko in all of these nuclear . . . nuclear meetings—excellent. Right on top of that subject matter. And I'll bet you that Gromyko went back to the Soviet Union saying, "Hey, listen. This president is calling the shots; we'd better move."

Bush as an Effective Rebuttalist

The first example to support the claim that Bush was an effective rebuttalist was, oddly enough, an instance in which Bush was wrong but presented a much more appealing image as an advocate. In the final rebuttal over Jack White's question on civil rights, Bush argued, contrary to the facts, that "spending for food stamps is way, way up under the Reagan administration. AFDC is up under the Reagan administration. And I am not going to be found wrong on that. I am sure of my facts, and we are trying to help, and I think we're doing a reasonable job." Then, Bush added, "But we are not going to rest until every American that wants a job gets a job, and until this prosperity and this recovery that's benefitting many Americans, benefits all Americans." The rebuttal, even though based on erroneous facts, contributed to an image of confidence and optimism in the Reagan administration. Despite Ferraro's more accurate use of the facts, the impression that resides in the text of the debate is one that dominates Ferraro's less incisive analysis of the issues.

In Bush's rebuttal over the issue of separation of church and state, he easily dismissed Ferraro's claim that Jerry Falwell would have undue influence over Reagan's appointments to the Supreme Court and federal courts when he explained that the only evidence to assess Reagan's performance thus far had been his "outstanding" appointment of Sandra Day O'Connor—and that this had displeased Jerry Falwell. Ferraro's evidence, in contrast to Bush's, seemed rather insubstantial. Despite reminding the audience that the Republican platform took the position that the abortion issue would be a "litmus test" for court appointments, Ferraro could produce no tangible evidence of Reagan violating the separation of church and state. Thus, when Bush stated that "we want justices who will interpret the Constitution, not legislate," his position seemed more appealing than Ferraro's.

Bush as a Partisan Advocate: Characterizing the Democratic Ticket in Negative Terms

In Bush's rebuttal during the first exchange, he criticized the Carter administration for delivering malaise and then asserted that Reagan had delivered leadership:

The other day she [Ferraro] was in a plant and she said to the workers why are you voting for . . . the Reagan-Bush ticket? And there was a long, deathly silence, and she said "Come on, we delivered." That's the problem. . . . They delivered 21.5 percent interest rates. They delivered what they called "malaise." They delivered interest rates that were right off the charts. They delivered take-home paychecks that were shrinking. And we've delivered optimism. People are going back to work—6 million of them—and 300 thousand jobs a month being created. That's why there was that deathly silence out there in that plant. They delivered the wrong thing. Ronald Reagan is delivering leadership.

Even though Ferraro criticized Bush's use of statistics and defended the Carter administration's record, she did not address the characterization of the Carter administration as one of malaise.

In the final exchange, Bush declined an opportunity to ask Ferraro a question and instead chose to define the choice for the audience:

The Reagan-Bush administration is so different from the Carter-Mondale administration, that the American people are going to have the clearest choice. It's a question of going back to the failed ideas of the past, when we came in—21.5 percent on those interest rates, inflation, despair, malaise, no leadership, blaming the American people for failed leadership. Or, another option—keep this recovery going until it benefits absolutely everybody. Peace at home, peace abroad, prosperity—opportunity. I'd like to hear her talk on those things.

Again, Ferraro ignored the characterization of past Democratic leadership in negative terms. Although she did defend the Carter administration's record on human rights, the more general characterization of Democratic leadership as political despair, economic woe, and spiritual malaise remained unchallenged. This negative characterization of Democratic leadership contextualized the debate in two important ways. First, the two strongest statements criticizing the Carter-Mondale term in office occurred in the first and last exchanges of the debate. In both instances, the image of malaise was never challenged by Ferraro—either as being false or irrelevant to the Mondale-Ferraro ticket. This framed the Democratic ticket, and Ferraro as its representative, in a most undesirable way. Second, Bush reinforced that frame of reference for the audience in the closing statement when he stated, "And the choice is, do we move forward with strength and with prosperity, or do we go back to weakness, despair, disrespect?" Obviously, no member of the political community would choose weakness, despair, and disrespect. Since Ferraro never countered this general impression of the Carter-Mondale administration, nor effectively created a distinct political identity apart from the legacy of Democratic malaise under which Mondale labored throughout the campaign, the desirability of the Democratic ticket was in serious question.

Ferraro's Strongest Moment

Bush made his most serious mistakes in the course of his rebuttal on the issue of terrorism in exchange five. First, he misrepresented Ferraro's position on covert activities, asserting that he "heard Mrs. Ferraro say that she would do away with all covert action." That was not Ferraro's position, and her rebuttal noted that error. Second, Bush invoked a patronizing attitude toward Ferraro when he said, "But let me help you with the difference, Ms. Ferraro, between Iran and the Embassy in Lebanon." Ferraro needed no help and chastized Bush for his patronizing attitude. Third, Bush then asserted, incorrectly, that "our two opponents have, [suggested] that these men [the marines serving in Lebanon when the terrorists attacked] died in shame—they better not tell the parents of those young marines. They gave peace a chance." Ferraro rebuked Bush on all three counts:

Let me just say, first of all, that I almost resent, Vice President Bush, your patronizing attitude that you have to teach me about foreign policy. I've been a member of Congress for six years. I was there when the Embassy was held hostage in Iran, and I have been there, and I've seen what has happened in the past several months: 17 months of your administration. Secondly, please don't categorize my answers either. Leave the interpretation of my answers to the American people who are watching this debate. And let me say further that no one has ever said that those young men who were killed—through the negligence of this administration and others—ever died in shame. No one who has a child who is nineteen or twenty years old—a son—would ever say that about the loss of anybody else's child.

This exchange reestablished a relationship of equality between the two candidates, and Ferraro demonstrated that she could hold her own against a male advocate.[17] Although one could argue that the rebuttals revealed Ferraro's superiority over Bush—given the fact that Bush had erred so thoroughly in his rebuttal and that Ferraro's refutation was so devastating—the impact of this exchange was limited to defining the relationship between Ferraro and Bush. Although Ferraro proved herself to be a competent advocate in the sense that she prevented Bush from asserting a superior-subordinate relationship with her in the area of foreign policy, her answer did not contribute to the larger, more important task of defending the Mondale-Ferraro vision of leadership.

Ferraro's Qualifications for Office

One of Ferraro's goals was to demonstrate that women could function as competent candidates for national office. She demonstrated her qualifications in four instances in the debate. In the first exchange, she presented herself as a rational, analytical, decision maker when asked how her experience stacked up to Bush's: "If one has taken a look at my career, they'll [see] that I level with the people, that I approach problems analytically, that I am able to assess the various facts with reference to a problem, and I can make hard decisions." On the separation of church and state, Ferraro revealed her understanding of a fundamental principle on which the nation was founded when she stated: "If you go back to the 1600s when people came here, the reason they came to this country was to escape religious persecution." She also stated that the same was true in the 1940s and 1980s, noting that "our country is founded on the principle that our government should be neutral as far as religion is concerned."

In the follow-up question, Quarles asked Ferraro if she thought that the Catholic church was treating her unfairly over her stand on the issue of abortion. Here Ferraro answered in personal terms clearly distinguishing between her private beliefs as dictated by the Catholic church and her obligations as a public official. More importantly, she indicated that if she found that her private beliefs interfered with her role as a public official, she would resign. This position suggested that she understood the importance of separating church and state and communicated her commitment to that fundamental principle as a candidate for public office.

Ferraro gave evidence that she understood the risks inherent in the use of military force in response to the question concerning what circumstances would justify the use of American combat forces in Central America: "I would advocate the use of force when it was necessary to protect the security of our country, protect our security interest or protect our people or protect the interests of friends and neighbors." Additionally, Ferraro indicated that the course of action that she and Mondale would pursue in Central America would be negotiation with the use of force as a last resort—a position that reflected an awareness of the serious risks involved in introducing United States military forces into any region of the world.

Finally, in the last exchange concerning whether the Soviet Union would take advantage of her because she was a woman, many media commentators extracted Ferraro's statement indicating that "if the Soviet Union were to ever believe that they could challenge the United States with any sort of nuclear forces or otherwise—if I were in a position of leadership in this country, they would be assured that they would be met with swift, concise, and certain retaliation." But the part of her answer that was more revealing of her leadership skills was her conclusion when she stated: "The most important thing, though, I think, as a leader, that what one has to do, is get to the point where you're not put into that position. And the way you get to that position of moving away from having to make a decision—on force or anything else—is by moving toward arms control." Even though Ferraro advocated what might be considered a controversial solution to the problem of avoiding nuclear confrontation, her initial response reflected a style of proactive leadership, of looking ahead to anticipate where or how problems might arise and then taking action before such circumstances escalated into a crisis.

In these exchanges, Ferraro described her approach to problems as analytical, revealed her understanding and commitment to the fundamental principle of separation of church and state, explained under what circumstances U.S. military forces should be used in Central America, and displayed a proactive style of leadership in heading off potential threats to national security. On these grounds, Ferraro appeared qualified for the vice presidency.

Drawing Conclusions as a Dimension of Leadership: Ferraro as Teacher Versus Ferraro as Political Leader

Despite the strong performance on leadership issues in domestic and foreign affairs, Ferraro's refutational skills lacked an incisive and direct style necessary to illustrate the weaknesses in Bush's answers. In her rebuttal in the first exchange, Ferraro had the correct statistics to refute Bush's claim that the Reagan administration had done a better job on the economy than Carter and Mondale had. However, after correcting Bush's statistics, Ferraro failed to state directly that Bush was wrong, that the Reagan administration was far less effective than the Carter-Mondale administration had been on job creation, interest rates for home loans, and economic opportunity for the poor, and that given a comparison of the two administrations, a rational audience would prefer the Carter-Mondale administration because of its more desirable track record on economic issues. Instead, Ferraro concluded her rebuttal by saying that "you can walk around saying things are great, and that's what we're going to be hearing. We've been hearing that on those commercials for the past couple of months. I expect they expect the American people to believe that. I'll become a one-woman truth squad, and we'll start tonight." The problem with Ferraro's position is that she never directly stated what the truth was. Correcting Bush's statistics without explaining how that altered the truth value of his claim left the counterargument incomplete. After Ferraro's rebuttal, the audience is left to its own knowledge of the issues to tell it what was true. In this respect, Ferraro missed an important opportunity to create doubt about Bush's claim that the Reagan administration had delivered four years of prosperity.

In the second exchange when Bush defended the Reagan administration's record on helping the poor and minorities, Ferraro corrected Bush's facts but again failed to assess the implications for the vice president's claim. Ferraro's language choices in this rebuttal suggested an image of a teacher correcting minor errors in a student's work:

The vice president indicates that the president signed the Voting Rights Act....
he did not support it while it was in the Congress, in the Senate. It was passed
despite his opposition, and he did sign it because he was required to do so. In
the civil rights cases that he mentioned, the great number of cases that they
have enforced, the reason they enforced them is because under the law they're
required to do that—and I'm delighted that the administration is following the
law.... I just have to correct, in my thirty seconds that are left, the comment
that the vice president made with reference specifically to a program like the
AFDC. If you take AFDC, if you take food stamps, if you take, oh, go down
the line on poor people's programs, those are the programs that suffered considerably under this administration's first budget cuts, and those are the ones
that, in the second part of their term—we were able to restore some of those
terribly, terribly unfair cuts to the poor of this country.

Ferraro never evaluated Bush's inability to use correct facts, nor did she
explain the implications of her interpretation of the facts. Ferraro needed
to state directly that all of Bush's claims were true only because of the
efforts of the Democratic party and that if Reagan had had his way, all
of these programs would have been eliminated. Again, this crucial aspect
of reconstituting Bush's claims in terms that were more favorable for
her view of the issues remained undeveloped.

Ferraro's refutational skills reflected a similar degree of unfulfilled
form in her initial answer to John Mashek's question on terrorism. In
her answer, Ferraro criticized Reagan for taking the position that the
United States would stand tall against terrorism but then failed to act
after three terrorist attacks on U.S. positions in the Middle East. This
was a valid criticism of the Reagan administration's inability to act with
some warning of imminent attack, but Ferraro's answer was an inconcise
ramble, ultimately leaving the audience more impatient with her inability
to make her point rather than with Reagan's inability to counter terrorist
threats.

In the exchange over Central America, Jack White asked Bush "if it
was right for the United States to be involved in mining the harbors of
Nicaragua, a country we're not at war with, and to subsequently refuse
the World Court to adjudicate that dispute and the complaint from
Nicaragua?" This was a tough question for Bush and, in fact, he sidestepped it by indicating that he supported what the United States did,
thought that it was supported by Congress and the law, but never
answered if it was right to mine the harbors of a country with which
we were not at war. This was a significant opportunity for Ferraro, and
in her rebuttal she did refute Bush's statement by saying "I did not
support the mining of the harbors in Nicaragua. It is a violation of
international law. Congress did not support it, and, as a matter of fact,
just this week the Congress voted to cut off covert aid to Nicaragua
unless and until a request is made and there is evidence of need for it

and the Congress approves it again in March." Again, however, the judgment of Bush's position given Ferraro's data was never developed. If what Ferraro said was true, then she should have pressed the attack one step further and argued that the Reagan administration, despite having what some would view as an admirable goal, had violated international law, subverted the process of Congressional oversight, and attempted to destabilize the government of a country with which we were not at war. Ferraro needed to explain that whether one supported the contra "freedom fighters" was irrelevant to the more fundamental question of U.S. conduct in foreign affairs, and that if the Reagan administration was disobeying national and international law, such actions constituted good reason for change.

Finally, in the last exchange before the closing statements, Ferraro missed two opportunities to challenge Bush. First, when asked if she had a question for her foe, she indicated that she did not have a single most important question she wanted to put to Bush. This revealed that Ferraro lacked a single, critical issue that could crystallize Bush's greatest weakness for the audience. Instead, Ferraro asked for "a commitment that pretty soon they're going to do something about making this a safer world for all of us," a rather bland attempt to focus an objection to the Republican ticket. Second, when Bush described the choice in the campaign as being between the failed ideas of the past and the prosperity of the Reagan administration, again, Ferraro presented evidence to support the claim that the Carter administration had achieved more than the Reagan administration but failed to state that conclusion in direct terms for her audience.

In all of these exchanges, Ferraro's ability to refute Bush's claims and reconstitute an understanding of the last eight years in more favorable terms for her ticket was seriously lacking. Had Ferraro been more effective in developing the implications of her data and in directly refuting Bush's claims concerning the records of the Carter and Reagan administrations, reactions to the debate might have been different. But because Bush was able to maintain two illusions—that the Carter-Mondale administration had been one of malaise and that the Reagan administration had delivered peace and prosperity, the Republican ticket appeared more desirable than it actually was. Both of these understandings were suspect given Ferraro's more accurate command of the facts. But by not developing a coherent and persuasive interpretation of those facts capable of directly challenging the opposing party's understanding of the past eight years, the audience was left with the impression that Bush represented a ticket that could deliver peace and prosperity. In contrast, and by implication, it appeared as though Ferraro represented a party that had failed in the past and offered little hope for the immediate future.

The analysis of Ferraro's refutational skills revealed that her command of the facts was insufficient to challenge Bush's defense of the Reagan administration. In all of the examples presented here, Ferraro appeared to be correcting Bush in the same manner as a teacher might correct a student.[18] But instead of simply presenting the correct information, Ferraro needed to illustrate how one would draw dramatically different conclusions about the past eight years, conclusions that would yield favorable judgments of Democratic leadership and unfavorable judgments of Republican leadership. In this sense, the key element that would have defined effective leadership in this debate would have been Ferraro's judgment and interpretation of the last eight years. Instead, despite the fact that Bush used whatever he thought the facts were to formulate his own judgments and interpretation of the facts, the important difference was that he used his facts to develop his political judgments and interpretations for the audience. Thus, the ability to develop plausible evaluations and coherent interpretations of the facts in a political debate appeared to be defining characteristics of appealing leadership.

The Closing Statements

Bush's closing statement, as already noted, reinforced a particularly favorable framework for evaluating the Republican ticket: Should we move forward with strength and prosperity, or return to weakness and despair? Having framed the decision for the audience in this way, Bush returned to praising Reagan and then, by contrast, portraying Mondale as a potential mistake for the nation. After framing the decision and then sketching briefly what the audience might expect under each option, Bush attempted to identify with all young Americans "who have a dream," and also to identify with all those Americans who remembered war. The range of his appeal was wide in scope, suggesting that he was a candidate who represented much of what we saw in ourselves. Bush concluded by appealing to our sense of closure, our need to finish something that we had begun in earnest when he stated, "Now we do have some unfinished business. We must continue to go ahead." The portrayal of the past as "vacillation and weakness" reinforced yet again the negative image of the Democratic ethos. And, finally, Bush closed by directing our attention somewhere ahead of us in time and above our present place. The image of bright, upward progress toward "America's greatest dreams" suggested a divinely ordained destiny and closed the debate nicely on the most positive terms describing the Republican ticket. In these respects, Bush's closing statement condensed the most essential aspects of the Republican vision for the audience in an efficient, appealing, and persuasive lens for the audience to view both the debate and the campaign.

Ferraro's closing statement began awkwardly but developed an extremely powerful theme of patriotism, a theme that redefined what it meant to be an American, and one that directly challenged the political identity that the Reagan administration had been attempting to develop in its national television advertisements.[19] When it was her turn to begin, she stated "I hope somebody wants to applaud," communicating an odd sense of insecurity, as though no one would support her or the values she represented. She then indicated the values that she and Mondale stood for—fairness and equality—but these values by themselves were insufficient to counter Bush's characterization of them as weak and despairing. From this point, however, the character of the closing statement began to change dramatically. Ferraro began to present as examples individuals whom she had met with over the past two months of the campaign. She used each of the examples to present a different problem that confronted ordinary citizens. But the problems were not limited to these few families. As Ferraro continued her report, one could feel the sense of identification developing between one's self and the people she had spoken with, as well as the realization that despite what Bush had been arguing, there were several problems threatening the well-being of the nation.

Over the last two months, I've been traveling all over the country, talking to people about the future. I was in Kentucky and I spoke to the Dyhouse family. He works for a car dealer, and he's worried about the deficits and how high interest rates are going to affect his job. Every place I go, I see young parents with their children, and they say to me, "what are we going to do to stop this nuclear arms race?" I was in Dayton, Ohio, a week and a half ago, and I sat with the Allen family, who live next door to a toxic dump, and they're very, very concerned about the fact that those toxics are seeping into the water that they and their neighbors drink.

The specifically named families communicated a sense of intimacy that Ferraro appeared to share with the nation. The fact that she named the families, remembered where they worked, and when she visited them reinforced a sense of genuine contact as well as concern with their needs, an impression that could not be communicated through a message manufactured for the ostensible purpose of persuading the audience to believe in a candidate who had campaigned with less than total commitment to the people. This sense of intimacy, once established, set up Ferraro's next move, which was to redefine patriotism, from the "feel good" invocation of cultural symbols displayed in the Republican TV advertisements to a concept of patriotism that was, in her words, "not only a pride in the country as it is, but a pride in this country that is strong enough to meet the challenges of the future." Ferraro's concept of patriotism, then, deflected the Republican characterization of the concept as a reaction to cultural symbols and defined the concept in terms of a reflective, rather than a reactive, ability. By sizing up the challenges facing the nation and moving to face those challenges before they can threaten the well-being of the national community, Americans demonstrated their patriotism. And that was what Ferraro did in the next section of the closing statement:

Do you know, when we find jobs for the 8.5 million people who are unemployed in this country, you know we'll make our economy stronger, and that will be a patriotic act. When we reduce the deficits, we cut interest rates. And I know the president doesn't believe that, but it's so—we cut those interest rates— young people can buy houses. That's pro-family. And that will be a patriotic act. When we educate our children—good Lord, they're going to be able to compete in a world economy, and that makes us stronger and that's a patriotic act. When we stop the arms race, we make this a safer, saner world, and that's a patriotic act. And when we keep the peace, young men don't die, and that's a patriotic act.

In sizing up the challenges that faced the nation, Ferraro enacted a form of patriotism that was distinct from and superior to the type of patriotism being peddled by the Reagan administration. Thus, the closing statement portrayed her as a candidate with a sincere, genuine concern for the nation as well as a candidate who could identify shallow, self-serving ploys to seduce the electorate into accepting a less desirable political identity for themselves.

After arguing that Mondale was the key to the nation's future, Ferraro concluded with a promise to continue the fight. The overall effect was dramatic. In this short speech, Ferraro had seized the underlying premise of the Republican campaign theme and redefined it to fit the Democratic party's interpretation of the last four years. She had articulated a concept of patriotism that was at once consistent with what the Republicans believed but sublimated their reactive impulse in favor of a more reflective attitude toward the nation's circumstances, an attitude that was capable of stimulating critical appraisal of the conditions in the nation. And if Ferraro could direct the nation's attention to a reflective appraisal of the nation's problems, she could then control the lens through which the voters evaluated the desirability of the candidates.

The last two sentences of the closing statement contained, potentially, substantial emotional impact. Mondale and Ferraro's position in the polls at this point in the campaign, in spite of Mondale's strong showing against Reagan in the first debate, revealed what some experts might have described as an almost impossible situation from which they could recover. Moreover, as I have argued above, Bush, for the most part, dominated this debate. Yet in the closing moments of the debate, Ferraro demonstrated her ability to strike at the heart of the Republican campaign. The text of the debate revealed two Ferraros in this debate: one who posed no threat to Bush and whose words in this debate were easily dismissed as mere "corrections," and another, who, after taking as many rhetorical hits in the course of the debate, suddenly became transformed into an advocate who could initiate devastating strikes at will. Thus, when Ferraro closed by saying, "This campaign is not over. For our country, for our future, for the principles we believe in, Walter Mondale and I have just begun to fight," she struck a chord of hope for Democratic supporters and revealed that she was capable of transforming the Democratic ticket into a viable, rhetorically competitive vision of leadership. Ferraro's closing statement, then, refuted the perception of Democratic leadership as "malaise." Only a strong and resourceful leader could muster a viable strategy when the future seemed in doubt. And because Ferraro's closing statement enacted a dynamic image of leadership, her resolve to pursue her principles despite overwhelming odds against her inspired her supporters to recommit themselves to the fight.[20]

Summary of Findings in the 1984 Vice Presidential Debate

Potentially, the vice presidential debate could have altered the outcome of the campaign. At least, Democratic strategists thought this to be the case. Before the debate, the *Washington Post* reported that "Geraldine A. Ferraro today began preparing in earnest for the Thursday night debate against Vice President Bush, with Democratic strategists now convinced that the stakes in the Philadelphia face off have increased dramatically."[21] Additionally, the *New York Times* noted: "Strategists on both sides say that while the election will turn on Presidential preferences, the outcome of the first and only Vice-Presidential debate of the 1984 campaign could further alter the dynamics of the race at a time when some voters, could be ready to reassess their feelings toward President Reagan and his Democratic challenger, Walter F. Mondale."[22] Just a day later, the *New York Times* indicated, that "in the view of both Democratic and Republican strategists, the ultimate reaction to the Vice-Presidential debate may play a substantial role in determining the pace and tone of the Presidential contest."[23] And in the days following the debate, both Mondale and Ferraro attempted to focus the public's attention on the debates as signs of weakness in Republican leadership.[24]

The dramatic impact anticipated by both Republican and Democratic strategists was tempered, however, by the uneven performances of the debaters and by the substantially different objectives each debater brought to the debate. *Time* magazine said that "Bush provided a helping hand to Reagan in one of the few moments of his presidency when he needed it."[25] *Newsweek* too had a similar impression of Bush's defense of the Republican ticket: "After Ronald Reagan's listlessness in Louisville, Republicans had reason to be buoyed by Bush's perkiness—especially his command of administration foreign policy. And on domestic issues he presented the Reagan case far more clearly than had the President himself."[26] Perhaps the most crucial element of Bush's performance was his attempt to restore some measure of confidence in Reagan's leadership, prompting Howell Raines to observe that "for Mr. Bush, the motif of his performance was his defense of Mr. Reagan, which seemed designed to counter charges that Mr. Reagan might be getting too old for his job and had a shaky hold on complex subjects such as arms control and relations with the Soviet Union."[27] Also, according to Jack Germond and Jules Witcover, Bush was able to divert attention from Reagan's age issue.[28] Certainly, the analysis of the text revealed several instances in which Bush defended Reagan's abilities as a leader. In a different vein, however, *Newsweek* suggested that Bush's performance only called attention to the fact that Reagan appeared to be disengaged from the day-to-day activities of managing the country and only served to raise the stakes for the second presidential debate.[29]

Ferraro's impact was beneficial to the Democratic ticket. According to *Newsweek*, "While she did not dominate the debate as Democrats had hoped, Ferraro did nothing to jeopardize Mondale's momentum."[30] Despite the fact that polls indicated that the public viewed Bush as the winner, the *Washington Post* interview of Peter Hart revealed that Ferraro helped the Democratic ticket more than Bush helped his: "You had two winners. Bush's positives are up 9 points. Ferraro's are up 13 points and her negatives are down 10. She may have boosted the ticket a bit more than he (Bush) did."[31] In more positive terms, Democratic consultant Robert Squier "argued that Ferraro had made a breakthrough. 'She is now in a position to project herself to all voters and especially women voters,' he said. 'Women are reluctant to offer their votes to a woman until she has proved she will not embarrass them. We're at that point.' "[32] But overall, the debate did not seem to have altered the campaign in ways that some of the strategists had predicted. Some commented that the debate was a draw in the sense that there was no clear reason for preferring one candidate over another.[33] *Newsweek* reported that "there was scant evidence that the veepstakes sweepstakes profoundly altered the dynamics of the presidential race. A CBS/*New York Times* poll found that the debate verdicts closely correlated with the presidential preferences of those surveyed."[34] According to the *Washington Post*, "The judgment of many political professionals was that the vice-presidential debate will not have much impact on the outcome of the Nov. 6 election."[35] And, as the *Washington Post* put it on October 12, "Both managed to do basically what they had set out to do. Ferraro managed to hold the stage with Bush and, to that extent at least, show that she was not out of her league. And Bush managed to be firm and aggressive without ever beating up on the lady. With that result, chances are that the spotlight will shift quickly back to Mondale and Reagan."[36]

The reason for this lack of dramatic impact on the presidential campaign might be found in the analysis of the text. As I have argued, Ferraro needed to go beyond "correcting" her opponent's facts to the point at which she assessed the implications of his errors. Ferraro needed to draw conclusions for her audience and reinterpret the facts of the debate to present an alternative vision of leadership. And that alternative vision of leadership needed to be as coherent and persuasive as her closing statement. The ability to make sound judgments, to draw appropriate conclusions from a set of facts, then, was found to be an important dimension of political leadership lacking in the language choices of Ferraro in the 1984 vice presidential debate. Perhaps it was because of these shortcomings in her ability to refute the Republican vision of leadership that political commentators have focused more on Ferraro's impact as the first female candidate for high office.

Instead of altering the course of the campaign, then, the debate had more impact for the political image of the debaters. As for Bush, "He appeared to have avoided the kind of upstaging by Ferraro that Reagan suffered at Mondale's hands in Louisville. Such an event would not only have compounded Republican problems in holding the lead in the election but clouded Bush's chances of gaining the presidential nomination in 1988."[37] As for Ferraro, "Her credible performance quieted critics who had doubted whether Ferraro—or any women—had the experience, depth and temperament to hold high office. Ferraro took pains to defuse the nervous Nellie factor; the prejudice that a woman would not be tough enough to handle foreign policy."[38]

In conclusion, the analysis of the text reveals that the vice presidential candidates were called upon to function in dual roles—as an advocate for the presidential ticket and as an advocate defending their own qualifications for office. Although Bush's defense of Reagan's leadership abilities was vulnerable to attack, the analysis of the text reveals the ways in which Ferraro's refutation skills failed to develop coherent objections to the Republican program. But although Bush's qualifications for high office were never in doubt, Ferraro's were. Examination of the text reveals that Ferraro proved that she was qualified for high office given her knowledge of fundamental principles of leadership, her ability to stand up to Bush when he attempted to patronize her, and her ability to develop an appealing vision of patriotism in the closing statement. In these ways, despite drawbacks in both performances, the need to fulfill dual objectives of defending one's self and one's party suggests that both candidates can be judged to have been successful. Defending the ticket became Bush's primary objective; defending herself as a credible candidate for high office became Ferraro's primary objective. Had either candidate been able to integrate these two objectives in a more effective way, the debate might not have been regarded as a draw, and its impact on the presidential campaign might have been more noteworthy.

THE 1988 VICE PRESIDENTIAL DEBATE: LLOYD BENTSEN VERSUS DAN QUAYLE

The most significant issue in this debate concerned doubts about Dan Quayle's ability to lead. This became evident when four of the panel's questions were devoted to discovering what Quayle would do if he became president. Although these questions were hypothetical in nature, they related directly to the nation's doubts about Quayle's competence as a potential president. The most important aspect of the debate, then, concerned Quayle's ability to remove doubts about his competence to serve as president if the time came for him to step into office.[39] The analysis of the debate demonstrates that Quayle's ability to attack the Democratic candidates and defend the Republican ticket was evident but quite limited.[40] Although this ability was not present as a characteristic pattern throughout the debate, it did suggest that Quayle's rhetorical qualifications for office were sufficient enough to demonstrate that he had a fundamental understanding of the values and policy he and George Bush represented.[41] In this respect, I argue that Quayle's performance, even though less desirable than Lloyd Bentsen's, failed to constitute a controversy sufficiently serious enough to cast doubt on Bush's decision to place him on the ticket.[42]

Is Dan Quayle Presidential Material?

Doubts about Quayle's presidential competence were raised in the first, eighth, thirteenth, and seventeenth questions asked by the panel. Quayle's answer to these four questions created the most doubt about his ability to serve as president. Even though Jon Margolis asked a question late in the debate concerning Quayle's character and suggested that Quayle had engaged in "overstatement and exaggeration" and was not "forthcoming" about his summer jobs in college, his grades, and his coauthor of the Job Training Partnership Act, Quayle's answer defused doubts about his trustworthiness when he explained who the coauthor of the Job Training Partnership Act was and why he still claimed credit for that legislation. Because competence, not trustworthiness, was the central issue for Quayle in this debate, the analysis focuses on the four exchanges that asked Quayle to explain what he would do if he became president.

The first question from Judy Woodruff asked Quayle to respond to doubts issued from within his own party: "Just last week former Secretary of State Haig said that your pick was the dumbest call George Bush could have made. Your leader in the Senate . . . Bob Dole said that a better qualified person could have been chosen. Other Republicans have been far more critical in private. Why do you think that you have not made a more substantial impression on some of these people who have been able to observe you up close?"

Quayle did not directly address the question but answered by interpreting the question as one concerned with qualifications for the vice presidency and the presidency: "The question goes to whether I am qualified to be vice president, and in the case of a tragedy, whether I'm qualified to be president." After defining the issue in terms of qualifications, Quayle presented his qualifications along the lines of three issues: national security and arms control, jobs and education, and the federal budget deficit. Quayle concluded his answer by asserting that Bush had more qualifications than Dukakis and Bentsen combined.

Although this can be considered a good answer in that it outlined Quayle's qualifications, he failed to explain why these particular credentials did not impress those who, in Woodruff's words, "have been able to observe [him] up close." By failing to respond to Republican doubts suggested in Tom Brokaw's question, Quayle's answer left the impression that both Republicans and Democrats doubted his ability. Dramatically, then, after only the first question, doubts about Quayle's abilities had widened to include members of his own party.

Bentsen argued in his response that the debate was not about qualifications for the vice presidency but the presidency. After referring to Woodruff's statement that the vice president has a fifty-fifty chance of assuming office, he concluded his answer by saying: "Now, the debate tonight is a debate about the presidency itself, and a presidential decision that has to be made by you. The stakes could not be higher." Although this frame of reference was more favorable for Bentsen given his greater experience, it created a difficult comparison for the audience. Even if the audience had decided that it liked Bentsen better than Bush at the end of this debate, it would still, at best, get Dukakis if it voted Democratic. For Bentsen to convince the audience that a Democratic ballot was in order, he would have to perform so skillfully that Quayle would appear completely unfit for the office.

Brit Hume's question in the eighth exchange brought up the issue of competence in an even more direct way. Hume pursued the issue by saying, "I want to take you back if I can to the question Judy asked you about some of the apprehensions people may feel about your being a heartbeat away from the presidency. And let us assume if we can for the sake of this question that you become vice president and the president is incapacitated for one reason or another, and you have to take the reins of power. When that moment came, what would be the first steps you'd take, and why?"

Quayle answered by saying that he would first say a prayer and then assemble Bush's people and talk. This first part of the answer was appealing because it showed a degree of humility and respect for the office and it showed that Quayle would base his first decision as president on dialogue with Bush's people. In this sense, Quayle reassured the audience that his actions would not depart radically from the direction set by the Bush administration. But Quayle abruptly shifted the answer back to his original response to Woodruff's question, arguing that it was a question about qualifications: "And I think this question keeps going back to the qualifications and what kind of a vice president in this hypothetical situation, if I had to assume the responsibilities of president, what I would be." From here, Quayle replayed his argument that he had served successfully in Congress for twelve years but added that he had made a difference and that he had more experience on the three issues of national security, jobs and education, and the budget deficit than Dukakis did. Although Quayle's strategy of developing a comparison between his qualifications and Dukakis' is potentially persuasive, his answer did not address the problem posed by the question, specifically, what can we expect Quayle to do if he became president. In this second opportunity to solve his rhetorical problem, then, Quayle failed to provide a satisfactory response to the hypothetical question on everyone's mind: Can Quayle be entrusted with the office of the Presidency?

In the thirteenth question of the debate, Hume came back to the issue: "Senator, I want to take you back to the question that I asked you earlier about what would happen if you were to take over in an emergency, and what you would do first and why. You said you would say a prayer, and you said something about a meeting. What would you do next?" This question underscored Quayle's rather limited understanding of what would be required of him if he were to assume the presidency. Quayle sidestepped the issue by asserting that it was not proper for him to "get into the specifics of a hypothetical situation like that." Then, Quayle again returned to his argument that his twelve years of experience qualified him to serve as president. Again, Quayle's qualifications did not directly address doubts about his future actions.

In failing to reveal a deeper understanding of what would be required of him to fulfill the duties of the presidency, Quayle left the panel unsatisfied. So Brokaw followed up on Hume's second attempt to discover what Quayle would do if he became president: "Senator Quayle, I don't mean to beat this drum until it has no more sound in it. But to

follow-up on Brit Hume's question, when you said that it was a hypothetical situation, it is, sir, after all, the reason that we're here tonight,
because you are running not just for the vice president. And if you cite
the experience you had in Congress, surely you must have some plan
in mind about what you would do if it fell to you to become president
of the United States, as it has to so many vice presidents just in the last
25 years or so."

Brokaw's question defined the issue for Quayle most precisely. The
question was, should he assume office, what was Quayle's vision of leadership for the nation. Each of Quayle's previous answers had tried to interpret the question in terms of qualifications for office. But this final
version of the question asked Quayle to reveal his personal vision of leadership for the country. Quayle's strategy, then, to defend himself in
terms of his qualifications, failed to reveal a personalized vision of leadership. And although Quayle's answer to Brokaw's question gave the audience a better sense of how Quayle would function within the Bush
administration, and thus be prepared to step into the presidency, the
strategy of presenting his qualifications ultimately led him to compare
himself to John F. Kennedy in the conclusion of his answer: "I have far more
experience than many others that sought the office of vice president of this
country. I have as much experience in the Congress as Jack Kennedy did
when he sought the presidency. I will be prepared to deal with the people
in the Bush administration, if that unfortunate event would ever occur."

In each of the previous questions to Quayle about what he would do
if he became president, Bentsen had never criticized Quayle's qualifications. Instead, Bentsen had simply suggested that it was a question
of maturity and breadth of experience. So when Quayle compared himself to Kennedy, the standard of measure became not the number of
years in Congress, but the character and vision of leadership Quayle
could offer. When Quayle compared himself to Kennedy, he set himself
up for Bentsen's dramatic rebuttal: "Senator, I served with Jack Kennedy, I knew Jack Kennedy, Jack Kennedy was a friend of mine. Senator,
you are no Jack Kennedy."

This moment defined the essential difference between the two candidates and fulfilled the audience's expectation that Quayle would somehow be unmasked as the weak candidate that many claimed him to be.
And Quayle's response, "That was really uncalled for, Senator," not
only highlighted the fact that Bentsen had put him in his place, but gave
Bentsen the opportunity to explain why his rebuke was justified: "You
are the one that was making the comparison, Senator—and I'm one who
knew him well. And frankly I think that you're so far apart in the objectives you choose for your country that I did not think the comparison was
well taken." Although Quayle's comparison might have been factually
true, Quayle's decision to compare himself to Kennedy was risky given

the audience's image of Kennedy as a dynamic and competent leader and given the fact that Bentsen would be one of the few individuals with the age, maturity, and personal experience to directly refute the comparison. In the end, if the comparison to Kennedy was not "well taken," and if Quayle could not persuade the audience that he knew what to do or explain what he would do if he became president, there was no reason to think of Quayle as presidential material.[43]

Bentsen's Defense of the Democratic Presidential Ticket

In addition to the fact that Bentsen refuted Quayle's comparison of himself with John F. Kennedy and that Quayle's explanation of what he would do if he became president was unsatisfactory for the panelists, Bentsen demonstrated his ability to defend the Democratic ticket in the fourth, eleventh, and twelfth exchanges.

The fourth exchange constituted a good comparison between Quayle's and Bentsen's abilities to attack the opposition while defending their tickets. Margolis asked Quayle if he considered himself to be an environmentalist given his record of "voting against environmental protection legislation about two-thirds of the time." Initially, Quayle's answer reflected a skillful response to the question from Margolis. Structurally, Quayle's answer did three things: It answered criticisms of his environmental record, it praised the Reagan administration's efforts to reduce ozone depletion, and it attacked Dukakis' image as an environmentalist. Despite these initial points, Quayle's answer was vulnerable on several grounds. Although he claimed that he had "a very strong record on the environment in the United States Senate," he was able to offer only two examples of supporting environmental legislation—the Superfund and the Clean Water Act. Bentsen's answer refuted Quayle's facts and was able to claim a more favorable environmental image when he stated:

This late conversion [by Quayle to environmentalism] is interesting to me. I must say, when they talk about Boston Harbor and he [Quayle] says he [Dukakis] hasn't done anything, the facts are he has a $6 billion program under way on waste treatment. And it was this administration—their administration—that cut out the money early on to be able to clean up water, and made it impossible to move ahead at that time on Boston Harbor. We are the authors, the Democratic Party, of Clean Air, of Clean Water, of the superfund. I am one who has played a very major role in passing the superfund legislation. And every environmental organization that I know—every major one—has now endorsed the Dukakis-Bentsen ticket. And I am one who has just received the environmental award in Texas for the work I've done to clean up the bays, to clean up the water, off the coast of Texas. No, I think we know well who's going to clean up this environment.

Bentsen's answer defended Dukakis with "the facts," placed the blame for Boston Harbor on the Reagan administration, claimed the Democratic Party as the party of leadership on environmental legislation, noted how environmental organizations had endorsed the Dukakis-Bentsen ticket, and announced that he had won an award for his environmental activities in Texas. Comparatively, Quayle did not appear to offer a credible commitment to the environment. He failed to refute the facts in Margolis' question indicating a record of opposition to environmental legislation, he could not claim the endorsement of a single environmental organization but Dukakis and Bentsen could, and he could not claim leadership on any major piece of legislation while Bentsen could claim not only leadership and an award for his work, but also the leadership of the Democratic Party on environmental issues.

Brokaw's question in the eleventh exchange constituted an important opportunity for Bentsen to explain why the American public should vote Democratic. Brokaw asked why the public should vote Democratic if the Republicans had achieved lower interest rates, lower unemployment, lower inflation, and arms control with the Soviet Union. Bentsen attacked the Republican administration on the grounds that it had written "$200 billion worth of hot checks every year," and that he too could create an illusion of prosperity if you allowed him to do that. Quayle's response was disappointing in the sense that it did not defend the Reagan administration against the charge of "writing bad checks." Instead, Quayle attacked Dukakis for increasing debt in Massachusetts but failed to provide any support for his claim. Although Quayle restated the accomplishments of the Reagan administration, he ignored the argument that it was based on an illusion of prosperity. In these respects, Quayle's ability to represent and defend the Republican ticket on the state of the economy seemed less adequate than Bentsen's defense of the Democratic ticket.

In the following exchange, Brokaw asked Quayle if he would be in favor of using the military to go after South American drug cartels since he had been in favor of the Reagan administration's use of force in Grenada. The question provided a good test of Quayle's thinking skills because it compared the two purposes behind the use of military force and concluded that the use of force seemed more justified in the case of fighting drugs, a problem that Quayle acknowledged was "the number one issue in this country." However, the question also contained a potential pratfall for Quayle. If, as a vice presidential candidate, he advocated the use of military force, he might appear as though he was stepping outside the bounds of his role and advocating a policy Bush would be unwilling to support. Furthermore, unless Quayle could provide good reasons relating to issues of national security, advocating the use of military force might reveal that

Quayle was unqualified to serve as president because of his willingness to use military force when it appeared unjustified.

The first part of Quayle's answer to the question described the role of the military in terms of "a coordinated effort, in reconnaisance" and Quayle stated that he did not "believe that we are going to turn the Department of Defense into a police organization." After he related some of the administration's successes in stopping the flow of drugs into the country, Quayle's answer became confusing in substance:

And it's heading up the effort to try and create a drug-free America, which is a challenge and a goal of all of us. Not only will we utilize national defense and the Department of Defense, but we've got to get on the demand side of the ledger; we've got to get to education. And education ought to begin at home, and it ought to be reinforced—reinforced in our schools. And there's another thing that will be more important than the premise of this question on a hypothetical of using troops. We will use the military assets,—we will use military assets—but we need to focus on another part of this problem, and that problem is law enforcement.

After telling the audience that we would not turn the military into a police force, Quayle indicated that we would "use the military assets" and then said that we were not going to, and then shifted back again to the position that we would use military assets. Based on his answer, it was unclear whether he would be in favor of using the military to fight against South American drug cartels, or if he were in favor of such a policy, what the nature of that action would entail. Also, Bentsen's ironic tone undercut Quayle's commitment to fight drugs:

It's interesting to see that the senator from Indiana, when we had a resolution on the floor of the United States Senate sponsored by Senator Dole, that this government would make no deal with Noriega—that the senator from Indiana was one of the dozen senators that voted against it. It's also interesting to see that one of his campaign managers that's trying to help him with his image was also hired by Noriega to help him with his image in Panama.

These two observations by Bentsen questioned Quayle's commitment to fight against South American drug suppliers and suggested that Quayle's image had somehow been "manufactured" by a campaign manager. Both points created doubt about Quayle's image as a candidate committed to the fight against drugs and as a candidate capable of carrying out that commitment.

Finally, Bentsen defended Dukakis well, first by criticizing the Reagan administration's inability to unite its efforts against drug abuse, and then by explaining how Dukakis-Bentsen would unify those efforts. Bentsen's argument was appealing because he provided evidence to suggest that Dukakis would be more effective in fighting drugs than the Republicans would:

We would put one person in charge of the war against drugs, and we'd commit the resources to get that job done. Now, Mike Dukakis has been able to do that type of thing in the state of Massachusetts by cutting the drug use in high schools while it's going up around the rest of the country, by putting in a drug educational program that the Drug Enforcement Agency said was a model to the country.

These programs are exactly what Quayle called for except that Bentsen was able to prove that Dukakis had done them while Quayle was unable to demonstrate that Reagan or Bush had. In summary, Quayle was confused over the use of military force in the war against drugs and was unable to describe a specific policy for what he described as the number one issue in the country. On the other hand, Bentsen created doubt about Quayle's commitment to the war against drugs and about his ability to contribute to that fight. Additionally, Bentsen demonstrated that Dukakis was more effective than Bush or Reagan had been in the fight against drugs by proving that Dukakis' policies in Massachusetts were successful.

Quayle's Failure to Exploit Bentsen's Vulnerabilities

Bentsen's arguments were not without weaknesses, however. On two critical issues in the debate—accepting PAC money and his fairness in criticizing Quayle's qualifications for office—Bentsen's answers were vulnerable. Quayle, however, was unable to adapt his arguments to the opportunities presented by Bentsen. For example, questions about the ethics of accepting PAC money were raised by Hume when he asked if Bentsen was embarrassed by Dukakis' refusal to accept any PAC money for his campaign. Bentsen argued that he complied with the law in these activities, was in favor of campaign reform, and charged that the Republicans had opposed campaign finance reform in the last session of Congress. Quayle indicated that he also was in favor of campaign finance reform but added that Bentsen "used to have a $10,000 breakfast club" for lobbyists. Although the nature of the format prevented an immediate response from Bentsen, in the next exchange, when he was allowed to respond to Quayle's second attempt to explain what he would do if he became president, Bentsen ignored Quayle's qualifications and instead addressed Quayle's statement about the $10,000 breakfast club. Arguing that "it's the same law that lets you invite high priced lobbyists down to Williamsburg, and bring them down there and entertain them playing golf, playing tennis, and bringing Republican senators down there, to have exchanged for that contributions for their campaign," Bentsen suggested that there was no difference in the way the two parties operated under the law. On a personal level, Bentsen argued that "[i]t's the same kind of law that lets you have honorariums—and you've collected over a quarter of a million dollars of honorariums now, speaking to various interest groups. And there's no control over what you do with that money."

Although these two exchanges demonstrated that Bentsen was no worse than Quayle in his dealings with lobbyists, Hume's follow-up question in the fourteenth exchange created a potentially serious issue for Bentsen. Hume asked that "if the *Washington Post* had not broken that story [about the $10,000 breakfast club] and other media picked up on it . . . why should we not believe that you would still be having those breakfasts to this day?" This question underscored doubts about Bentsen's philosophical integrity by suggesting that had he not been "caught" by the media, he would still be accepting the lobbyists' money.

Bentsen needed to give the audience a personalized explanation of his actions, a reason to believe that he would have done the right thing had he not been caught, but his answer fell short in this regard. Even though he acknowledged that it had been an error, and that the perception was bad, he also noted that it was perfectly legal. He gave no reason to believe that he would have disbanded the club had he not received negative publicity, nor did he defend the virtue of his actions given the fact that they were legal. Had Quayle adapted his response to Bentsen's answer, he could have noted how Bentsen avoided the issue in the question. But Quayle did not criticize Bentsen for his poor judgment in starting the club in the first place and, consequently, missed an opportunity to reinforce doubts about Bentsen's character.

Quayle missed another opportunity to develop arguments against Bentsen's candidacy later in the debate when Hume noted that Quayle's qualifications as a vice presidential candidate were comparable to Bentsen's qualifications at the time he ran for president in 1976, and asked if it was fair for him to criticize Quayle. Bentsen sidestepped the issue of fairness by shifting the comparison to "experience and maturity," a comparison that favored him over Quayle. When Quayle responded to Bentsen's answer, though, he neglected to criticize Bentsen's failure to address the double standard and instead reviewed his role in the Job Training Partnership Act. Even though Bentsen's answer in this exchange did not directly address Hume's question, Quayle's failure to criticize Bentsen's double standard constituted another instance in which Quayle was unable to adapt to the rhetorical opportunities created by Bentsen. Since the weaknesses of Bentsen's political image were not revealed in Quayle's arguments, Bentsen appeared more desirable than Quayle as a vice presidential candidate.

Quayle's Defense of the Republican Ticket

Despite Quayle's inability to explain what would he do if he became president and his failure to exploit opportunities to attack Bentsen, there were points in the debate when he demonstrated his ability to attack the Democratic ticket and defend the Republican ticket against attacks. For example, in the fifth exchange when Brokaw asked Quayle about his commitment to the poor, Quayle defended the Republican administration by arguing that

we have backed the homeless bill, the McKinney Act, which is the major piece of legislation that deals with the homeless—the Congress has cut the funding that the administration recommended . . . the biggest thing that we have done for poverty in America is the Tax Simplification Act of 1986: six million working families got off payroll.

Bentsen claimed that Quayle had been of no help when it came to passing "the most major welfare reform bill in the history of our country" but did not identify which bill this was. For the members of the audience who knew what bill Bentsen was referring to, this was a good attack on Quayle. But Bentsen did not refute the two examples in which Quayle defended the Reagan administration. On the issue of poverty, then, Quayle presented a defense of the Reagan administration that went unrefuted by Bentsen. Even though Bentsen did an effective job of revealing how Quayle was not committed to the poor, Quayle's answer suggested that he was capable of defending the Republican record.

In the next question, Brokaw asked Bentsen about his differences with Dukakis on contra aid. Bentsen provided an excellent response by acknowledging that he and Dukakis had differences but then focused the answer on the differences between Bentsen and the Reagan administration. This strategy sidestepped the tension between Dukakis and Bentsen and allowed Bentsen to criticize the opposition. Bentsen's answer outlined a clear and desirable approach to policy-making in the entire region.

Quayle refocused the issue on contra aid, arguing that "there's no doubt in a Dukakis administration that the aid would be cut off to the democratic resistance in Nicaragua," attacked Dukakis by arguing that the Monroe Doctrine had not been superseded, and proved that Dukakis' opposition to the invasion of Grenada was out of step with 85 percent of the American public who supported the "rescue mission." Although none of these moves directly criticized the approach to policy-making outlined by Bentsen, they focused attention on the more widely accepted political belief that our military ventures in Central America were justified because of a perceived Communist threat.

Perhaps the best example of Quayle's advocacy skills were evident in his answer to Margolis' question concerning the enforcement of Occupational Safety and Health Administration laws. When asked "would you acknowledge to the hundreds of injured and maimed people in Nebraska, Iowa, and elsewhere in the Midwest that in this case deregulation may have gone too far and the government should reassert itself in protecting workers' rights?" Quayle attacked the premise of the question:

The premise of your question, Jon, is that somehow this administration has been lax in enforcement of OSHA regulations. And I disagree with that. And I'll tell you why. If you want to ask some business people that I talk to periodically, they complain about the tough enforcement of this administration. . . . When we have found violations in this administration, there has not only been tough enforcement, but there have been the most severe penalties—the largest penalties in the history of the Department of Labor.

The second part of Quayle's answer addressed the policy of deregulation, and here Quayle defended its success:

Now, the broader question goes to the whole issue of deregulation and has deregulation worked or has deregulation not worked. In my judgment deregulation has worked. We have a deregulated economy and we have produced, through low taxes, not high taxes, through deregulation—the spirit of entrepreneurship, . . . 17 million jobs in this country since 1982.

Finally, Quayle summarized the differences in political philosophy between the two parties:

Deregulation as a form of political philosophy, is a good philosophy. It's one that our opponents disagree with. They want a centralized government. But we believe in the market, we believe in the people and yes, there's a role of government and the role of government is to make sure that . . . the welfare of the people is taken care of. And we'll continue to do that.

This was perhaps Quayle's best answer. He demonstrated his ability to recognize the premise of a controversial question, refute it, and then develop a defense of his party's policy based on its outcomes and political philosophy. Bentsen's response was disappointing. Even though he noted that the Reagan administration did not have its heart in the enforcement of the laws, Bentsen did not draw attention to the fact that Quayle's answer failed to refute Margolis' facts that "the budget for the agency has been cut by 20 percent and the number of inspections and manufacturing plants has been reduced by 33 percent." And when Bentsen shifted the discussion from the enforcement of OSHA laws to the enforcement of environmental laws, and then back again to OSHA without connecting the two topics clearly or developing an indictment of Quayle, Bush, or Reagan, he lost an opportunity to dispute the desirability of deregulation as a political philosophy.

Bentsen provided a much better argument against the Reagan administration in the next exchange where he attacked the Republican administration for driving 220 thousand farmers off the land and cutting farm assistance to rural areas by 50 percent. Although Quayle did not defend the Reagan administration against these attacks, he attacked the Democratic party on a broader scale by reminding the audience of Jimmy Carter's grain embargo and stating that the farmer did not want supply management. These two positions pushed the audience away from Democratic solutions to the problems faced by farmers and toward the Republican policies. Finally, Quayle ridiculed Dukakis for suggesting that American farmers grow Belgian endive, a tactic that suggested that Dukakis was out of touch with the traditional crops produced by American farmers.

There were two final exchanges in which Quayle provided evidence of his ability to defend his ticket and attack the opposition's. In Quayle's rebuttal in the twenty-second exchange, in which Margolis asked Bentsen what programs he would eliminate to reduce the budget deficit, Quayle created doubt about Bentsen's commitment to reduce the deficit when he noted that "Senator Bentsen voted against Gramm-Rudman, the very tool that has been used to bring the federal budget deficit down." In the twenty-third exchange in which Bentsen was asked about his differences with Dukakis, Quayle listed all of the military programs opposed by Dukakis and concluded with Schlesinger's open question to Dukakis published in *Time* magazine, "Are you viscerally antimilitary?" By identifying examples of antimilitary policies and using testimony from a former secretary of defense who had served in a Democratic administration, Quayle's argument suggested quite persuasively that Dukakis was, indeed, antimilitary.

SUMMARY

This chapter has demonstrated the need for vice presidential candidates to present a rationale for change or a justification for the party's political programs and values. Failing to justify the approach to leadership reflected in the party platform or the presidential candidate's program can create doubt about the ticket's capacity to provide effective leadership as was the case with Dole in 1976, with Ferraro in individual exchanges with Bush in 1984, and in Quayle's inability to take advantage of weaknesses in Bentsen's answers in 1988.

Additionally, these treatments of the debates demonstrated the importance of advocacy skills on the part of the vice presidential candidates when they are called upon to defend the presidential candidate or program after those candidates and programs have been challenged by other events in the campaign; for example, when Bush needed to defend Reagan after his dismal showing in the first debate with Mondale and when Ferraro needed to justify continued interest in, and support for, the Mondale-Ferraro ticket despite a substantial deficit in the polls. The debates also give us a sense of what kind of vice president and potential president the candidates might make. From the debates we can see how well Bush worked with the Reagan administration given his enthusiasm and strong ability to defend Reagan's leadership and programs. We could infer that Dole had not really considered his role in a prospective Ford administration although Mondale had thought about how he would contribute to a prospective Carter administration. Ferraro's performance reassured us that women were competent for high office, and Quayle made us nervous about his being a heartbeat away from the presidency— but not nervous enough to reject Bush for his decision to put Quayle on the ticket given the fact that he had a minimal understanding of the presidency and a limited ability to defend the Republican ticket.[44]

The analysis of the vice presidential debates also showed how single exchanges can dramatically clarify a candidate's political image; specifically, in 1976 it showed how a single exchange spotlighted the rhetorical problem of Dole as an uncharitable partisan "hatchet man" and in 1988 how Quayle's comparison of himself to Kennedy, though factually accurate, reflected an immaturely developed sense of political judgment because it was presented in a debate in which the opponent was in a much superior position to evaluate its probative value as a qualification for office. For the 1984 debate, however, Ferraro's response to Bush's patronizing tone in the fifth exchange over terrorism was less important as a defining moment than it was as an action that redefined her role with Bush after his attempt to establish a superior-subordinate relationship with her in his answer. This showed how a candidate's language use can implicitly question or in extreme cases—especially when women compete with men for political office—erode a candidate's status as a competent, rational, analytical, and informed competitor for office. Additionally, the analysis revealed how a candidate can use language to reassert a role of equality, call the strategy into question, and demonstrate the skills of leadership implicitly being questioned by the opponent.

This chapter also identified some of the ways in which verbal style can complement or contradict a candidate's substantive claim about himself or his programs as was the case in Dole's closing statement, and how a candidate can transcend previous limitations in the debate and reenergize a candidacy as Ferraro did in the conclusion of her closing

statement against Bush. In both instances, the closing statements functioned in significant ways in shaping the candidate's images. In Dole's
case, the closing statement confirmed his limitations; in Ferraro's case,
both the verbal style and content of the closing statement refuted the
implicit image reflected in weak performances in some of the individual
exchanges.

Finally, the chapter showed how vice presidential candidates can neglect important aspects of presidential leadership. For example, the analysis of the 1984 debate pointed out how candidates must do more than
correct an opponent's facts but also draw conclusions as a necessary
aspect of demonstrating leadership rhetorically, a limitation revealed in
Ferraro's performance when she had better evidence in some of her
exchanges with Bush but failed to press the implications for her audience. Or, in 1988, how Quayle might have been overcoached to the
point of preventing him from seeing the the vulnerabilities in Bentsen's
answers. All of this suggests that vice presidential debates are important
to the vice presidential candidates, the presidential candidates, and potentially to the outcome of the campaign.

NOTES

1. Jack Germond, "Running in Place," *New York Times Magazine*, October 10,
1976, 15. Germond noted how Dole's rhetoric in the campaign differed from his
reputation as a "slashing" partisan. In the debate, however, Dole returned to
his more familiar image.

2. David E. Rosenbaum, *New York Times*, October 17, 1976, A–28. Rosenbaum
observed that Ford chose Dole because he could appeal to conservative elements
in the Republican party.

3. Linda Charlton, *New York Times*, October 15, 1976, B–5; Germond, 109.

4. Charlton, *New York Times*, B–5: Mondale's role was to defend Carter and
his own liberal record, defend the Democratic ticket, and to defend himself by
showing that he understood the issues and could handle them competently.

5. Linda Charlton, *New York Times*, October 17, 1976, IV, 3.

6. Douglas E. Kneeland, *New York Times*, October 15, 1976, B–5. Kneeland
reported that Dole had not taken the debate seriously. Also, Germond found
Dole relying on one-liners, some of which found their way into the debate. See
Germond, "Running in Place," *New York Times Magazine*, October 10, 1976, 108.
Germond quoted Dole as calling "the debate a 'throw away' by the League of
Women Voters, a bone tossed to the number two candidates. . . . "

7. In two separate articles, Douglas E. Kneeland, reported that Dole had
been avoiding answering any question that called for a specific position on policy
matters. *New York Times*, October 15, 1976, B–5 and October 17, 1976, VI, 3.

8. Germond wrote that the candidates had been reminded that they could
not help the ticket but only hurt if they made some serious error; see "Running
in Place," *New York Times Magazine*, October 10, 1976, 15. The analysis of the
debate suggests that this view was only partially correct. Mondale successfully

defended Carter, the ticket, and himself, thus improving the chances of the Carter-Mondale ticket's victory in a close election, but Dole's partisan attacks hurt the Republican ticket.

9. *New York Times*, October 11, 1984, A–1: "In the wake of the first Presidential debate, which rejuvenated Mr. Mondale's candidacy and left the Reagan campaign in a defensive posture, Mr. Bush is under pressure, as one Republican strategist put it, to 'win one for the Gipper' and slow the opposition's new-found momentum."

10. *New York Times*, October 12, 1984, B–7: "The 90 minute debate, once regarded as a campaign sidelight, assumed added importance after the debate Sunday between Mr. Reagan and Mr. Mondale. In that meeting, Mr. Reagan's performance knocked the Republican campaign off stride and started a run of good luck for the Democrats in their strongest week so far."

11. *New York Times*, October 11, 1984, A–1: "Political analysts say the performances turned in by Mr. Bush and Mrs. Ferraro could have a greater effect on their own political futures than on the outcome of this year's Presidential contest. . . . The impression each makes in 90 minutes before a national television audience that night could shape the political identity of each debater more than anything they do on the campaign trail." The *Washington Post*, October 11, 1984, A–23: "Despite the differences in their styles, Bush and Ferraro have a lot in common in that each has a lot at stake in tonight's proceeding—their political futures." See also, William A. Henry III, *Visions of America: How We Saw the 1984 Election* (Atlantic Monthly Press: Boston, 1985), 251.

12. *Christian Science Monitor*, October 15, 1984, A–21: "Mr. Bush set out to reaffirm his boss's achievements, to showcase his experience in foreign affairs, and to shore up his own standing among the GOP's Southern and Western conservative wings."

13. *Time*, Oct. 22, 1984, 30: "All along it was to be the first time that a woman contender for national office had trod on the dueling ground of televised debate. Then, after Ronald Reagan's unexpectedly weak performance against Walter Mondale, the match-off between running mates also became a potential benchmark scoring opportunity for Democratic Ferraro. The challengers had a chance to claim two underdog victories in quick succession and keep their comeback momentum rolling." *Christian Science Monitor*, October 15, 1984, A–21: "Ms. Ferraro aimed to show herself informed, collected, competent—to give her opponent no psychological edge on the platform, and to give those distrustful of a woman a step away from the Oval Office no excuse to dismiss her for reasons of gender." *New York Times*, October 11, 1984, B–11: "As the first woman to be Vice-Presidential candidate on a major ticket, Mrs. Ferraro has the opportunity to erase any doubts about her capacity to serve in the nation's second highest office, and as Mr. Mondale did last Sunday, to improve her favorable rating with the voters."

14. For a discussion of the problems faced by female rhetors, see Karlyn Kohrs Campbell and E. Claire Jerry, "Woman and Speaker: A Conflict in Roles," in *Seeing Female: Social Roles and Personal Lives*, ed. Sharon S. Brehm (Westport, CT: Greenwood Press, 1988): 123–133. Also, see Geraldine Ferraro with Linda Bird Francke, *Ferraro: My Story* (New York: Bantam, 1985): 240–242.

15. The text used for analysis came from the *New York Times*, October 12, 1984, B 5–6. All quotations are from this transcript.

16. Ferraro described Bush as a cheerleader for Reagan. See Ferraro, *My Story*, 257.

17. Ibid., 260. Ferraro felt insulted by Bush's condescending tone.

18. Ibid., 241. The fact that Ferraro did not argue more directly and completely might be attributed to the problems faced by female rhetors, that the role of woman and speaker conflict. This problem led her advisers to suggest that she round out her more "fiesty" image.

19. Ferraro decided to make the theme of patriotism an important part of her remarks because she had been frustrated with the way the Republicans had defined patriotism in terms of "invading the tiny island of Grenada, escalating the tension with the Soviet Union by bluster and bravado, proposing to spend billions on arming space with nuclear missiles, supporting a covert war run by the CIA in Nicaragua" 255 (*My Story*). What was interesting about her definition of patriotism was how it reflected a distinctly feminist view of the world and that it functioned so dramatically to refocus the meaning of the term and the nature of the campaign.

20. Ferraro felt that her debate performance energized her Democratic supporters: *My Story*, 267.

21. *The Washington Post*, October 10, 1984, A–4.

22. *New York Times*, October 11, 1984, A–1.

23. *New York Times*, October 12, 1984, B–7.

24. *Christian Science Monitor*, October 15, 1984, 1: "But the strategy for the Democratic challengers to get their own trailing campaign on track is not big rallies. It is debates. Both Mondale and Ferraro last week continually reminded voters of Mondale's strong showing in his first debate with Reagan."

25. *Time*, October 22, 1984, 31.

26. *Newsweek*, October 22, 1984, 29.

27. *New York Times*, October 12, 1984, B–7.

28. Jack Germond and Jules Witcover, *Wake Us When It's Over* (New York: Macmillan, 1985), 522.

29. *Newsweek*, October 22, 1984, 30.

30. *Newsweek*, October 22, 1984, 29.

31. The *Washington Post*, October 13, 1984, A–7.

32. Ibid.

33. See *New York Times*, October 13, 1984, A–8; Ellen Goodman, The *Washington Post*, October 13, 1984, A–16; *Christian Science Monitor*, October 15, 1984, A–21.

34. *Newsweek*, October 22, 1984, 29.

35. The *Washington Post*, October 13, 1984, A–7.

36. The *Washington Post*, October 12, 1984, A–20.

37. The *Washington Post*, October 12, 1984, A–20.

38. *Newsweek*, October 22, 1984, 29.

39. E. J. Dionne, Jr., *New York Times*, October 7, 1988, B–6; Maureen Dowd, *New York Times*, October 1, 1988, 8.

40. Gerald M. Boyd, New York Times, October 5, 1988, A–30.

41. Dionne, B–6.

42. E. J. Dionne, Jr., *New York Times*, October 5, 1988, 1, 30.

43. Jack W. Germond and Jules Witcover, *Whose Broad Stripes and Bright Stars: The Trivial Pursuit of the Presidency 1988* (New York: Warner, 1989), 437, 441. Quayle was told by his advisers not to use the comparison with Kennedy in the debate.

44. Ibid., 444. Germond and Witcover noted that despite the public's uneasiness with Quayle being only a heartbeat away from the presidency, the fact that he was on the ticket did not seem to reflect poorly enough on Bush's judgment for them to shift their support to Dukakis.

Chapter Nine

Reassessing the Rhetorical Functions of Political Debates

More than three decades ago, Harold Lasswell recognized two problems confronting scholars interested in presidential debates.[1] The first problem was a conceptual one; it asked simply what was the best way to conceptualize a political debate. In short, since presidential debates were not traditional debates over policy matters, nor press conferences, but an altogether different type of rhetorical event occurring in the campaign and combining several functions, previous criteria for evaluating the debates yielded unsatisfactory results. The second problem stemmed from the first. Since debates combined different forms of interaction, how could we rationally evaluate the discourse of the candidates? This study has attempted to solve those two problems by viewing debates as opportunities for candidates to present and defend desirable images of political character specifically in the area of presidential leadership. Although the case for considering debates as tests of political character was presented in Chapter 1, this chapter discusses argument as a strategy of enactment, considers the ways in which the debates shaped perceptions of presidential character by summarizing the ways in which the debates contributed to deliberative and epideictic purposes in the campaigns, and concludes with a discussion of the ways in which this approach to the debates can enlarge and improve our understanding of debates as opportunities to enact presidential character.

POLITICAL DEBATES AS VIRTUAL CONTAINERS OF PRESIDENTIAL CHARACTER

Political debates enact images of leadership because they contain presidential character virtually. Suzanne K. Langer described the idea of a virtual entity in *Problems of Art*:

Anything that exists only for perception, and plays no ordinary, passive part as common objects do, is a virtual entity. It is not unreal; where it confronts you, you really perceive it, you don't dream or imagine that you do. The image in a mirror is a virtual image. A rainbow is a virtual object. It seems to stand on the earth or in the clouds, but it really "stands" nowhere; it is only visible, not tangible.[2]

The same may be said for images of presidential candidates that arise out of the confrontation inherent in a political debate. Unlike artistic expression, which gives form to subjective emotional feeling, however, political debates give form to dynamic images of leadership potential. In this respect, political character is not tangible but is perceived in the dramatic interaction of opposing candidates.

The closest analogue to political debates as virtual phenomena is drama, or the enactment of virtual future.[3] In both drama and political debate, character is enacted. Both enactments occur through speech as symbolic action. Both are illusory in that they present an image of the future, although they are not really future events. Debates, like dramas, are viewed in their entirety so that the audience apprehends both as enactments of character. Finally, the suspense of formal development occurs in both, although in different ways.

In drama, the characters are bound by the script that places them in strategic relationships with one another; the interaction gives form to the action and ultimate development of each character.[4] But in political debate, the script is not set; each candidate chooses the image he or she will present to the audience. The suspense of formal development in character is heightened by the fact that the words of the characters, despite any rehearsal or advice prior to the performance, are indeed their own. Because the image of each candidate is not fixed but formed in the dialectical exchange, the audience perceives the candidate's leadership potential only as an outcome of the dramatic ordeal, and they use these performances to deliberate about the future leadership ability of the candidates. The audience recognizes not the dramatic form of destiny but the nature of each candidate's character under the stress of symbolic attack.

Political debates are virtual "containers" of political character in that candidates can shape whatever image they desire due to the plastic nature of the dramatic form. But a rhetorical conceptualization of political image must be based on how candidates create, maintain, and change their images through the use of language. Not only would the image enacted by a candidate depend on his or her skillful use of language, but also that dynamic element of enactment would remain in the debate as a structure of its verbal pattern. Debates, because they are composed of words with political purpose in mind, have internal formal structures that yield verbal patterns of language action by the candidates. Given this description of debates, critics can consider the ways in which candidates use argument to enact an image of political character for the community.

In these respects, an audience apprehends a debate in its entirety, as a dramatic conflict of character, not as a discursive argument over policies. The role of the critic is to reveal the meaning of the patterns found in political debates, patterns that can be understood as performances of leadership potential instead of evaluating the truthfulness of the candidate's arguments. This is not to say that the truthfulness of a candidate's discourse cannot be considered in developing an argument about the nature of character that inheres in a candidate's language choices. Individual arguments in specific exchanges can be assessed, but they derive meaning from the larger pattern containing them. Because the debate is a dramatic development, audiences apprehend a virtual image of a candidate's presidential qualities only in relation to an opposing candidate's rhetorical action. The nature of the image is understood not as a discursive argument in the sense of an assertion about character, but as character, enacted through argumentative response to symbolic threats. Having witnessed the debate, audiences of undecided voters can deliberate over how well each candidate fulfilled the formal expectations of leadership created by the dramatic exchange of symbolic threats. In these ways, debates, as linguistic structures, form images of character for consideration by the audience.

DELIBERATIVE DIMENSIONS OF POLITICAL DEBATES

Not all critics agree that debates provide important information about the candidates' leadership abilities. James Klumpp has argued that campaigns in particular fail to establish the leadership qualities of the candidates because the discourse, including the debates, is controlled to a large degree by the campaign managers.[5] J. Michael Hogan has criticized the media in the 1988 debates on the grounds that the panelists, unable to trick candidates into making mistakes on substantive issues, asked questions that were irrelevant to matters of governance.[6] Celeste Michelle Condit has suggested that in the debates, epideictic functions have replaced deliberative ones altogether.[7] Other studies have chosen to emphasize the epideictic dimension exclusively over deliberative considerations.[8] But the analysis of the debates suggests that these events really function in both deliberative and epideictic ways and that to consider one dimension at the exclusion of the other unnecessarily limits our understanding of these rhetorical transactions. Political debates perform deliberative functions because they test candidates rhetorically and reveal the nature of each candidate's political character.[9] What the audience witnesses is a dramatic encounter in which images of political character are confirmed, created, or transformed in significant ways.[10] Because debates bring about dramatic fulfillment or reversal of political images, undecided voters can watch and judge the character of the candidates based on their performances. It is precisely because so much of the campaign discourse is controlled by campaign managers that debates are important places to look for clues to presidential leadership potential.[11] Despite the fact that they are coached extensively prior to debates, candidates must perform without the aid of a manager or script for a sustained period of time during which they have no control over the questions that will be asked. Although many of the panelists' questions may seem irrelevant to matters of governance, they are often designed to provide a glimpse of the character behind the mask created by campaign managers. So we have questions about who the candidates perceive as heroes, what books they have read recently, and what they think about their opponent, as well as questions designed to focus debate over policy matters. And although the candidates' discourse does include appeals to values, the texts of the debates also revealed that the candidates justified policies, substantiated claims, and refuted attacks. Specifically, chapters 2 through 8 revealed the ways in which debates, as argumentative enactments of character, synthesized a variety of potential issues into contrasting images of potential presidential ability. Whether the viewing audiences perceived these differences is not my claim here, but I am arguing that these visions of presidential character reside within the texts of the debates and that these analyses suggest the ways in which the language choices of the candidates could have worked for the audiences as well suggesting ways in which critics can locate important differences in political images. In short, debates offer opportunities for audiences to watch, comprehend, and deliberate over the images of presidential leadership enacted in the debates. In these ways, the debates can provide audiences with crucial information for their decision in the presidential campaign. This section summarizes the findings of the analyses for each of the campaigns and shows how the debates might have contributed to audiences' deliberations over the candidates' leadership abilities.

Near the end of the campaign, and most evident in the fourth debate, the key difference between Kennedy and Nixon had become Kennedy's image of a vital and vigorous candidate. In the literature devoted to the study of ethos, this characteristic has been described as dynamism or charisma. The development of Kennedy's image and the subsequent erosion of Nixon's can be traced in the debates.

Of the four debates, the first was the most important because it changed dramatically the nature of the campaign. Kennedy articulated and enacted a specific concept of the presidency, defused Nixon's charge that he was immature and inexperienced, and made the Democratic vision of leadership credible. By contrast, Nixon failed to sustain his best attack on Kennedy, offered no competing vision of desirable leadership, accepted Kennedy's criteria for evaluating the choices before the public, and then failed to defend the Republican platform in the specific exchanges over farm surpluses, teacher salaries, and political leadership. Furthermore, Nixon corroborated doubts about his fitness for office when he fell into a rhetorical trap set by Sander Vanocour and revealed his inability to solve a complex rhetorical problem.

The first debate featured significant stylistic differences between the candidates. Kennedy's refutation was concise, thorough, specific, and well grounded in facts, but Nixon's answers were awkward, inept, qualified, and inelegantly complex. Kennedy's rhetoric suggested a polished and vibrant image of leadership. Nixon's did not.

Although these elements were present in some degree in the other debates, they were most evident in the first debate. Because the first debate altered the character of the campaign, the other debates functioned as opportunities for Nixon to rebuild a desirable image of leadership.

Analysis of the other debates revealed that Nixon never developed a coherent and distinct vision of leadership to challenge Kennedy's, nor did Nixon ever regain the credibility of a more experienced candidate that he lost in the opening exchanges with Kennedy. Most importantly, Nixon never disputed Kennedy's frame of reference for understanding the meaning of the 1960 campaign as a question of vigorous leadership in time of crisis. This frame of reference established a favorable context for interpreting Kennedy's rhetorical actions in the campaign and in subsequent debates.

Nixon performed well in the second debate, especially the first half. But two factors diminished the effect of his improvements. None of the exchanges featured a dramatic reversal of what had occurred in the first debate; the question Kennedy posed for the audience was still phrased in his terms, not Nixon's. In two key exchanges, on the issue of party labels and responsible advocacy, Kennedy's answers embodied a more desirable image of character. Although Nixon's answers might have reinforced partisan supporters, they did not affect the change that had been developing in Kennedy's image.

In the third debate, Kennedy's ability to avoid rhetorical traps on the defense of Berlin, oil depletion allowances, and Truman's language provided Nixon with opportunities to attack Kennedy's image. But the analysis of those exchanges revealed Nixon's inability to exploit vulnerabilities in Kennedy's answers. The rhetorical effect of Kennedy's performance can be seen in the exchanges over labor unions and economic growth. Nixon poorly imitated Kennedy's words, argued inconsistently that we have moved adequately with the current administration but must move faster in the future, and asked Kennedy for the credibility he lacked.

The strongest evidence for the claim that Kennedy had successfully developed an image of a vital and vigorous candidate can be found in the opening and closing statements of the fourth debate. The analysis revealed that in those speeches, Nixon used Kennedy's theme and style, not his own; the result was a hollow imitation of Kennedy. Thus, by the end of the fourth debate, Nixon's image had been transformed from that of the more experienced vice president to a dim version of the more vital and vigorous Kennedy. Taken as a series of rhetorical acts, the debates shaped the nature of the decision for the public, suggesting a choice between a candidate who had developed a vital and vigorous image of leadership reminiscent of FDR versus a candidate who could not develop a competing image of desirable leadership, appeared to be speaking as a vice president instead of a presidential candidate, and could not embody the image of the challenger in a more appealing way.

In 1976, the issue before the public was trustworthiness, not dynamism as it was in 1960. Although a substantial portion of the debates was devoted to specific exchanges over policy issues, the focus of the debates concerned perceptions of fairness, integrity, and trust. In all three debates, the candidates designated trust as the key issue in the closing statements. The panelists raised questions about Watergate in the first and third debate. In the second debate, Carter's strategy was to focus the audience's attention on Ford's secrecy in foreign policy. Because doubts about Ford's trustworthiness constituted a major obstacle to his bid for the presidency, and because both the candidates and the panelists identified trust and integrity as significant issues, questions relating to Watergate, Nixon's pardon, and openness in government suggested that these were the key issues in the campaign.

An examination of the first debate reveals a close contest. Ford refuted Carter's credentials for office by presenting evidence of Carter's poor record as governor and demonstrated that he was one step ahead of Carter in proposing a national energy policy. Ford's refutation of Carter's attacks on his domestic policy also indicated that Ford was capable of defending his record. But Ford faltered twice when he failed to explain an apparent inconsistency in his actions toward Nixon and draft evaders and tried to argue with insufficient evidence that there was integrity in the White House but corruption in Congress. Although Carter never answered Ford's criticism of his record in Georgia, he demonstrated strong advocacy skills in attacking Ford's record on taxes, the economy, and vetoes. In their closing statements, both candidates focused the audience's attention on the issue of trust.

In the second debate, Ford made the mistake of arguing that eastern

Europe generally and Poland specifically were not under Soviet domination. Although research indicated that the public did not perceive this as a significant error at the time of the debate, the press seized on it as a sign of Ford's intellectual limitations. Reading the reviews by the press, many members of the audience doubted Ford's competence. More important, analysis of the text revealed Carter's criticism of Ford's secrecy and integrity in foreign policy. Thus, Carter's strategy of emphasizing doubts about Ford's trustworthiness dominated the second debate.

Ford did not develop a concept of presidential character in the third debate. Without a significantly different way of understanding his rhetorical actions, doubts about Ford's competence and trustworthiness remained. When Ford was unable to explain satisfactorily his involvement in limiting an initial investigation of Watergate, he missed his last opportunity to put aside doubts about his integrity and direct attention to Carter's limited credentials for presidential office. But by this time, what had been implicitly developing as a doubt had become explicitly stated as an issue: Ford's limited trustworthiness was confirmed in his answers to questions about Watergate. Ford could not present a personalized defense of his character and thus could not fulfill the rhetorical prerequisite for office—trust. Carter did not need to become "presidential" rhetorically if the president himself was unable to present himself in a trustworthy light.

Although Carter convinced the public he was an outsider to Washington politics and untainted by Watergate in 1976, that was not the issue in 1980. Because Carter needed to defend his record and because presidential political debates were uniquely suited to test the quality of a candidate's programs as well as the candidate's ability to defend them, Carter needed to perform well in his debate against Reagan. Although some research has demonstrated that Reagan argued better in many exchanges, the most significant test of presidential ability was selected by Carter—the issue of nuclear weaponry.

Throughout his administration, Carter seemed to react to events rather than control them. For Carter to elevate nuclear weaponry above all other issues was an attempt to control the ground of the debate and to demonstrate symbolically his ability to master a threatening situation. His strategy was well-founded. Given Reagan's strident remarks on foreign policy, he was most vulnerable on the issue of war and peace. But Carter failed to answer seven of Reagan's attacks on his defense policies and then concluded with an image of him turning to his daughter for counsel concerning what was the most serious problem confronting humanity. The failure to defend himself and the need to turn to his daughter symbolized his inability, and by contrast, Reagan appeared more competent to serve as president.

The Anderson-Reagan debate shaped a contrasting image of an optimism developed by Reagan versus one of cynicism embodied by Anderson. What was interesting about this debate was Anderson's failure to demonstrate the "Anderson difference." Given the potential for dramatic reversal inherent in the dialectic, a good performance by Anderson could have generated the kind of doubt that Mondale was able to create in his first debate with Reagan. No such action occurred, and it is interesting to note that after the debate, Anderson's standing in the polls began to decline. One might infer that those who had been disillusioned with Reagan and Carter, and who had been interested in seeing the "Anderson difference" enacted in significant political discourse, became disenchanted with what appeared to be little more than political consciousness-raising espoused by a cynical candidate.

Where dynamism, trustworthiness, and competence had been the key issues formulated in the 1960, 1976, and 1980 debates, respectively, reliability was the key issue after Mondale successfully challenged Reagan's command of the facts in the first 1984 debate. Unfortunately, Mondale's strong attack on Reagan's use of the facts became translated into a question of Reagan's age rather than a question of leadership ability measured in terms of reliability.

Reagan's age was not interfering with his performance. He was just at a loss to counter Mondale's arguments. By phrasing the issue in terms of Reagan's age, the media implicitly deemphasized Mondale's leadership ability and suggested an easy standard for Reagan to meet to justify a second term. Reagan needed to appear only as though he were not senile. Mondale needed another dramatic success to challenge Reagan's image as a reliable candidate.

In the second debate, Reagan's argumentative performance improved; Mondale's did not. To dismiss repeated unproven claims, Reagan used his strategy of one-liners to highlight the weaknesses of Mondale's attacks. On the age issue, Reagan used humor to attack the "youth" of his candidate. If Mondale had created doubts about Reagan's ability to control a threatening situation in the first debate, those doubts evaporated in the course of the second. Reagan defended his administration against Mondale's criticisms, attacked Mondale's programs, and defused the age issue with humor. Reagan's faculties had not left him, and he could be relied on for continued leadership in a second term.

In 1988, Bush needed to overcome doubts about his ability to present a coherent line of thinking in his answers to questions in the debate. When there had been shortcomings in the first debate, his answers in the second debate were much improved stylistically. In Dukakis' case, even though the polls indicated that he had won the first debate, he failed to indicate where he would lead the country. The analyses of the 1988 debates revealed how perceptions of winning cannot necessarily be equated with a successful performance. In both debates, Dukakis was

unable to describe his vision for the country or demonstrate an inspiration for leadership. So the debates revealed rather clearly that Dukakis
either did not know where he would lead the country or that he did
not know exactly or that he was reluctant to describe his vision for the
nation. In any of these cases, a continuation of Republican leadership
seemed a safer bet for many Americans.

Vice presidential debates serve deliberative functions most clearly
when the panelists focus on presidential candidates' programs. But the
vice presidential debates provide us with information about the vice
presidential candidates' leadership potential as well as information about
the viability of the presidential candidates' platform. This was clearly
the case in the 1976 vice presidential debate between Dole and Mondale.
But both the 1984 and 1988 vice presidential debates functioned a bit
differently in the campaign. In 1984, Bush was called upon to defend
Reagan after his poor showing in the first debate while Ferraro was
occupied with the task of demonstrating that she was capable enough
for the office. Both candidates had substantially different problems to
address in the debates. What I found interesting in the 1984 vice presidential debate was how much of Bush's performance was designed to
bolster Reagan's image and how limited Ferraro's performance in the
individual exchanges were, but how well she transcended her shortcomings in the closing statement. Finally, the vice presidential debate
can have direct bearing on the presidential candidate as in 1988 when
Quayle's lack of experience was the central focus, and his performance
was interpreted as a statement about Bush's decision-making ability.

With the exception of the vice presidential debates, these analyses
support the claim that the debates crystallized key issues to be resolved
concerning the nature of presidential character in each campaign. This
position assumes a dynamic concept of presidential ethos: that differences in personal character are revealed in rhetorical choices peculiar to
a given campaign, debate, and exchange. Because these differences are
distilled in the course of the debates and yield contrasting images of
political ability, audiences can tune in and watch the ways in which the
candidates attempt to solve the rhetorical problems created by the
panelists.

EPIDEICTIC DIMENSIONS OF POLITICAL DEBATES

The idea that political debates perform an epideictic or ceremonial
function has already received some attention from those who study
political debates. After the 1976 debates, George Bishop, Robert
Meadow, and Marilyn Jackson-Beeck noted that "from this perspective,
then, the debates signify social and cultural events whose greatest impact
may be felt at the level of systems and institutions. Furthermore, the

felt impact is not seen so much as a matter of change, but rather as a fix or boost for the common political consciousness."[12] Gladys Engel Lang has described debating as "an accepted ritual, a routine part of the political process" that has shown signs of becoming a "political institution."[13] In a broader sense, Gronbeck has suggested that campaign discourse functions as an enactment of our collective self.[14] Others have argued that debates can best be approached as examples of epideictic rhetoric.[15] Noting the distinction between consummatory and instrumental rhetoric in his analysis of the 1988 debates, John Lucaites has suggested that debates serve primarily consummatory functions, that is, they are ritualistic opportunities for candidates to enact the <public trust>.[16] Implicit in Lucaites' conceptualization of the <public trust> is the assumption that candidates must measure up to some standard of rhetorical or argumentative excellence in order for the <public trust> to be enacted in the debates. However, when Lucaites concluded his analysis of the 1988 debates, he was at a loss to explain why Dukakis failed to enact the <public trust> for the audience. This failure to fulfill the expectations of the public was not due to the nature of the debates but was a function of Dukakis' inability to reveal his capacity for presidential leadership. In fact, Lucaites' analysis proves that debates work not so much as consummatory rhetoric exclusively but also instrumentally in the sense that the debates showed us Dukakis' limitations as a leader. All of this points back to my claim that debates function in both ways, giving us information about candidates' character and assuring us that the democratic system is working. Whether we like what we see in the debates is less important than the fact that we can measure both candidates against one another as they are called upon to solve the problems posed for them by the panelists.[17] Although debates might not help everyone to decide whom to vote for, they do constitute one moment in the campaign when the audience can watch the representatives of the two parties argue over what is best for the community. And the public nature of the ordeal provides the audience with an opportunity to see how democratic values of rational dialogue are played out. In these ways, debates serve as models for reasoned discussion of political issues and celebrate the fact that the system invites participation in the way of watching the debates.

Debates not only enact the political values of rational dialogue for the community but also may constitute a way of dealing with unexpressed communal insecurities. During the 1960 campaign and in the debates, both Nixon and Kennedy argued that we were in a life or death struggle with the Soviet Union. Additionally, the fear of communism manifested itself in various aspects of American culture.[18] In these ways, Americans were invited by politicians to see their world threatened by Communist advances. Debates, then, revealed not only the qualities of the candidates but also gave evidence of the political system's capacity to generate candidates capable of standing up the the Communist threat. In a more direct way, the 1976 debates may have functioned to both reassure the public that the political system could produce candidates of good character and demonstrate that the democratic process of resolving political disagreements through dialogue was still intact. The tension created by the residual divisiveness of Nixon's pardon coinciding with the bicentennial celebration further underscored the need to renew the democratic ethos of the community. The only way to show the public that the system was still working was to return to a form of political discourse that demonstrated not only the qualities of the candidates but also enacted the political values of the community in the process. In these ways, debates can restore political confidence when the community collectively experiences a perception of political weakness. Thus, when Carter refused to debate Reagan in 1980 after the prolonged hostage ordeal in Iran, the public indicated their readiness to reject Carter at the polls. This made the refusal to debate a potent campaign issue in itself.[19] At the very minimum, then, it seems reasonable to say that candidates risk substantial public disapproval when they refuse to debate during periods when American leadership or status seems to have fallen short of implicit standards of manifest destiny inherent in our political and cultural myths. This may explain Reagan's willingness to debate in 1984 when he enjoyed a substantial lead in the polls.[20] Somehow it would have seemed incongruous for the person who had restored confidence in American leadership to dodge an opportunity to reenact his role of president. Lurking in the background, however, may have been doubts about Reagan's competence, and it may have been less risky for him to accept the debates than avoid a confrontation with Mondale. Thus, increasingly, candidates are expected to accept debates despite wide margins in the polls because the refusal to debate in itself constitutes a powerful and unfavorable message to the electorate communicating not only the candidate's inability to defend himself but that he does not share the same democratic values as the rest of the community. The fact that vice presidential debates occurred in 1976 and 1984 also seem to indicate that debates address insecurities on the part of the electorate. Although assassinations and impeachment proceedings of U.S. presidents have tended to be historical exceptions to the rule, the public had witnessed both since the first series of debates in 1960.[21] Thus, it made sense for vice presidential candidates to debate in 1976 so that the public could get a look at their potential leadership abilities should something happen to the president. And the attempted assassination of Reagan as well as the unique candidacy of Geraldine Ferraro renewed interest in the vice presidential candidates of 1984.[22] Finally, the doubts about Dan Quayle's leadership skills were so enormous that only a debate could have assured the public that Quayle could, at least in a marginal way, fulfill the basic expectations for office. In these ways, debates may be functioning on an epideictic level. By allowing the public to witness democracy in action, debates symbolize the core values of the democratic community and communicate to the audience the idea that the system works.

THE RELATIONSHIP BETWEEN POLITICAL ARGUMENT AND PRESIDENTIAL CHARACTER

The question of "Who won?" dominates postdebate discussions and, with rare exceptions, this discussion is conducted and controlled by media journalists so that the commentary received by the public reflects the inherent limitations of the media's purpose, scope, and detail.[23] Hogan and Condit have gone so far as to suggest that the commentary provided by journalists lacks substance and is thus uninformative for the public.[24] Others have noted how media commentators minimize detailed rationale assessments of candidates' performance by relying on a "sports" or "horse race" metaphor emphasizing oversimplified judgments of who won and lost.[25] Donn W. Parson has argued that the very nature of the question "Who won?" forces an either/or commentary, which, although fitting within the confines of modern media air time and newspaper space, is at odds with the purpose of criticism that seeks to investigate and explain the many ways in which the debates shape candidates' images and audiences' perceptions of the candidates.[26]

The question itself presupposes a shared set of standards that can be applied to the debates when, in fact, David Vancil and Sue Pendell have demonstrated that audiences may often use different criteria in evaluating candidates' debate performances.[27] The issue is further complicated by the fact candidates may have multiple objectives in a debate so that a perception of having won, say on stronger refutational skills, would be insufficient to carry the audience as in the case of the first 1976 debate when Ford could not respond to doubts about his fairness and in the first 1988 debate when Dukakis was unable to convey a personable or inspiring style in his answers. In these ways, asking "Who won?" narrows the range of options available to critics and leaves us dependent on the capsulated summaries of journalists who, according to Robert Meadow, "take on the powerful role of interpreter of the debate providing meaning and a framework for interpreting an otherwise incomprehensible event."[28]

Although it may be impossible to dislodge the media from their role as interpreters of debates, the need for enlarging the discussion of what the debates mean for audiences, that is, function rhetorically to shape candidates' images and potentially influence an audience's perception of a candidate seems clear if only for the purpose of offering media commentators a more sophisticated way of approaching the debates.[29] But studies of the ways in which candidates enact roles of leadership are also informative in the sense that they contribute to a public's understanding of what candidates are trying to accomplish in the debate and because they give the public a way to consider some of the rhetorical implications of political argument.[30] After all, this is the reason the public watches the debates: to understand where candidates stand on the issues and to see what the candidates are like.[31] In these ways, rhetorical critics can contribute to the public's understanding of the debates by identifying the ways in which the political images of the candidates are shaped by the debates.[32]

Together, the analyses of the debates suggest several possibilities for assessing the ways in which political argument contributes to images of political character. Initially, critics can look at the debates to determine whether a candidate's discourse reflects a particular concept of the presidency or vision of leadership. For example, Kennedy's opening statement in the first debate revealed his perception of the role of president as someone who places the nation's needs before the audience and asks that the people vote for him on the basis of his ability to recognize what needs to be done to make the nation stronger as well as his ability to move vigorously in the direction of those solutions. Lacking experience and a particular vision of leadership, Carter offered a concept of leadership based on moral identity in his theme of "a government as good as the people." After Carter's first term in office, the need for patriotic inspiration was evident to the Reagan camp in the 1980 campaign, and his actions in the debates were devoted to constructing a desirable patriotic image for the political community. And Reagan's debate with Anderson in 1980 showed us that political consciousness-raising was the limit to Anderson's understanding of the office. Or we may find that a candidate is unable to articulate a vision of leadership, as was the case with Dukakis in 1988. In any of these cases, a concept of leadership was made available or unarticulated by the candidates. Critics can contribute much to evaluating the capacity for leadership exhibited by the candidates when they identify and explain the candidates' view of office reflected in their rhetoric.

We can also measure how well a candidate understands the nature of the office by examining the way they conduct themselves in the debate. Examining the 1960 debates revealed Kennedy's ability to justify change and Nixon's inability to locate a style or substantive message that suggested him in the role of a leader able enough to carry on in the tradition of Eisenhower. An excellent example of how debates mark a candidate's knowledge of the office was found in Mondale's superior performance in his vice presidential debate with Dole. Mondale's performance reflected his understanding that the vice presidential candidate could help the ticket if the debate could be used to defend himself, the presidential candidate, and the party platform; Dole's performance revealed that he did not take the debate seriously. The first 1984 debate showed how a candidate can take a single dimension of presidential character and illustrate how the opposing candidate is vulnerable to an attack along that line as Mondale did to Reagan concerning the deficit. The second debate showed how important it is for a candidate to control the key issue that defines an important difference between the candidates so that in the second debate we found Mondale unable to sustain criticism of Reagan's positions and unable to counter Reagan's use of humor. Or the debates can reveal how enthusiasm for the office is an insufficient qualification for leadership as was the case in 1988 when Dukakis indicated he was ready to lead but could not explain the direction in which he wanted to take the country. Each of these examples underscores the need for presidential candidates to defend their values, programs, and visions of leadership through argument. By looking at the ways these choices are defended rhetorically, critics can reveal the candidates' capacity for national leadership in office.

Critics need to be able to discuss the ways in which language shapes and transforms a candidate's political image in the debates. We should pay more attention to the ways in which a candidate's verbal style complements or contradicts his or her substantive message. Focusing on stylistic aspects of a candidate's performance helped to explain the implicit appeal in Kennedy's rhetoric in the 1960 debates as well as why Nixon seemed less appealing in contrast. Kennedy sounded like someone who was strong, vibrant, dynamic, and thus ready to lead; Nixon did not. Giving consideration to verbal style also helped to explain why Dole's rhetoric seemed less appealing than Mondale's in the 1976 vice presidential debate. Dole's verbal style contradicted his substantive message that he and the Republican party trusted and cared for the people. Looking at verbal patterns also helped explain how Ford failed to solve his rhetorical problem—his answers in the debates reflected a pattern of impersonal response to a very personal issue. Reagan's pattern of attacking Carter and defending himself implicitly reinforced an impression of competence in advocacy; Carter's repeated failure to defend against Reagan's attacks confirmed the audience's doubts about his competence. One of the more interesting aspects of the 1984 debates was Mondale's ability to justify his candidacy in the face of polling results that put him out of the race. However, by arguing that the debates served as the vehicle to communicate his message while simultaneously testing its validity as a rationale for change, Mondale was able to remain consistent within his definition of leadership—that a president has to confront the facts—and prove to the American public that change was justified since Reagan was performing poorly in the first debate. And Ferraro's closing statement showed how a candidate's rhetoric can redefine a previous image, recontextualize the meaning of previous actions, and a renew a party's commitment to a candidate who was behind in the polls. In these respects, the 1984 campaign showed how the polls can be altered by a candidate's performance in the debates. But Ferraro's performance also revealed the problem that female politicians face in enacting desirable images of leadership. By working hard to appear less than "feisty," Ferraro sacrificed an essential component of leadership in her answers—the ability to draw conclusions, to make inferences for the audience, and to press the implications of her opponent's answers. In considering the kinds of roles that political candidates rely on in shaping their image, critics can explain rhetorical shortcomings and clarify what constitutes important dimensions of presidential leadership in a given campaign. Finally, examining stylistic aspects of a candidate's performance can reveal a particular candidate's rhetorical problem such as Bush's lack of presidential polish in 1988 or the fact that every time Dukakis gave what might have been regarded as a strong argument, he reinforced the audience's negative impression of him as a passionless technocrat. Identifying these rhetorical problems explains what each candidate must do to perform successfully in the debate. And these kinds of observation also allow us to talk about how both candidates could be successful (or fail) rather than defining the discussion in terms of one winner and one loser.

Identifying a candidate's rhetorical problem and analyzing the ways he attempts to solve it can by itself constitute an important way to compare presidential and vice presidential aspirants. For example, it may be the case that a particular aspect of a candidate's political image might be in question prior to a debate. This was the case in the first 1960 debate when questions were put to Kennedy concerning his limited experience and qualifications for office or when Nixon was asked what he had contributed to the Eisenhower administration that would suggest that his experience as vice president qualified him for higher office. Ford's failure to develop more appealing ways to answer questions about his association with Nixon became a critical difference between him and Carter. Reagan's use of one-liners in his second debate with Mondale showed how important humor was as a rhetorical strategy: It relieved the tension associated with the expectation that Reagan might fail his second and last test for office while simultaneously reasserting his ability to take charge of and control a threatening situation. And although it became clear that Quayle's ability to explain what he would do if he became president was very limited, his defense of the Republican ticket, though minimally competent, received little consideration from critics in terms of assessing his qualifications for office. Debates, then, are events during which panelists create rhetorical problems for candidates to solve, candidates can create rhetorical problems for their opponents to solve, and solving one's rhetorical problem can shift the focus of the campaign. This was the case in 1960 when Kennedy's lack of experience evaporated as an issue and the focus shifted to Nixon's limitations, in 1976 when the focus shifted from Ford's competence to Ford's motive in pardoning Nixon, in 1984 when the focus of the campaign shifted from Mondale's poor showing in the polls to concerns about Reagan's age, and in 1988 when the focus shifted from the content of Dukakis' answers to the passion with which he communicated his message to the people. In these instances, the performance of the candidates contributed to a shift in focus on the campaign discourse. Critics can identify these rhetorical problems, provide detailed assessments of how well the candidates solve them, and thus gauge more effectively the ways in which the debates contribute to the outcome of the campaign.

Critics can also give more attention to the rhetorical and argumentative strategies in the debates. Kennedy's use of Lincoln's and Roosevelt's personae in his opening statement of the first debate was particularly effective in suggesting Kennedy in the role of an experienced leader. The argument that we needed to get America moving again was difficult for Nixon to refute. When Nixon agreed with Kennedy that we cannot stand still, the substantive difference between their positions in the campaign seemed negligible. Reducing the substantive differences between the candidates helped Kennedy because the public was not necessarily dissatisfied with the record of Republican leadership. And by defining the difference between himself and Nixon primarily as stylistic in nature, Kennedy shaped the comparison between himself and Nixon in the most favorable terms for himself. Here, argumentative substance turns back into a consideration of argumentative style; when Kennedy justified his criticism of the Republican party on the exchanges over farm surpluses, teachers' salaries, and legislative enactment, his arguments were stylistically more preferable to Nixon's. Thus, a candidate's rhetorical style and substance are reflexively related: one reinforces the other so that issue and image are inseparable. Mondale's performance in the 1976 vice presidential debate and in the first 1984 debate also showed how important argumentative strategy was in shaping a political image. Mondale understood how to develop a rationale for change based on the incumbent's record in office in the vice presidential debate. Dole never developed the kind of specific defense of the Ford administration or of the Nixon administration that was needed to justify a rational decision in his favor. Additionally, in Dole's performance, we saw that a defense based on ideological grounds was insufficient against arguments that challenged the values underpinning the political philosophy used by Dole. In 1984, Mondale successfully connected several of the panelists' questions to measuring leadership, defined leadership in terms of dealing with facts, and showed how Reagan was out of touch with the facts on the issue of the deficit. It was this particular strategy that accounted for Reagan's poor showing in the first debate, yet few commentators have given this strategy detailed consideration.

Critics can also give attention to the unique way in which argumentation works in a political debate. For example, the fact that a candidate uses facts that are inaccurate, makes invalid comparisons, or uses statistics incorrectly does not necessarily cost the candidate anything in terms of his credibility unless the opposing candidate points out the error. And even when the opposing candidate points out the error, unless the appropriate conclusion is drawn for the audience, the impact of the correction can go unnoticed as was the case with Ferraro in her debate with Bush. When "weak" arguments are left unrefuted by a candidate, we should ask why, especially if the rhetorical failure occurs on a critical issue as was the case with Dukakis in the second debate when Bernard Shaw asked him if he would change his position on capital punishment if Kitty Dukakis were raped and murdered. The Dukakis debate team had prepared him for this issue with a personalized defense of his position on the issue of crime, yet Dukakis did not use this answer. And we should consider potential vulnerabilities in candidates' answers so that we probe weaknesses in substantive appeals by candidates. For example, Bentsen's performance in the vice presidential debate seemed strong only in relation to Quayle's failure to attack some of his more vulnerable answers. In his second debate with Reagan, Mondale failed to refute Reagan's justifications for his positions and thus appeared to be repeating his claims rather than reasoning his way to his conclusions. In both of these instances, part of the explanation for one candidate's success in the debate can be found in the failure of the other candidate's skill. However, the relationship between individual exchanges and the overall impression of a candidate's image needs to be considered in relation to crucial questions of presidential character. For example, in the 1960 debates, even though some of Nixon's arguments seemed stronger than Kennedy's in the second, third, and fourth debates, none of the answers reversed the gains Kennedy made on the critical issues of presidential character from the first debate. When we discuss argumentation in political debates, we need to connect advocacy skills to key issues and key exchanges in the debate to explain how a particular exchange or pattern of response reveals a candidate's potential for leadership. In this way, for example, we can identify when images of presidential character are forged as was the case in the exchanges on leadership and experience in the first 1960 debate, in Ford's failure to respond to questions about Watergate in the third 1976 debate, in the exchange over arms control in the 1980 Reagan-Carter debate, in Dole's claim that the Democrats were responsible for all of the wars in the twentieth century in the 1976 vice presidential debate, in Ferraro's rebuke of Bush for his patronizing tone to her in the 1984 debate, and in Bentsen's stern reproach of Quayle for comparing himself to Kennedy in the 1988 debate. All of these are key moments in the debate in which a candidate's language choices revealed something important about the kind of political judgment the candidate might bring to office.

Another way in which candidates reveal their qualities for office can be found in the way they shape arguments designed to appeal to a national community. The very nature of the debate situation implies the existence of two alternatives and the need to appeal to a majority or consensus of opinion. In 1960, Nixon argued from a relatively narrow Republican perspective, as did Dole in the 1976 vice presidential debate; Kennedy in 1960 and Mondale in the 1976 vice presidential debate attempted to develop rationales for office based on more objective, argumentative appeals. Part of Kennedy's and Mondale's successes, then, can be attributed to the fact that their language choices took into account the presence of a divided audience and sought to appeal to both sides on the basis of arguments designed to transcend narrow political interests. Looking at the first 1960 debate and the 1976 vice presidential debate reveals the way in which argument was used to defend each candidate's party platform. In both instances, one can also see how Kennedy and Mondale responded to the implicit understanding that because they were calling for change, they had the burden of proof; they needed to develop a case for change. In the 1976 presidential debates, even though Ford defended his record relatively well, I found that the more important issue to consider was Ford's trustworthiness. Thus my analysis of the debates focused on illustrating how Carter had developed an effective rhetorical strategy of weaving concerns about trusting Ford in all three of the debates and how Ford failed to respond directly to these concerns. Analysis of the 1984 debates revealed how a candidate like Mondale could achieve a dramatic victory in the first debate of a series but, by relying on a strategy of repetition, fail in a subsequent debate specifically because he neglected to develop detailed arguments capable of refuting the incumbent's immediate defense of his administration. One important aspect of the debates, then, is to consider the way challengers respond to the problem of developing a case for change.

SUMMARY

This chapter has argued that political debates can be considered virtual containers of political character in the sense that candidates have the opportunity to enact any image of leadership they desire. The element of choice is particularly revealing of character since whatever image a candidate chooses to offer can be attacked by the opposing candidate. In this way, debates test each candidate's language choices to reveal strengths and weaknesses in the political image presented for the audience's deliberation. The findings of the analyses of the 1960, 1976, 1980, 1984, and 1988 debates were used to show how debates served deliberative and epideictic functions in presidential campaigns. The debates can be considered deliberative rhetorical transactions in the sense that the audience watches the ways that both candidates respond to symbolic attacks on their character and solve rhetorical problems in the course of the debate. In witnessing the debate, an audience evaluates the ways in which each candidate's language choices reflect presidential character. Also, the debates can be considered epideictic rhetorical transactions because the act of arguing political issues before the public enacts the political value of rational dialogue, the cornerstone of a democratic system of government. Given the importance of debates in presidential campaigns, critics need to consider the ways in which political argument and presidential character are related. Critics can examine the debates to discover what a candidate's concept of the presidency entails, a candidate's understanding of the office, the way in which language can shape and transform a candidate's image in the debates, the ways in which a candidate solves rhetorical problems in the debates, the ways in which rhetorical and argumentative strategies can account for the development of images of presidential character, the ways in which advocacy skills can be used by a candidate to build a case for change or defend against attacks on the incumbent administration, and the ways in which a candidate develops rationales for his or her candidacy based on argumentative appeals that transcend narrow political interests. One or more of these considerations may become relevant in explaining the ways in which candidates attempt to present themselves as leaders, capable of serving as the president. What a critic chooses to focus on will depend on the candidates, the issues, and the developments in any given campaign. My hope, however, is that by focusing on the ways in which presidential character is dramatically enacted in a political debate, we can develop a better understanding of how political debates serve democratic values.

NOTES

1. Harold Lasswell, "Introduction," in *The Great Debates*, ed. Sidney Kraus (Bloomington, IN: Indiana University Press, 1962), 19–24.

2. Suzanne Langer, *Problems of Art* (New York: Charles Scribner's Sons, 1957), 7.

3. Suzanne Langer, *Feeling and Form: A Theory of Art* (New York: Charles Scribner's Sons, 1953), chap. 7, "The Dramatic Illusion," 306–325.

4. Ibid., 306–325.

5. James F. Klumpp, "W(h)ither Civic Discourse(?)!" in *Spheres of Argument: Proceedings of the Sixth SCA/AFA Conference on Argumentation*, ed. Bruce Gronbeck (Annandale, VA: SCA, 1989), 149.

6. J. Michael Hogan, "Media Nihilism and the Presidential Debates," *Argumentation and Advocacy* (Spring 1989): 223.

7. Celeste Michelle Condit, "Feminized Power and Adversarial Advocacy: Leveling Arguments or Analyzing Them?" *Argumentation and Advocacy* (Spring 1989): 227.

8. David Werling, Michael Salvador, Malcolm O. Sillars, and Mina A. Vaughn, "Presidential Debates: Epideictic Merger of Issues and Images in Values," in *Argument and Critical Practices: Proceedings of the Fifth Conference on Argumentation*, ed. Joseph W. Wenzel (Annandale, VA: SCA 1985), 229–238.

9. Bruce Gronbeck, "The Functions of Presidential Campaigning," *Communication Monographs* 45 (1978): 268–280.

10. Orrin Klapp, *Symbolic Leaders: Public Dramas and Public Men* (Chicago: Aldine, 1964), 31.

11. W. Lance Bennett, "Where Have All the Issues Gone? Explaining the Rhetorical Limits in American Elections," in *Spheres of Argument: Proceedings of the Sixth SCA/AFA Conference on Argumentation*, 133.

12. George F. Bishop, Robert G. Meadow, Marilyn Jackson-Beeck, eds., *The Presidential Debates: Media, Electoral, and Policy Perspectives* (New York: Praeger, 1978), xvii.

13. Gladys Engel Lang, "Still Seeking Answers," *Critical Studies in Mass Communication* 4 (June 1987): 211.

14. Bruce Gronbeck, "Functional and Dramaturgical Theories of Presidential Campaigning," *Presidential Studies Quarterly* 14 (Fall 1984): 496.

15. Condit, "Feminized Power," 227; Werling et al., "Presidential Debates."

16. John Louis Lucaites, "Rhetorical Legitimacy, <Public Trust> and the Presidential Debates," *Argumentation and Advocacy* (Spring 1989): 231–238.

17. Lang goes so far as to argue that the substance of what the candidates say in these debates is not as important as how well they communicate and project the intended image. See "Still Seeking Answers," 213.

18. Eric F. Goldman, *The Crucial Decade and After: America, 1945–1960* (New York: Vintage, 1960), 307–346; Marty Jezer, *Life in the United States: 1945–1960* (Boston: South End Press, 1982), 77–106.

19. Robert G. Meadow, "A Speech by Any Other Name," *Critical Studies in Mass Communication* 4 (June 1987): 208.

20. Lang, "Still Seeking Answers," 211.

21. See William C. Spragens, "Political Impact of Presidential Assassination and Attempted Assassinations," *Presidential Studies Quarterly* 10 (Summer 1980): 336–347.

22. For a discussion of the media's interest in Ferraro, see Sidney Kraus, *Televised Presidential Debates and Public Policy* (Hillsdale, NJ: Lawrence Erlbaum Associates, 1988), 111–112.

23. Dennis K. Davis, "Television and Political Debates," *Critical Studies in Mass Communication* 4 (1987): 201, cited in Kraus, *Televised Presidential Debates and Public Policy*, 76.

24. Hogan, "Media Nihilism and the Presidential Debates," 224; Condit, "Feminized Power," 228. See also John T. Morello, "Who Won? A Critical Examination of Newspaper Editorials Evaluating Nationally Televised Debates," *Argumentation and Advocacy* 27 (Winter 1991): 124.

25. Kraus, *Televised Presidential Debates*, 88–92; Klumpp, "Civic Discourse," 149; Morello, "Who Won?" 114–115. Dennis K. Davis, "Review and Criticism," *Critical Studies in Mass Communication* 4 (June 1987): 201; Kathleen Hall Jamieson and David Birdsell, *Presidential Debates* (New York: Oxford University Press, 1988): 170–173.

26. Donn W. Parson, "On the Education of a TV Debate Critic," *Argument and Social Practice: Proceedings of the Fourth Conference on Argumentation*, ed. J. Robert Cox, Malcolm O. Sillars, and Gregg B. Walker (Annandale, VA: 1985), 216.

27. David Vancil and Sue E. Pendell, "Winning Presidential Debates," *Western Journal of Speech* 48 (1984): 62–74.

28. See Meadow, "A Speech by Any Other Name," 209. Meadow develops the case for "dispensing with the so-called presidential debates," 207.

29. See Jamieson and Birdsell, *Presidential Debates*, 170–172, 214–215; Morello, "Who Won?" 124.

30. Gronbeck has called for studies analyzing the ways in which candidates enact roles in political campaigns. See "Functional and Dramaturgical Theories of Presidential Campaigning."

31. K. Lang and G. E. Lang, *Politics and Television* (Chicago: Quarterly Press, 1968), cited in Lang, "Still Seeking Answers," 213.

32. See David S. Birdsell, "Introduction," *Argumentation and Advocacy* 27 (Winter 1991): 99.

Selected Bibliography

Alexander, Herbert E., and Margolis, Joel. "The Making of the Debates." In *The Presidential Debates: Media, Electoral, and Policy Perspectives*. Edited by George F. Bishop, Robert G. Meadow, and Marilyn Jackson-Beeck. New York: Praeger, 1978, 18–32.

Anderson, James A., and Avery, Robert K. "An Analysis of Changes in Voter Perception of Candidates' Positions." *Communication Monographs* 45 (November 1978): 354–361.

Aristotle. *Politics*. Translated by Ernest Baker. London: Oxford University Press, 1977.

———. *Rhetoric*. Translated by W. Rhys Roberts. New York: Modern Library, 1954.

Auer, J. Jeffrey. "The Counterfeit Debates." In *The Great Debates*. Edited by Sidney Kraus. Bloomington, IN: Indiana University Press, 1962, 142–150.

———. "Great Myths about the Great Debates." *Speaker and Gavel* 18 (Winter 1981): 14–21.

Balthrop, V. William. "Argument as Linguistic Opportunity." *Proceedings of the Summer Conference on Argumentation*. Edited by Jack Rhodes and Sara Newell. Annandale, VA: SCA/AFA, 1980, 184–213.

Bechtolt, Warren E., Jr., Hilyard, Joseph, and Bybee, Carl R. "Agenda Control in the 1976 Debates: A Content Analysis." *Journalist Quarterly* (Winter 1977): 674–681.

Becker, Lee B., Sobowale, Idowu A., Cobbey, Robin E. and Eyal, Chaim H. "Debates' Effects on Voters' Understanding of Candidates and Issues." In *The Presidential Debates: Media, Electoral, and Policy Perspective*. Edited by Georgy F. Bishop, Robert G. Meadow, and Marilyn Jackson-Beeck. New York: Praeger, 1978, 126–139.

Becker, Samuel and Lower, Elmer W. "Broadcasting in Presidential Campaigns." In *The Great Debates*. Edited by Sidney Kraus. Bloomington, IN: Indiana University Press, 1962, 25–55.

Bennett, W. Lance. "Where Have All the Issues Gone? Explaining the Rhetorical Limits in American Elections." In *Spheres of Argument: Proceedings of the Sixth SCA/AFA Conference on Argumentation.* Edited by Bruce Gronbeck. Annandale, VA: SCA/AFA, 1989, 128–135.

Berquist, Goodwin F., and Golden, James L. "Media Rhetoric, Criticism and the Public Perception of the 1980 Debates." *Quarterly Journal of Speech* 67 (1981): 125–137.

Birdsell, David S. "Introduction." *Argumentation and Advocacy: Journal of the American Forensic Association* 27 (Winter 1991): 97.

Bishop, George F., Meadow, Robert G., and Jackson-Beeck, Marilyn, eds. *The Presidential Debates: Media, Electoral, and Policy Perspectives.* New York: Praeger, 1978.

Bitzer, Lloyd. "The Rhetorical Situation." *Philosophy and Rhetoric* 1 (January 1968): 1–14.

———, and Rueter, Theodore. *Carter v. Ford: The Counterfeit Debates of 1976.* Madison, WI: University of Wisconsin Press, 1980.

Black, Edwin. "A Note of Theory and Practice in Rhetorical Criticism." *Western Journal of Speech* 44 (Fall 1980): 331–336.

———. *Rhetorical Criticism: A Study in Method.* Madison, WI: University of Wisconsin Press, 1965; reprinted 1978.

Blankenship, Jane, and Kang, Jong Geun. "The 1984 Presidential and Vice Presidential Debates: The Printed Press and 'Construction' by Metaphor." *Presidential Studies Quarterly* 21 (Spring 1991): 307–318.

Blume, Keith. *The Presidential Election Show: Campaign :84 and Beyond the Nightly News.* South Hadley, MA: Bergin and Garvey, 1985).

Blumenthal, Sidney. *Pledging Allegiance: The Last Campaign of the Cold War.* New York: Harper Collins, 1990.

Bowes, John E., and Strentz, Herbert. "Candidates' Images: Stereotyping and the 1976 Debates." In *Communication Yearbook II.* Edited by Brent Ruben. New Brunswick, NJ: Transaction, 1978, 391–406.

Boyd, Gerald M. *New York Times,* October 5, 1988, A–30.

Bradlee, Benjamin C. *Conversations with Kennedy.* New York: W. W. Norton, 1975.

Brehm, Sharon, ed. *Seeing Female: Social Roles and Personal Lives.* Westport, CT: Greenwood Press, 1988.

Breslin, Rosemary, and Hammer, Joshua. *Gerry! A Woman Making History.* New York: Pinnacle, 1984.

Brockriede, Wayne. "Rhetorical Criticism as Argument." *Quarterly Journal of Speech* 60 (1974): 459–467.

Brydon, Steven R. "The Two Faces of Jimmy Carter: The Transformation of a Presidential Debater, 1976 and 1980." *Central States Speech* 36 (Fall 1985): 138–151.

Burke, Kenneth. *A Grammar of Motives.* Berkeley, CA: University of California Press, 1969.

Campbell, Karlyn Kohrs. "Criticism: Ephemeral and Enduring." *Speech Teacher* 22 (January 1974): 9–14.

———. "The Nature of Criticism in Rhetorical and Communicative Studies." *Central States Speech* 30 (Spring 1979): 4–13.

———, and Jamieson, Kathleen Hall. "Form and Genre in Rhetorical Criticism:

An Introduction." in *Form and Genre: Shaping Rhetorical Action*. Falls Church, VA: SCA, 1977, pp. 9–32.

——. "Inaugurating the Presidency." *Presidential Studies Quarterly* 15 (Spring 1985): 394–411.

Campbell, Karlyn K. and Jerry, E. Claire. "Woman and Speaker: A Conflict in Roles." In *Seeing Female: Social Roles and Personal Lives*. Edited by Sharon S. Brehm. Westport, CT: Greenwood Press, 1988, 123–133.

Campbell, Kathleen. "Enactment as a Rhetorical Strategy in 'The Year of Living Dangerously.' " *Central States Speech Journal* 39 (Fall/Winter 1988): 258–268.

Carlin, Diana Prentice. "A Defense of the 'Debate' in Presidential Debates." *Argumentation Advocacy: The Journal of the American Forensic Association* 25 (Spring 1989): 208–213.

——, Howard, Charles, Stanfield, Susan, and Reynolds, Larry. "The Effects of Presidential Debate Formats on Clash: A Comparative Analysis." *Argumentation and Advocacy: The Journal of the American Forensic Association* 27 (Winter 1991): 128–136.

Carter, Richard F. "A Very Peculiar Horse Race." In *The Presidential Debates: Media, Electoral, and Policy Perspectives*. Edited by George F. Bishop, Robert G. Meadow, and Marilyn Jackson-Beeck. New York: Praeger, 1978, 3–17.

Carter, Douglass. "Notes from Backstage." In *The Great Debates*. Edited by Sidney Kraus. Bloomington, IN: Indiana University Press, 1962, 127–131.

Chaffee, Steven H. "Presidential Debates—Are They Helpful to Voters?" *Communication Monographs* 45 (November 1978): 330–353.

Charlton, Linda. *New York Times*, October 15, 1976, B–5.

——. *New York Times*, October 17, 1976, IV, 3.

Christian Science Monitor, October 15, 1984, 1.

——, October 15, 1984, A–21.

Clevenger, Theodore, Jr., Parson, Donald W., and Polisky, Jerome B. "The Problem of Textual Accuracy." In *The Great Debates*. Edited by Sidney Kraus. Bloomington, IN: Indiana University of Press, 1962, 341–347.

Combs, James E. *Dimensions of Political Drama*. Santa Monica, CA: Goodyear, 1980.

Condit, Celeste Michelle. "Feminized Power and Adversarial Advocacy: Leveling Arguments or Analyzing Them?" *Argumentation and Advocacy: The Journal of the American Forensic Association* 25 (Spring 1989): 226–230.

Consigny, Scott. "Rhetoric and Its Situations." *Philosophy and Rhetoric* 7 (Summer 1974): 175–186.

Davis, Dennis K. "Television and Political Debates." *Critical Studies in Mass Communication* 4 (June 1987): 201.

——. "Review and Criticism." *Critical Studies in Mass Communication* 4 (June 1987): 201.

Desmond, Roger Jon, and Donohue, Thomas R. "The Role of the 1976 Televised Debates in the Political Socialization of Adolescents." *Communication Quarterly* 29 (Fall 1981): 302–308.

Deutschmann, Paul J. "Viewing, Conversation, and Voting Intentions." In *The Great Debates*. Edited by Sidney Kraus. Bloomington, IN: Indiana University Press, 1962, 232–252.

Dionne, E. J., Jr. *New York Times*, October 5, 1988, 1, 30.

———. *New York Times*, October 7, 1988, B–6.

Dowd, Maureen. *New York Times*, October 1, 1988, 8.

Drew, Elizabeth. *Portrait of an Election: The 1980 Presidential Campaign*. New York: Simon and Schuster, 1981.

———. *Campaign Journal: The Political Events of 1983–1984*. New York: Macmillan, 1985.

Drucker, Susan J., and Hunold, Janice Platt. "The Debating Game." *Critical Studies in Mass Communication* 4 (June 1987): 202–206.

Edelman, Murray. *The Symbolic Uses of Politics*. Urbana, IL: University of Illinois Press, 1967.

Ellsworth, John W. "Rationality and Campaigning: A Content Analysis of the 1960 Presidential Campaign Debates." *Western Political Science Quarterly* 18 (December 1965): 794–802.

Fairlie, Henry. *The Kennedy Promise: The Politics of Expectation*. Garden City, NY: Doubleday, 1973.

Ferraro, Geraldine, with Linda Bird Francke. *Ferraro: My Story*. New York: Bantam, 1985.

Fish, Duane R. "Image and Issue in the Second Bush-Dukakis Debate: The Mediating Role of Values." *Spheres of Argument: Proceedings of the Sixth SCA/AFA Conference on Argumentation*. Edited by Bruce Gronbeck. Annandale, VA: SCA/AFA, 1989, 151–157.

Fisher, Walter. "Rhetorical Fiction and the Presidency." *Quarterly Journal of Speech* 66 (April 1980): 118–126.

Friedenberg, Robert V. " 'We Are Present Here for the Purpose of Having a Joint Discussion': The Conditions Requisite for Political Debates." *Journal of the American Forensic Association* 16 (Summer 1979): 1–9.

———. " 'Selfish Interests,' or the Prerequisites for Political Debate: An Analysis of the 1980 Presidential Debates and the Implications for Future Campaigns." *Journal of the American Forensic Association* 18 (Fall 1981): 91–98.

Fry, Northrup. *Anatomy of Criticism: Four Essays*. Princeton, NJ: Princeton University Press, 1957.

Germond, Jack "Running in Place," *New York Times Magazine*, October 10, 1976, 15.

———, and Witcover, Jules. *Blue Smoke and Mirrors: How Reagan Won and Why Carter Lost the Election of 1980*. New York: Viking, 1981.

———. "Presidential Debates: An Overview." *The Past and Future of Presidential Debates*. Edited by Austin Ranney. Washington, DC: American Enterprise Institute, 1979.

———. *Wake Us When It's Over: Presidential Politics of 1984*. New York: Macmillan, 1985.

———. *Whose Broad Stripes and Bright Stars: The Trivial Pursuit of the Presidency 1988*. New York: Warner Books, 1989.

Gold, Ellen Reid. "Ronald Reagan and the Oral Tradition." *Central States Speech Journal* 39 (Fall/Winter 1988): 159–176.

Goldman, Eric F. *The Crucial Decade and After: America, 1945–1960*. New York: Vintage, 1960.

Goldman, Peter, and Mattews, Tom. *The Quest for the Presidency 1988.* New York: Touchstone, 1989.

Goodman, Ellen. The *Washington Post,* October 13, 1984, A–16.

Graber, Doris A. "Problems in Measuring Audience Effects of the 1976 Debates." In *The Presidential Debates: Media, Electoral, and Policy Perspectives.* Edited by George F. Bishop, Robert G. Meadow, and Marilyn Jackson-Beeck. New York: Praeger, 1978, 105–125.

———, and Kim, Young. "Why John Q. Voter Did Not Learn Much from the 1976 Presidential Debates." *Communication Yearbook II.* Edited by Brent D. Ruben. New Brunswick, NJ: Transaction—International Communication Association, 1978, 407–422.

Greenfield, Jeff. *The Real Campaign: How the Media Missed the Story of the 1980 Campaign.* New York: Summit, 1982.

Gronbeck, Bruce E. "The Functions of Presidential Campaigning." *Communication Monographs* 45 (1978): 268–280.

———. "Functional and Dramaturgical Themes of Presidential Campaigning." *Presidential Studies Quarterly* 14 (Fall 1984): 486–499.

———. "The Presidential Campaign Dramas of 1984." *Presidential Studies Quarterly* 15 (Spring 1985): 386–393.

Hagner, Paul R., and Rieselbach, Leroy N. "The Impact of the 1976 Presidential Debates: Conversion or Reinforcement?" In *The Presidential Debates: Media, Electoral, and Policy Perspectives.* Edited by George F. Bishop, Robert G. Meadow, and Marilyn Jackson-Beeck. New York: Praeger, 1978, 157–178.

Halberstam, David. *The Best and the Brightest.* New York: Random House, 1972.

Halloran, S. Michael. "Doing Public Business in Public." In *Form and Genre: Shaping Rhetorical Action.* Edited by Karlyn Kohrs Campbell and Kathleen Hall Jamieson. Falls Church, VA: SCA, 1977, 118–137.

Hart, Roderick P. *Verbal Style and the Presidency: A Computer-Based Analysis.* New York: Academic Press, 1984.

———. "A Commentary on Popular Assumptions about Political Communication." *Human Communication Research* 8 (Summer 1982): 366–389.

Hartman, Robert T. *Palace Politics: An Inside Account of the Ford Years.* New York: McGraw Hill, 1980.

Hellweg, Susan A., and Phillips, Steven L. "A Verbal and Visual Analysis of the 1980 Houston Republican Presidential Primary Debate." *Southern Speech Communication* 47 (Fall 1981): 23–38.

Henry, William A., III. *Visions of America: How We Saw the 1984 Election.* Boston: Atlantic Monthly Press, 1985.

Hess, Stephen. *The Presidential Campaign.* rev. ed. Washington, DC: The Brookings Institution, 1978.

Hillbruner, Anthony. "Rhetoric and Politics: The Making of the President 1960." *Western Journal of Speech* 29 (Spring 1965): 91–102.

Hinck, Edward A. "Enacting Leadership through Political Debate: A Rhetorical Analysis of the 1980 Presidential Debate between Ronald Reagan and Jimmy Carter." Paper presented at the Doctoral Honors Seminar, Ohio University, Athens, Ohio, May 1984.

———. "Enacting the Presidency: A Rhetorical Analysis of Twentieth Century Presidential Debates." Ph.D. Diss., University of Kansas, 1987.

Hogan J. Michael. "Media Nihilism and the Presidential Debates." *Argumentation and Advocacy: The Journal of the American Forensic Association* 25 (Spring 1989): 220–225.

Hughes, Emmet John. *The Living Presidency.* New York: Coward, McCann and Geoghegan, 1972.

Jackson-Beeck, Marilyn, and Meadow, Robert G. "The Triple Agenda of Presidential Debates." *Public Opinion Quarterly* 43 (1979): 173–180.

Jamieson, Kathleen Hall. *Packaging the Presidency: A History and Criticism of Presidential Campaign Advertising.* New York: Oxford University Press, 1984.

———. "Antecedent Genre as Rhetorical Constraint." *Quarterly Journal of Speech* 61 (December 1975): 406–415.

———, and Birdsell, David. *Presidential Debates: The Challenge of Creating an Informed Electorate.* New York: Oxford University Press, 1988.

Jamieson, Kathleen Hall, and Campbell, Karlyn Kohrs. "Rhetorical Hybrids: Fusions of Generic Elements." *Quarterly Journal of Speech* 68 (May 1982): 146–157.

Jezer, Marty. *The Dark Ages: Life in the United States, 1945–1960.* Boston: South End Press, 1982.

Karayn, James. "Presidential Debates: A Plan for the Future." In *The Great Debates: Carter vs. Ford, 1976.* Edited by Sidney Kraus. Bloomington, IN: Indiana University Press, 1962, 209–222.

Katz, Elihu, and Feldman, Jacob J. "The Debates in Light of Research: A Survey of Surveys." In *The Great Debates.* Edited by Sidney Kraus. Bloomington, IN: Indiana University Press, 1962, 173–223.

Katz, Lee Michael. *My Name is Geraldine Ferraro: An Unauthorized Biography.* New York: New American Library, 1984.

Kauffman, Charles. "Poetic as Argument." *Quarterly Journal of Speech* 67 (November 1981): 407–415.

Kelley, S. "Campaign Debates: Some Facts and Issues." *Public Opinion Quarterly* 26 (1962): 351–366.

Klapp, Orrin E. *Symbolic Leaders: Public Dramas and Public Men.* Chicago: Aldine, 1964.

Kneeland, Douglas E. *New York Times*, October 15, 1976, B–5.

———. *New York Times*, October 17, 1976, VI, 3.

Kondracke, Morton. *The New Republic*, September 20, 1980, 5.

Kraus, Sidney, ed. *The Great Debates: Carter vs. Ford, 1976.* Bloomington, IN: Indiana University Press, 1979.

———. "Voters Win." *Critical Studies in Mass Communication* 4 (June 1987): 214–216.

———. *Televised Presidential Debates and Public Policy.* Hillsdale, NJ: Lawrence Erlbaum Associates, 1988.

———, and Davis, Dennis K. "Political Debates." *Handbook of Political Communication.* Edited by Dan D. Nimmo and Keith R. Sanders. Beverly Hills: Sage, 1981, 273–298.

Kraus, Sidney, and Smith, Raymond G. "Issues and Images." In *The Great Debates.* Edited by Sidney Kraus. Bloomington, IN: Indiana University Press, 1962, 289–312.

Lang, Gladys Engel. "Still Seeking Answers." *Critical Studies in Mass Communication* 4 (June 1987): 211–213.

———, and Lang, Kurt. "Immediate and Delayed Responses to a Carter-Ford Debate: Assessing Public Opinion." *Public Opinion Quarterly* 42 (1978): 322–341.

———. "The Formation of Public Opinion: Direct and Mediated Effects of the First Debate." In *The Presidential Debates: Media, Electoral, and Policy Perspectives*. Edited by George F. Bishop, Robert G. Meadow, and Marilyn Jackson-Beeck. New York: Praeger, 1978, 61–80.

———. "Polling on Watergate: The Battle for Public Opinion." *Public Opinion Quarterly* 44 (1980): 530–547.

Lang, Kurt, and Lang, Gladys E. "Ordeal by Debate: Viewer Reactions." *Public Opinion Quarterly* 25 (1961): 277–341.

———. "Reactions of Viewers." In *The Great Debates*. Edited by Sidney Kraus. Bloomington, IN: Indiana University Press, 1962, 313–330.

Langer, Suzanne. *Feeling and Form: A Theory of Art*. New York: Charles Scribner's Sons, 1953.

———. *Problems of Art*. New York: Charles Scribner's Sons, 1957.

Lasswell, Harold D. "Introduction." In *The Great Debates*. Edited by Sidney Kraus. Bloomington, IN: Indiana University Press, 1962, 19–24.

Leff, Michael. "Textual Criticism: The Legacy of G. P. Mohrmann." *Quarterly Journal of Speech* 72 (1986): 377–389.

———, and Sachs, Andrew. "Words the Most Like Things: Iconicity and the Rhetorical Text." *Western Journal of Speech Communication* 54 (Summer 1990): 252–273.

Leff, Michael C., and Mohrmann, Gerald P. "Lincoln at Cooper Union: A Rhetorical Analysis of the Text." *Quarterly Journal of Speech* 60 (October 1974): 346–358.

Lemert, James B., Elliott, William R., Nestvold, Karl J., and Rarick, Galen R. "Effects of Viewing a Presidential Primary Debate." *Communication Research* 10 (April 1983): 155–171.

Leuthold, David A., and Valentine, David C. "How Reagan 'Won' the Cleveland Debate: Audience Predispositions and Presidential Debate 'Winners.'" *Speaker and Gavel* 18 (Winter 1981): 60–66.

Lubell, Samuel. "Personalities V. Issues." In *The Great Debates*. Edited by Sidney Kraus. Bloomington, IN: Indiana University Press, 1962, 151–162.

Lucaites, John Louis. "Rhetorical Legitimacy, <Public Trust> and the Presidential Debates. *Argumentation and Advocacy: The Journal of the American Forensic Association* 25 (Spring 1989): 231–238.

McCall, Jeffrey M. "The Panelists as Pseudo-Debaters: An Evaluation of the Questions and Questioners in the Presidential Debates of 1980." *Journal of the American Forensic Association* 21 (Fall 1984): 97–104.

McClain, Thomas B. "Secondary School Debate Pedagogy." *Argumentation and Advocacy: Journal of the American Forensic Association* 25 (Spring 1989): 203–204.

McCloskey, H. "Consensus and Ideology in American Politics." *American Political Science Review* 58 (1964): 361–382.

Madsen, Arnie. "Partisan Commentary and the First 1988 Presidential Debate."

Argumentation and Advocacy: The Journal of the American Forensic Association 27 (Winter 1991): 100–113.

Martel, Myles. *Political Campaign Debates: Images, Strategies and Tactics.* New York: Longman, 1983.

Mazo, Earl, Moos, Malcolm, Hoffman, Hallock, and Wheeler, Harvey. *The Great Debates: An Occasional Paper on the Role of the Political Process in the Free Society.* Santa Barbara, CA: Center for the Study of Democratic Institutions, 1962.

Meadow, Robert G. "A Speech by Any Other Name." *Critical Studies in Mass Communication* 4 (June 1987): 207–210.

———, and Jackson-Beeck, Marilyn. "A Comparative Perspective on Presidential Debates: Issue Evolution in 1960 and 1976." In *The Presidential Debates: Media, Electoral, and Policy Perspectives.* Edited by George F. Bishop, Robert G. Meadow, and Marilyn Jackson-Beeck. New York: Praeger, 1978, 33–50.

———. "Candidate Political Philosophy: Revelations in the 1960 and 1976 Debates." *Presidential Studies Quarterly* 10 (Spring 1980): 234–243.

Mehling, Ruben, Kraus, Sidney, and Yoakum, Richard D. "Pre-Debate Campaign Interest and Media Use." In *The Great Debates.* Edited by Sidney Kraus. Bloomington, IN: Indiana University Press, 1962, 224–231.

Merelman, Richard M. "The Dramaturgy of Politics." *The Sociological Quarterly* 10 (1969): 216–241.

Messaris, Paul, Eckman, Bruce, and Gumpert, Gary. "Editing Structure in the Televised Versions of the 1976 Presidential Debates." *Journal of Broadcasting* 23 (Summer 1973): 359–369.

Meyer, John. "Ronald Reagan and Humor: A Politician's Velvet Weapon." *Communication Studies* 41 (Spring 1990): 76–88.

Middleton, R. "National TV Debates and Presidential Voting Decisions." *Public Opinion Quarterly* 26 (1962): 426–429.

Miller, A. H., and MacKuen, M. "Learning about the Candidates: The 1976 Presidential Debates." *Public Opinion Quarterly* 43 (1979): 326–346.

Minnow, Newton, and Sloan, Clifford M. *For Great Debates: A New Plan for Future Presidential TV Debates.* New York: Priority Press, 1987.

Mohrmann, Gerald P., and Leff, Michael C. "Lincoln at Cooper Union: A Rationale for Neo-classical Criticism." *Quarterly Journal of Speech* 60 (December 1974): 459–467.

Mollenhoff, Clark R. *The Man Who Pardoned Nixon.* New York: St. Martin's Press, 1976, chap. 8.

Moore, Jonathan, ed. *The Campaign for President: 1980 in Retrospect.* Cambridge, MA: Ballinger, 1981.

Morello, John T. "Visual Structuring of the 1976 and 1984 Nationally Televised Debates." *Central States Speech Journal* 39 (Fall/Winter 1988): 233–243.

———. " 'Who Won?' A Critical Examination of Newspaper Editorials Evaluating Nationally Televised Presidential Debates." *Argumentation and Advocacy: The Journal of the American Forensic Association* 27 (Winter 1991): 114–127.

Murphy, John. "Presidential Debates and Campaign Rhetoric: Text Within Context." *The Southern Communication Journal* 57 (Spring 1992): 219–228.

Neustadt, Richard E. *Presidential Power, The Politics of Leadership*. New York: Wiley, 1961.

New York Times, September 28, 1960, 1.

————, September 10, 1976, A–19.

————, September 19, 1976, VI, 1.

————, October 13, 1976, A–20.

————, October 15, 1976, B–4.

————, October 28, 1976, 48.

————, October 31, 1976, IV, 1.

————, November 1, 1976, 49.

————, October 10, 1984, A–4.

————, October 11, 1984, A–1.

————, October 11, 1984, B–11.

————, October 12, 1984, B–5–6.

————, October 12, 1984, B–7.

————, October 13, 1984, A–8.

————, October 5, 1988, A–1, A–30.

————, October 13, 1988, A–1.

————, October 13, 1988, B–10.

Newsweek, August 25, 1940, 22.

————, October 22, 1984, 29.

————, October 22, 1984, 30.

Nimmo, Dan. *The Political Persuaders: The Techniques of Modern Election Campaigns*. Englewood Cliffs, NJ: Prentice-Hall, 1970.

————. *Political Communication and Public Opinion in America*. Santa Monica, CA: Goodyear, 1978.

————, Mansfield, Michael, and Curry, James. "Persistence and Change in Candidate Images." In *The Presidential Debates: Media, Electoral, and Policy Perspectives*. Edited by George F. Bishop, Robert G. Meadow, and Marilyn Jackson-Beeck. New York: Praeger, 1978, 140–156.

————, and Savage, Robert. *Candidates and Their Images: Concepts, Methods, and Findings*. Pacific Palisades, CA: Goodyear, 1976.

O'Brien, Lawrence F. *No Final Victories*. New York: Doubleday, 1974.

Parson, Donn W. "On the Education of a TV Debate Critic." In *Argument and Social Practice: Proceedings of the Fourth Conference on Argumentation*. Edited by J. Robert Cox, Malcolm O. Sillars, and Gregg B. Walker. Annandale, VA: SCA/AFA, 1985, 211–218.

————. "Congregation by Segregation: An Analysis of Argument Strategies in the First 1988 Presidential Debate." In *Spheres of Argument: Proceedings of the Sixth SCA/AFA Conference on Argumentation*. Edited by Bruce Gronbeck. Annandale, VA: SCA/AFA, 1989, 136–139.

Perelman, Chaim, and Olbrechts-Tyteca, L. *The New Rhetoric*. Translated by John Wilkinson and Purcell Weaver. Notre Dame, IN: Notre Dame University Press, 1969.

Pfau, Michael. "Criteria and Format to Optimize Political Debates: An Analysis of South Dakota's 'Election '80' Series." *Journal of the American Forensic Association* 9 (Spring 1983): 205–214.

Pike, Kenneth L. "Etic and Emic Standpoints for the Description of Behavior."

In *Communication and Interaction*. Edited by Alfred G. Smith. New York: Holt, Rinehart and Wilson, 1966, 152–163.

Polsby, Nelson W. "Debatable Thoughts on Presidential Debates." In *The Past and Future of Presidential Debates*. Edited by Austin Ranney. Washington, DC: American Enterprise Institute, 1979, 184.

Ranney, Austin. *The American Elections of 1984*. Durham, NC: American Enterprise Institute: Duke University Press, 1985.

———, ed. *The Past and Future of Presidential Debates*. Washington, DC: American Enterprise Institute, 1979.

Rathbun, John. "The Problem of Judgment and Effects in Historical Criticism: A Proposed Solution." *Western Journal of Speech* 33 (Summer 1969): 146–159.

Reedy, George E. *The Twilight of the Presidency*. New York: Mentor, 1970.

Riley, Patricia, and Hollihan, Thomas A. "The 1980 Presidential Debates: A Content Analysis of the Issues and Arguments." *Speaker and Gavel* 18 (Winter 1981): 47–59.

———, and Cooley, David. "The 1976 Presidential Debates: An Analysis of the Issues and Arguments." Paper presented at the Central States Speech Association Convention, Chicago, April 1980.

Ritter, Kurt. "American Political Rhetoric and the Jeremiadic Tradition: Presidential Nomination Acceptance Addresses, 1960–1976." *Central States Speech* 31 (Fall 1980): 153–171.

———, and Hellweg, Susan A. "Televised Presidential Primary Debates: A New National Forum for Political Debating." *Journal of the American Forensics Association* 2 (Summer 1981): 1–14.

Rosenbaum, David E. *New York Times*, October 17, 1976, A–28.

Rosenfield,, Lawrence. "The Anatomy of Critical Discourse." *Speech Monographs* 25 (March 1968): 50–69.

———. "The Experience of Criticism." *Quarterly Journal of Speech* 60 (December 1974): 489–496.

Rosenthal, Paul I. "The Concept of Ethos and the Structure of Persuasion." *Speech Monographs* 33 (June 1966): 11–26.

Rowland, Robert C. "The Substance of the 1980 Carter-Reagan Debate." *Southern Speech Communication* 5 (Winter 1981): 142–165.

———, and Garcia, Rey. "The 1984 Democratic Debates: Does Format Make a Difference?" In *Argument and Social Practice: Proceedings of the Fourth Conference on Argumentation*. Edited by J. Robert Cox, Malcolm O. Sillars, and Gregg B. Walker. Annandale, VA: SCA/AFA, 1985, 219–235.

Rowland, Robert C., and Voss, Cary R. W. "A Structural Functional Analysis of the Assumptions Behind Presidential Debates." In *Argument and Critical Practices: Proceedings of the Fifth Conference on Argumentation*. Edited by Joseph W. Wenzel. Annandale, VA: SCA/AFA, 1987, 239–248.

Runkel, Daniel R., ed. *Campaign for President: The Managers Look at 88*. Dover, MA: Auburn House, 1989.

Salant, R. S. "The Television Debates: A Revolution That Deserves a Future." *Public Opinion Quarterly* 26 (1962): 335–350.

Samovar, Larry A. "Ambiguity and Unequivocation in the Kennedy-Nixon Television Debates: A Rhetorical Analysis." *Western Journal of Speech* 29 (Fall 1965): 211–218.

Sarnoff, Robert W. "An NBC View." In *The Great Debates*. Edited by Sidney Kraus. Bloomington, IN: Indiana University Press, 1962, 56–64.

Schram, Martin. *Running for President 1976: The Carter Campaign*. New York: Sein and Day, 1977.

Sears, D. O., Fredman, J. L., and O'Connor, E. F., Jr. "The Effects of Anticipated Debate and Commitment on the Polarization of Audience Opinion." *Public Opinion Quarterly* 28 (1964): 615–627.

Sebald, Hans."Limitations of Communication: Mechanisms of Image Maintenance in Form of Selective Perception, Selective Memory and Selective Distortion." *Journal of Communication* 12 (September 1962): 142–149.

Seldes, Gilbert. "The Future of National Debates." In *The Great Debates*. Edited by Sidney Kraus. Bloomington, IN: Indiana University Press, 1962, 163–172.

Seltz, Herbert A., and Yoakum, Richard D. "Production Diary of the Debates." In *The Great Debates*. Edited by Sidney Kraus. Bloomington, IN: Indiana University Press, 1962, 73–126.

Sheehy, Gail. *Character: America's Search for Leadership*. New York: William Morrow, 1988.

Siepmann, Charles A. "Were They 'Great'?" In *The Great Debates*. Edited by Sidney Kraus. Bloomington, IN: Indiana University Press, 1962, 132–141.

Sigelman, Lee, and Sigelman, Carol K. "Judgments of the Carter-Reagan Debate: The Eyes of the Beholders." *Public Opinion Quarterly* 48 (1984): 624–628.

Smith, Hedrick. *New York Times*, August 11, 1980, A–1.

Spragens, William C. "Political Impact of Presidential Assassination and Attempted Assassinations." *Presidential Studies Quarterly* 10 (Summer 1980): 336–347.

Sorenson, Theodore C. *Kennedy*. New York: Harper and Row, 1965.

Stanton, Frank. "A CBS View." In *The Great Debates*. Edited by Sidney Kraus. Bloomington, IN: Indiana University Press, 1962, 65–72.

Steeper, Frederick T. "Public Response to Gerald Ford's Statements on Eastern Europe in the Second Debate." In *The Presidential Debates: Media, Electoral, and Policy Perspectives*. Edited by George F. Bishop, Robert G. Meadow, and Marilyn Jackson-Beeck. New York: Praeger, 1978, 65–72.

Tannenbaum, Percy H., Greenberg, Bradley S., and Silverman, Fred. "Candidate Images." In *The Great Debates*. Edited by Sidney Kraus. Bloomington, IN: Indiana University Press, 1962, 271–288.

terHorst, Jerald. *Gerald Ford and the Future of the Presidency*. New York: Third Press, 1974, 216–217.

"The Battle of the Button." *Newsweek*, September 1, 1980, 8.

Tiemens, Robert K. "Television's Portrayal of the 1976 Presidential Debates: An Analysis of Visual Content." *Communication Quarterly* 33 (Winter 1985): 34–43.

———. "The Visual Context of Argument: An Analysis of the September 25, 1988 Presidential Debate." In *Spheres of Argument: Proceedings of the Sixth SCA/AFA Conference on Argumentation*. Edited by Bruce Gronbeck. Annandale, VA: SCA/AFA, 1989, 140–146.

————, Hellweg, Susan A., Kipper, Phillip, and Phillips, Steven L. "An Integrative Verbal and Visual Analysis of the Carter-Reagan Debate." *Communication Quarterly* 33 (Winter 1985): 34–43.

Time, October 22, 1984, 30, 31.

Trent, Judith, and Friedenberg, Robert V. *Political Campaign Communication: Principles of Practice*. New York: Praeger, 1983.

Tugwell, Rexford G., and Cronin, Thomas E., eds. *The Presidency Reappraised*. New York: Praeger, 1974.

Vancil, David, and Pendell, Sue E. "Winning Presidential Debates." *Western Journal of Speech* 48 (1984): 62–74.

Wald, K. D., and Lupfer, M. M. "The Presidential Debate as a Civics Lesson." *Public Opinion Quarterly* 42 (1978): 342–353.

Wall, Victor, Golden, James L., and James, Herbert. "Perceptions of the 1984 Presidential Debates and a Select 1988 Presidential Primary Debate." *Presidential Studies Quarterly* 18 (Summer 1988): 541–564.

Ware, B. L., and Linkugel, W. A. "They Spoke in Defense of Themselves: On Generic Criticism of Apologia." *Quarterly Journal of Speech* 59 (October 1973): 273–283.

Washington Post, October 10, 1984, A–4.

————, October 11, 1984, A–23.

————, October 12, 1984, A–20.

————, October 13, 1984, A–7.

Weaver, Warren, Jr. *New York Times*, November 6, 1976, 8.

Werling, David, Salvador, Michael, Sillars, Malcolm O., and Vaughn, Mina A. "Presidential Debates: Epideictic Merger of Issues and Images in Values." In *Argument and Critical Practices: Proceedings of the Fifth SCA/AFA Conference on Argumentation*. Edited by Joseph W. Wenzel. Annandale, VA: SCA/AFA, 1987, 229–238.

White, Theodore, H. *The Making of the President—1980*. New York: Atheneum, 1961.

Yoder, Jess, and Mims, Howard. "The Significance of Written Texts." In *The Great Debates: Carter vs. Ford, 1976*. Edited by Sidney Kraus. Bloomington, IN: Indiana University Press, 1979, 449–452.

Zyskind, Harold. "A Rhetorical Analysis of the Gettysburg Address." *Journal of General Education* 4 (April 1950): 202–212.

DEBATE TEXTS

"Debate between the President and Former Vice President Walter F. Mondale in Kansas City, Missouri, October 21, 1984." *Public Papers of the Presidents, Ronald Reagan, 1984, Book II*. Washington, DC: Government Printing Office, 1987, 1589–1608.

"Debate between the President and Former Vice President Walter F. Mondale in Louisville, Kentucky, October 7, 1984." *Public Papers of the Presidents, Ronald Reagan, 1984, Book II*. Washington, DC: Government Printing Office, 1987, 1441–1462.

Joint Appearances of Senator John F. Kennedy and Vice President Richard M. Nixon:

Presidential Campaign of 1960. Washington, DC: Government Printing Office, 1961, 72–92; 146–165; 204–222; 260–278.

"Presidential Campaign Debate of October 6, 1976, San Francisco, CA." *Public Papers of the Presidents, Gerald R. Ford, 1976–77, Book III*. Washington, DC: Government Printing Office, 1979, 2408–2436.

"Presidential Campaign Debate of October 22, 1976, Williamsburg, VA. *Public Papers of the Presidents, Gerald R. Ford 1976–77, Book III*. Washington, DC: Government Printing Office, 1979, 2621–2649.

"Presidential Campaign Debate of September 23, 1976, Philadelphia, PA." *Public Papers of the Presidents, Gerald R. Ford 1976–77, Book III*. Washington, DC: Government Printing Office, 1979, 2283–2312.

"Remarks at the 1980 Presidential Campaign Debate, October 28, 1980, Cleveland, OH." *Public Papers of the Presidents, Jimmy Carter, Book III*. Washington, DC: Government Printing Office, 1982, 2476–2502.

Transcript of the 1980 Debate between Ronald Reagan and John Anderson. Washington, DC: 1980. League of Women Voters.

Transcripts of the 1988 Presidential and Vice Presidential Debates. Washington, DC: 1988. Commission on Presidential Debates.

Transcript of the 1984 Vice Presidential Debate between George Bush and Geraldine Ferraro. Washington, DC: 1984. League of Women Voters.

"Vice Presidential Debate: October 15, 1976, Houston." In *The Presidential Debates: Media, Electoral, and Policy Perspectives*. Edited by George F. Bishop, Robert G. Meadow, Marilyn Jackson-Beeck. New York: Praeger, 1978, 261–281.

Index

Mears, Walter, 175
Medicare, 128–29, 139–40
Middle East, 91, 181, 187
military force, 113
Minuteman missile system, 114, 118
Mohrmann, Gerald P., 7
Mondale, Walter, 180, 192, 207, 221, 223, 225–30; confronting the facts, 134; controlling the facts against Reagan, 133, 220; controlling key issue in first debate with Reagan, 226; definition of leadership, 131, 147; enactment of leadership, 131; inability to use public record, 145; strategy of enumeration, 137; use of evidence, 142; vision of leadership, 184
Monroe Doctrine, 204
Morton, Thruston, 51
MX missile, 100, 114, 118, 154

national defense, 145
national prestige: as an issue in the 1960 campaign, 59, 62, 64; as a test of Kennedy's character, 65
national security, 172–74, 186, 196–97, 200
National Security Council, 28
Nelson, Jack, 90, 91, 92, 93
Newman, Edwin, 73
Newsweek, 193
New York Times, 96, 163, 192
Nicaragua, 187, 204
Niven, Paul, 46
Nixon, Richard M., 76, 87, 92–96, 145, 160, 216–18, 222, 225–30; accepted Kennedy's definition of campaign issues, 22; as Chairman of Eisenhower's Committee on Price Stability, 26; closing statement in fourth debate, 68, 218; failure to refute Kennedy, 23–24, 217–18; inability to develop own sense of presidential style, 50, 52–53, 55, 57–58, 64, 68, 217; inability to enact presidential role, 17, 22–23; inconsistent argumentation, 17, 52, 55, 57, 68, 217; on the issue of

responsible advocacy, 45, 54; missed opportunities to attack Kennedy, 49–52, 217; opening statement in fourth debate, 54–58, 218; pardon of, 71–72, 79–82, 92–93, 96, 178–79, 223; in persona of vice president, 23–24, 26, 56, 218; on the role of party labels, 45, 47–49, 217
Nixon administration, 82, 91
nonpersonal persuasion, 8
Noriega, Manuel, 201
Novins, Stuart, 26

O'Connor, Sandra Day, 181–82
oil depletion allowance, 50
opening statements, 10; Dole's, 169–71; of the first Kennedy-Nixon debate, 17, 18–25, 225; of the fourth Kennedy-Nixon debate, 58–66; Mondale's, 168; as symbolic context for interpreting candidates' discourse, 20
OSHA, 205–6

PAC money, 202
Pakistan, 87
Panama, 201
Parson, Donn W., 224
patriotism, 190–92, 194, 225
pattern of response, 5, 9, 11, 113, 122, 175
peace, 54, 122, 168, 178, 183–84, 191
Pendell, Sue, 224
performance, candidates', 2
Persian Gulf, 101
personal persuasion, 8
phronesis, 4
Playboy, 91, 172
policies, presidential, 1
poor, the, 137–38, 177, 186–87, 204
populism, 72
presidential campaign advisers, 1
presidential debates: audiences, 2; purpose of, 2
presidential vision, 10–11; Anderson's, 109–11; Bush's (as vice presidential candidate), 189;

About the Author

EDWARD A. HINCK is Assistant Professor of Communications and Director of Forensics at Central Michigan University. He has coached debate for thirteen years and taught argumentation, public speaking, communication theory, and rhetorical theory and criticism.